WITH THE BARK OFF

WITH THE BARK OFF

A Journalist's Memories of LBJ and a Life in the News Media

NEAL SPELCE

with Thomas Zigal

BRISCOE CENTER
FOR AMERICAN HISTORY
THE UNIVERSITY OF TEXAS AT AUSTIN

Distributed by Tower Books, an Imprint of the University of Texas Press

Requests for permission to reproduce material from this work should be sent to:
Office of the Director
Dolph Briscoe Center for American History
University of Texas at Austin
2300 Red River Stop D1100
Austin, TX 78712-1426

♾ The paper used in this book meets the minimum requirements of ANSI/NISO z39.48-1992 (r1997) (Permanence of Paper).

Library of Congress Control Number: 2021935633

ISBN 978-1-953480-06-4 (hardcover)
ISBN 978-1-953480-07-1 (library ebook)
ISBN 978-1-453480-08-8 (nonlibrary ebook)

Cover: Neal Spelce with Lyndon B. Johnson in Hyannis Port, Massachusetts, July 30, 1960. *Photo by Vern Sanford*

It is all here: the story of our time—with the bark off. . . . I do not know how this period will be regarded in years to come. But that is not the point. This library will show the facts—not just the joy and triumphs, but the sorrow and failures, too.

—Lyndon Baines Johnson's remarks at the dedication of the LBJ Presidential Library on May 22, 1971

"From my decades of intimate knowledge of LBJ, I can tell you Neal Spelce absolutely nails LBJ's personality with these stories, many that have never been told. Reinforcing his powers of observation are the dozens of Neal's personal photographs he sprinkles throughout *With the Bark Off*. I've watched Neal firsthand throughout his career. He has no agenda but the truth.

His life in the news media runs the gamut from reporting on-the-air live during unrelenting gunfire on a college campus to following Vice President Johnson into a jungle village in Vietnam.

Neal Spelce tells his stories as if he's confiding in you in a personal conversation. And they are entertaining, much of the time with a self-deprecating sense of humor. It is a splendid memoir."

—Tom Johnson, former LBJ White House aide, former publisher of *Los Angeles Times*, former CEO, Cable News Network (CNN)

"Neal Spelce's memoir sparkles with stories, anecdotes, and characters recalled by a wide-eyed Texan who moved among the shakers and makers of his time but kept his feet on the ground and his notebook handy. It's a heckuva trip—starting deep in the heart of Texas that gave us mesmerizing figures like LBJ, John Connally, and Darrell Royal and stirred ambition among the rest of us like bluebonnets blooming in the spring."

—Bill Moyers, former LBJ White House press secretary and acclaimed PBS documentarian and commentator

"Over more than two-thirds of a century, Neal Spelce came to be on a first name basis with many powerful people, and he witnessed an impressive number of big events and change. Much of this was as a first-person, on-the-ground, there-when-it-happened chronicler of his time. As the years have added up, Neal's body of work is as much that of a historian as a reporter. But unlike many who write about history, he experienced it firsthand."

—Dan Rather, former award-winning CBS-TV news anchor, editor, and reporter

"Neal Spelce is one of those rare people who can't make a move without stepping into history, which is why his memoir is so fascinating and rewarding. He was on the scene when Lyndon Johnson shouted 'Yee-haw' in the Taj Mahal and when he was laid to rest on the Pedernales. In 1966, Spelce was also the newsman who alerted the world, under fire and in real time, to the then-unimaginable horrors of a mass shooting. He also consulted on Ann Richards's wardrobe at the 1988 Democratic convention, and he may very well be the only living soul to know the meaning of the word 'thermostrockimortimer.'"

—STEPHEN HARRIGAN, author of
Big Wonderful Thing: A History of Texas

"In the 1960s, America was hungry for 'someone to believe in,' and Neal Spelce was that someone for the next half-century. The press, the public, and my family trusted him for his honesty and integrity. In his long-awaited chronicle of those times, Neal takes us through his remarkable life at breakneck speed in the midst of world events and the great stories of our times. *With the Bark Off* is a marvelous read, from the year my father was selected as President Kennedy's running mate to Neal traveling across Asia with Daddy as vice president. In his long and abundant life, Neal has always been ethical, credible, informed, and beloved—a man of great professionalism with a big heart. His book shows he's still someone to believe in."

—LUCI BAINES JOHNSON, daughter of
President and Mrs. Lyndon Baines Johnson

"Neal Spelce is the journalistic Zelig of our times. From JFK and LBJ to the Bushes and John McCain, Spelce has had a front-row seat to the history between those bookends. And from that unique perch, he presents a unique view of the politics and news that have shaped our history. It's a fun ride, made all the better because Spelce tells it all with the bark off."

—MARK MCKINNON, chief media adviser to George W. Bush and
John McCain, creator and cohost of *The Circus* on Showtime

CONTENTS

FOREWORD

There was a time when a strong, frontier vision of Texas shaped many a young boy's life. We were taught to believe that it was imperative that we learn to "ride, rope, and shoot." The younger the better. This self-identity was rooted in the state's history, and even more strongly in its powerful mythology. It can be found in classics of American art and letters, in books like Larry McMurtry's *Lonesome Dove* and Cormac McCarthy's *All the Pretty Horses*, and movies like *The Searchers* and *Red River*. When Texas boys of yore grew older, there often came another rite of passage as childhood notions of cowboys gave way to a stint as an oil-field roughneck, which was depicted in Edna Ferber's classic *Giant*.

Neal Spelce, born in 1936, moved to Texas as a child when these kinds of teachings were much more widespread than they are today. As he grew up, this vision of Texas remained alive, but the state was changing. Texas was becoming more urban, and as the population exploded, the economy evolved along with the demographics. By the time Neal reached adulthood, he had become a living embodiment of a state that straddled the past and the future. He, like Texas, was steeped in the old ways and myths, and held dear to their value. But he could also see a state growing into a new era of modernity.

Neal believed the old cowboy code that a man's handshake should be his bond, and he understood the value of the hard, manual labor that was revered in the oil fields. But he also recognized that the new Texas, indeed the world, demanded better, longer schooling, more knowledge of critical thinking, and a premium put on new discoveries, no matter the field of study.

Deep within himself he was old Texan to the core, rawhide and one tough son-of-a-gun when he had to be, but he was also a gentleman and a scholar who in dress, speech, and style was thoroughly of the new Texas.

As with so many of his fellow young, professional counterparts, Neal felt no obligation to wear a big hat, an oversized belt buckle, or always have on cowboy boots. He respected and always got along well with those

Dan Rather offered congratulations to me at my wedding to Connie Davis on St. Patrick's Day, March 17, 1996, just before we tossed down too many glasses of green champagne. *Photo courtesy Neal Spelce*

who did, but it wasn't his way. Not his style. He brings to mind some of my favorite lyrics from that Terry Allen song "Amarillo Highway": "I don't wear no Stetson, but I'm willin' to bet, son, that I'm as big a Texan as you are."

At the University of Texas, Neal studied to master the fundamentals of the postwar expanding field of mass communications: journalism, radio, television, advertising, and the rest. He soon became a reporter, and that's where our paths first crossed, as he writes about in this book. It has led to an enduring friendship that I cherish.

I was not surprised to see Neal go on to become a superb reporter and broadcaster who also had success as an entrepreneur and writer. Over more than two-thirds of a century, he came to be on a first-name basis with many powerful people and he witnessed an impressive number of big events and change. Much of this was as a first-person, on-the-ground, there-when-it-happened chronicler of his time. As the years have added up, Neal's body of work is as much that of a historian as a reporter. But unlike many who write about history, he experienced it firsthand.

Neal is humble about all of this. Always has been. I think that's one reason he hasn't done this kind of book before. He didn't want to come off as bragging. We are lucky that he finally was persuaded, that he heard some version of "Hell, Neal, just rear back and tell it with the bark off." And that he was reminded of a well-known saying from the old Texas: "If it's true, it ain't bragging."

So here in these pages, the good guy, quiet man, and eyewitness to history opens up to tell us stories from his extraordinary life. And these stories have the added value of being true.

DAN RATHER
Austin, Texas
August 2020

PREFACE

A round lunchtime on August 1, 1966, listeners who tuned in to KTBC radio in Austin, Texas, were horrified to hear the frantic voice of the station's thirty-year-old news director, Neal Spelce, reporting from the campus of the University of Texas:

Another shot! The sniper fired three quick, successive shots. Apparently in the length of time it takes to cock the weapon and then . . . . Another shot! He just fired another shot and this time . . . . Another shot! That's the fifth shot now in about 20 or 30 seconds. He's still situated below the University of Texas clock on the south side. The clock now shows 12:32. And he's coolly and calmly sitting up there firing away . . . generally in our direction."

Neal Spelce's riveting on-the-scene reporting of a sniper murdering fifteen people and badly injuring thirty-one others was quickly hooked into the national radio and television networks and broadcast across the nation in real time. Neal covered an incident that was, up to that time, the deadliest mass shooting by a lone gunman in American history. His cool eyewitness reporting while a murderous shooter was rapidly firing—in his "general direction"—has forever linked him to a shocking and tragic event that sadly was a harbinger of even worse mass shootings to come.

But Neal Spelce's career has been so much more than his courageous reporting on that hot summer day in Texas. In a career spanning several decades, Neal has been an award-winning pioneering broadcast journalist, media producer, and publicist. He has interviewed or been associated with presidents Truman, Kennedy, Johnson, Nixon, Ford, Carter, Bush, Clinton, and Bush. The Society of Professional Journalists has honored Neal with the nation's highest award for radio reporting, and he has received the National Headliners award for "outstanding television news reporting." A graduate of the University of Texas at Austin's Moody College of Communication, the college has named its broadcast journalism studio in his honor. Neal also is a valued member of the Briscoe Center's Advisory Council.

A few years ago, Neal donated to the Briscoe Center his collection of correspondence, photographs, publications, and audio and video tape recordings documenting his illustrious professional career. That collection includes more than three hundred 90-second TV vignettes about America that Neal's company produced and placed in more than a hundred US markets under the titles of *An American Moment with Charles Kuralt* and then, following Kuralt's death, *An American Moment with James Earl Jones.* The Neal Spelce Collection joins the center's extensive archive of papers documenting the history of American journalism, which includes the papers of Neal's friend, Walter Cronkite, as well as those of Morley Safer, Molly Ivins, Joseph Wershba, Liz Smith, William P. Hobby Sr., Walter Winchell, Steve Kroft, George Crile, Robert Trout, and many other important figures in the history of the news industry.

Neal's many admirers have long hoped that he would write a memoir in which he would share with the public the "back stories" of the people and events with which he has been closely associated in his stellar career. With the skilled help of his collaborator, Tom Zigal, who is a well-known author in his own right, that hope has been fulfilled by *With the Bark Off,* which the Briscoe Center has the honor of publishing.

The Briscoe Center's publication of Neal Spelce's memoir is part of its mission as a history center to support, facilitate, and disseminate research based largely on its collections. The publication of *With the Bark Off* has been made possible by funds from the center's Dolph Briscoe Endowment. I want to thank Austin philanthropist and Briscoe Center Advisory Council member Michael Klein for his staunch support and encouragement of this project. The center's talented editor, Dr. Holly Taylor, skillfully guided the book's editing and production. I am indebted to Holly and to Alison Beck, the Briscoe Center's director of special projects, for their outstanding work.

DON CARLETON
Executive Director
Briscoe Center

INTRODUCTION

Through his ascending political leadership in Congress from the late 1930s and well into his presidency in the 1960s, Lyndon Baines Johnson laid the groundwork for Austin and the Texas Hill Country to become the dynamic and fascinating place it is today. I don't think it would've happened as quickly without the worldwide attention and prestige that the thirty-sixth president of the United States brought to a government-paycheck, small college town with no Fortune 500 companies, no large private industry, no major airport, and only one TV station—which was owned by him and his wonderful wife.

It was my good fortune to have gone to work for the Johnsons at KTBC when I was still a student at the University of Texas (UT). My relationship with their family lasted for the next fifty-plus years and continues today. Working directly with LBJ—"The Man" himself—was a once-in-a-lifetime experience, but it certainly had its ups and downs. I've lost count of how many times I was chewed out by the Master of Butt Chewings. But on several occasions I was with him when history came knocking on the door.

I was with Vice President Johnson when he visited South Vietnam for the first time in 1961. He reassured President Ngô Đình Diệm that the four hundred Green Beret "special advisers" the United States was giving him at that very moment would help him destroy the Viet Cong once and for all.

I worked with former president Johnson hands-on, and in minute detail, when he asked me to chair the committee that planned the dedication ceremony for his presidential library in 1971.

I oversaw his burial service at the Johnson ranch on a cold, rainy winter's day. And as the Johnson family spokesperson several years later, I rode in the funeral cortege when the hearse carried Mrs. Johnson to her resting place beside her husband. Thousands of people lined the city streets and highway to the ranch, removing their hats, placing their hands over their hearts, and bowing their heads out of respect for that remarkable lady.

I was with Vice President Johnson when he visited South Vietnam for the first time, in May 1961. He jumped out of his car to respond to the welcome he received in Saigon just as he did on the US campaign trail. *Photo by Neal Spelce*

During my career as a news reporter, I was involved in some of the most riveting and exhilarating experiences imaginable. I've told these stories for decades in lively conversations with friends, and they've always urged, "Neal, you need to write these stories down." On one occasion, an influential thought-leader told me I had an *obligation* to do so. While prize-winning journalists and historians have written volumes about Lyndon Johnson, few of the stories you're about to read have made it into print. Everyone has heard about LBJ talking to aides and cabinet members while he was using the toilet, but what living soul, besides me, experienced something even worse?

Many of us at age eighty-plus can look back on our lives and recall a seminal moment that shook us, enlightened us, changed us, and defined who we would become. That happened to me on August 1, 1966, when I was a thirty-year-old news director at KTBC in downtown Austin and I overheard a dispatch on the station's police scanner saying that gunshots were being fired from the University of Texas Tower. I will forever be known as the reporter who drove to campus in a big red station wagon and was the only one to broadcast live during those terrifying ninety minutes for the world to hear as that tragedy was unfolding.

Recently I spoke to a UT class about my experiences on that blazing hot day in the summer of 1966, and we walked together to where I was hunkered down with a radio mic in my hand, talking nonstop as the sniper's bullets were whizzing all around. Even though I don't recall being rattled at the time of the incident, I was surprised at how emotional I became as I told my story to students whose parents are too young to remember that dark moment, when the first mass school shooter in American history took deadly aim at so many innocent lives.

I teared up as we stood at the red granite memorial to the victims who died that day, and to my surprise, some of the students teared up as well. Their generation is keenly aware of mass gun violence and how it destroys entire communities of the young and vulnerable. The Tower tragedy is only one of the many stories I relate firsthand in this chronicle.

In my early experiences as a news reporter, the monumental figure of Lyndon Baines Johnson loomed large and only an arm's length away—sometimes as my employer, sometimes as the politician standing next to me as I shook President John F. Kennedy's hand. Like the aides and confidants surrounding LBJ in his public years, I saw the best of him and the worst, and almost always "with the bark off." I can still feel that long arm wrapped around my shoulders when he would draw me in and say, "Neal, there's somebody I want you to meet." Or "there's something I want you to do." I could bet the ranch that in the next few moments, something extraordinary was going to happen.

ALL THE WAY WITH LBJ

In May 1961, at the end of my year as a CBS Fellow at Columbia University, newly elected vice president Lyndon Johnson was planning his first trip to Southeast Asia, and he wanted to take journalists to report on the health conditions in the places he would visit. Someone backed out of the trip, and I received a call from LBJ's aide Warren Woodward, who invited me to participate in the two-week tour. I accepted the offer in a New York minute.

Woodward said, "We're going to make key stops in Vietnam, India, and Pakistan," and asked if I had a current passport. I didn't. I was twenty-five years old and my only "foreign travel" was to a Mexican border town when I was a child living in the Rio Grande Valley of Texas.

"Can you be here in Washington tomorrow?" he asked. "Pack your bags, come on down, and we'll walk you through the State Department to get your passport and your shots."

I owned one suit and two or three ties. I ran to the nearby laundry to pick up a few shirts being washed and pressed. My wife, Sheila, thought it was a great opportunity and completely supported the decision. The next day I was on a plane to Washington, DC, and an LBJ team met me at the airport and took me to the State Department. I was in a daze and full of questions, like "When do we leave?" and "What is our itinerary?"

The aides led me by the hand and put me on a Pan American charter flight, the press plane that followed Air Force Two. (Air Force One was the title given to the airplane when the president was flying in it, but the same plane was called Air Force Two when the vice president was using it.) I was designated as a medical reporter, although all I knew about medical reporting was that it hurt when I got a shot.

It turned out to be a fascinating and eye-opening journey for a rookie reporter from Texas, and historic in many ways. It wasn't my first experience with LBJ—he and Mrs. Johnson had been my bosses at KTBC Austin—but it was certainly the first assignment I'd had covering him up-close-and-personal on a diplomatic junket.

Our first official stop was in Manila, the Philippines. The State Department people said to us "medical reporters": "We've set up a meeting with the head of their medical school and the chief medical officer for their government. Please bear in mind that you're representing the United States of America."

To my surprise, I was the only reporter who attended the meeting. And I was completely out of my element. The Philippine health officials said, "Whatever you want to ask us about our medical facilities and health care in our country, we're happy to address it."

I didn't have a camera crew to do a television interview. It was just me and my little Argus C3 camera. So I sat there in a conference room with those learned, high-level health professionals and asked a number of questions, nodding at their replies. I'm sure they were stupid questions. "What's the general state of your health care? What about children's vaccinations? What about hygiene?" Broad questions that elicited various opinions and responses.

One of my key traits as a reporter was I always took a lot of notes. A businessman once told me, "Neal, every time you talk to me, I notice you write something down." He said, "That's very impressive. You may be writing down 'This guy is an idiot,' but it looks like you're really paying attention to what I'm saying."

Although I was taking notes, I'm sure the Filipinos were thinking, "What's this kid doing here?" I can't imagine how I could've impressed anybody in that room. I prayed that the meeting was not being recorded. At the conclusion, I said, "Thank you very much. I enjoyed this wonderful opportunity," and left quickly.

I went back to the hotel and, Eagle Scout that I was, asked my esteemed medical reporters, "Why didn't y'all go?" And they said, "We're not interested in all that crap. We'd rather tag along with the regular press corps, where the real action is."

Major political shifts were taking place in that part of the world, although I was unaware of them at the time. But I sensed that larger forces were at work, occupying Vice President Johnson's efforts, and from that point on, I tried my best to be attentive and follow the White House press corps to whatever they were covering.

After the Philippines, we traveled to Saigon, where LBJ met for the first time with Ngô Đình Diệm, the leader of South Vietnam, and his

War was being waged by the Vietnamese while we were there, but JFK had not yet increased US troops beyond the "adviser" level. *Photo by Neal Spelce*

sister-in-law, Madame Nhu, a fiery, outspoken aristocrat. At their meeting, LBJ declared President Diệm "the Winston Churchill of Asia."

Unbeknownst to me and the majority of the American people, the Kennedy administration had just sent four hundred Green Beret "special advisers" to aid South Vietnam in its battle against Viet Cong guerrillas. In the next few months, President Kennedy would deploy eight thousand combat soldiers to bolster the struggling South Vietnamese army, and the Vietnam War was underway.

Inexperienced though I was in the realm of international conflict, I could clearly see that it was a crucial time to be in Indochina—the beginning of a violent era—and I observed things that left indelible images in my memory.

The State Department staffed the press plane, and prior to landing they would brief us on the current situation and US diplomatic and military policies with the country we were visiting. "These are the players. This is what's going on. Here's where we stand." They were especially cautious in Vietnam, where a real war was being waged against the Viet Cong out in the countryside, and people were dying.

We stayed in the notorious Caravelle Hotel in Saigon, which housed two embassies and the Saigon bureaus of CBS, ABC, and NBC. The State Department told us that Vice President Johnson was going to meet with Vietnamese leaders in a private dinner that first night, "but we've set up a dinner for the press corps at a floating restaurant on the Mekong River."

Eager as ever, I jumped on the first van—no one else had shown up at that point—and I was driven way out to the floating restaurant. Several Vietnamese dignitaries were waiting there to entertain the press. I was proud to be a representative of the United States and shook everyone's hand, smiling. Then I looked around and realized that once again I was the only reporter who showed up. It was becoming a habit.

An American fellow walked up beside me and said, through pursed lips, "I'm going to be here with you, and you just do what I tell you and everything will be okay. Just follow my lead. Don't worry about a thing."

I didn't know if he was State Department, CIA, or what. He acted as my escort, but he was also giving me orders: "We're going to go eat over here. Do what I say and you'll be fine."

I had trouble hearing what he was saying because he was barely moving his lips. We all sat down and commenced to drinking beer and having fun, and by then our Vietnamese hosts had loosened up. They brought out a roasted pig on a platter, and my handler said, "Do as I tell you to do."

They set the platter down and everybody began to cheer. The back half of the pig was carved in little one-inch squares. The skin tasted like what we used to call *crackling* in Texas, otherwise known as pork rind, which is crispy fried pig skin. The Vietnamese version had been ladled with a delicious sauce as it roasted.

My handler mumbled, "Okay, grab the tail of the pig." I said, "Huh?" And he said, "the tail. Pick up the tail and eat it. Do it now."

Thanks to LBJ, this dorky young reporter found himself part of an international trip with the newly elected vice president in 1961. *LBJ Library photo by Republic of Vietnam*

I reached over and grabbed the little curlicue tail and the skin around the asshole of the pig, and the handler said, "Go ahead. Go ahead."

It tasted like crackling. Everyone cheered and I said, "What was that about?" My handler said, "I'll tell you later." But he never did. I don't know if it was a Vietnamese tradition of some sort, or if they thought, "Here's this dumb American, let's see if he'll really do this."

That floating restaurant was later blown up by the Viet Cong. I'm pretty sure it wasn't a negative food review of their roasted pig.

LBJ had been briefed by the Diệm regime about the military situation in Vietnam, and the next day we reporters accompanied him to watch a demonstration of an incendiary gelling agent called napalm—a weapon I was unaware of at the time. An airplane flew low over a field and released the agent, which whooshed with a frightening sound and spread in a wave of liquid fire. I took a photograph, shaken by its massive destruction and wondering how it would be used. It was a terrifying sight. One I will never forget.

Later that day, the press was on a bus behind the vice president's official motorcade when he suddenly stopped the trail of vehicles, got out

A wall of napalm fire blasting from a low-flying plane was a terrifying sight to see up close. *Photo by Neal Spelce*

of the car, and walked into a little village. Security went into panic mode. This was an area where the Viet Cong guerrillas were waging war. They were embedded in these villages. They would attack, then retreat and blend in with the people. This particular village hadn't been secured by the army or Secret Service, but LBJ went walking in to shake hands. "I'm going to go meet these people," he said.

We piled off the press bus thinking, "This is a bad idea. He's liable to get killed here." I took a photo of him shaking hands with the villagers.

LBJ was practicing what he preached. During that visit to South Vietnam in May 1961, he wrote a memorandum to President Kennedy saying,

Our mission people [the new military advisers] must, by example and by subtle persuasion, encourage the Saigon government from the president down to get close to the people, to mingle with them, to listen for their grievances and to act on them. Handshakes on the streets . . . is the concept that has got to be pursued. And shirt-sleeves must be the hallmark of Americans. Unless we get this approach, which we do not now have, on the part of Vietnamese offi-

Security went into panic mode when LBJ stopped his motorcade and walked into a village that could have been a haven for the Viet Cong. *Photo by Neal Spelce*

cials [Diệm's administration] or Americans, this effort is not going to succeed.

At the village, we reporters were rushing to catch up with the long-legged LBJ, and running through our minds was "guerrillas . . . attack US vice president . . . international incident."

A guy was racing in front of me, and his sports coat was on fire. Smoke was billowing out of his coat pocket. I caught up with him and grabbed the back of his coat, ripped it off him, threw it on the ground, and stomped out the blaze. And then I dashed off to see what was happening with LBJ.

That evening, as press people are wont to do, we were all sitting at the bar in the Caravelle Hotel, having drinks and telling stories about the day. I looked over and saw Peter Kalischer, the Far Eastern correspondent for

CBS News. Back then, funding seemed to be virtually unlimited and the network could afford to station its people all over the world.

I introduced myself and told him I was a CBS Fellow wrapping up my year in New York. I asked him, "Did you get here in time to see LBJ's trip out in that village?"

He said, "Yes, I did! I was there. And some damned fool ripped the coat off my back, threw it on the ground, and stomped on the pipe I'd stuck in the pocket."

I said, "Good lord, did you see who it was?"

He said, "No!"

"A pleasure to meet you, sir," I said. "Glad you're here. Let me know if you need anything, I'm always happy to help out a fellow CBS guy."

I headed back to nurse my drink. I don't know if Peter Kalischer ever figured out who ripped off his jacket and crushed his favorite pipe.

Fortunately, there was no incident at that village in the jungle. LBJ was happy to meet the villagers and talk with them through an interpreter. He exuded bravado and self-confidence, and he could always sense a great photo opportunity and a public stage to exhibit his man-of-the-people charisma and rugged charm.

It was on that trip in May 1961 that my wild ride with Lyndon Baines Johnson began in earnest. He would shape my career, change the course of American history with his aspirations for a Great Society, and put my adopted hometown of Austin, Texas, on a trajectory to become one of the most popular cities in the United States.

Although I didn't know it at the time, that ride had begun when I was twelve years old and running through a sunbaked field with my little brother in the small Texas town of Raymondville. Because that's where I first saw The Man himself descending like a god from the heavens in a thundering helicopter.

One summer day in 1948, my brother, Bennett, and I were playing outside near a softball field when we heard a helicopter flying over the area and a loudspeaker announcing, "Come on down to the softball field for a rally."

Bennett and I went running toward the field—I'm pretty sure I was barefoot and wearing shorts—and the helicopter circled low and then landed, and a very tall man named Lyndon Baines Johnson stepped out. He was campaigning for the US Senate and addressed the small crowd through a bullhorn. I don't recall a word he said, because I was more fascinated by the helicopter. I'd never seen a politician up close, delivering a speech. It was a completely new concept to me.

A few months later, when we were leaving Raymondville for good, my brother and I kept begging Mother to turn on the radio in the car because we wanted to hear the election results. We were curious if that tall man named Lyndon Johnson was going to win. By virtue of seeing him in the flesh in our own dinky, half-forgotten little corner of the country, a massive figure stepping out from a roaring helicopter, he had made a memorable impression on us.

It wasn't until years later that I realized he was walking the walk. As he said in that Vietnam memo to President Kennedy, LBJ was striving "to get close to the people, to mingle with them, to listen for their grievances and to act on them." He believed in wearing shirtsleeves and shaking hands on street corners and at softball fields. Even at twelve years old, I knew I wouldn't forget his unusual name. But little did I know that he would impact me in many life-changing ways for decades.

A MIGHTY BULWARK

For many years, outsiders had no idea that Austin and the Hill Country were hidden gems deep in the heart of Texas. Wasn't the Lone Star State all about cowboys, sagebrush, and rattlesnakes—the John Wayne western movie image? People elsewhere couldn't imagine bountiful lakes and rolling hills covered in green woodlands anywhere in Texas.

But LBJ grew up surrounded by those woods and grassy farmland, and that's where he felt at home. Soon after winning the seat in the sprawling Tenth US Congressional District of Texas in 1937, his first elected office, he made it a priority to support President Franklin Roosevelt's New Deal programs and bring hydroelectricity and power lines to rural Central Texas.

I had met LBJ historian Doris Kearns Goodwin on several occasions, and in her book *Leadership: In Turbulent Times*, she nailed what I heard LBJ say many times about "how he had brought electric power to the Hill Country, and how electricity had changed the daily lives of thousands of farm families, letting them enjoy such modern conveniences as electric lights, refrigerators, and washing machines for the first time."

As a young congressman, Lyndon Johnson worked behind the scenes to secure federal funding to complete four hydroelectric dams in the chain of Highland Lakes that stretches for eighty-five miles from Austin to the northwest. His most important project was what is now Mansfield Dam. Lake Travis, a reservoir formed by the dam, provides drinking water for more than a million people in the Austin area. The lake is also a scenic recreation area with expensive shoreline homes and restaurants overlooking the water. But Mansfield Dam's essential function is to control a sometimes raging Colorado River that for decades had flooded the capital city and smaller communities downriver.

It's hard to believe now, but a study from the US Army Corps of Engineers indicated that between 1900 and 1913, seventeen floods had caused $61.4 million in property damage and claimed sixty-one lives. That's a lot of damage in century-ago dollars and casualties. There are dramatic photographs of houses drifting through Austin's downtown floodwaters in the old days.

In his remarks at the dedication of Buchanan Dam on October 16, 1937, Johnson said, "Today we are gathered here before this magnificent structure, a mighty bulwark against the blind and raging forces of nature, better to make it do our will."

Less than a year later, after a great flood in July 1938, LBJ addressed a mass rally in Austin to reassure his constituents: "Yes, we are going to have four dams. They are going to hold back floodwater and they are going to pay for themselves with some electric power which doesn't have to run through the cash register of a New York power and light company before it gets to our lamps. . . . We are going to keep building these dams in a business way. When we store up floodwaters, we are going to release them through hydroelectric turbines and we are going to sell the electricity . . . to the people. It will be the people's electricity, and the people are going to get it at cost—for a small fraction of what they have been paying the power monopoly for twenty years."

My family and I personally benefited from the creation of those lakes. We bought a small condo on Lake Travis and a boat, and we all enjoyed water skiing and family outings thanks to LBJ's vision.

At the same time that LBJ was firming up the physical and economic infrastructure of his beloved homeland, the University of Texas was playing a leadership role in the emergence of technology research in the Austin area and in supporting the cultural and artistic ambience of "Athens on the Colorado."

At the end of World War II, a couple of UT engineering professors negotiating on behalf of their university, C. Read Granberry and J. Neils Thompson, leased an old magnesium plant on four hundred acres of prairie land north of the city, primarily to conduct military research and testing. In 1949, Senator Lyndon Johnson helped UT purchase the land from the federal government. There he was again, now a US senator and a forceful advocate for his Texas constituents, securing land for what would first be called the Balcones Research Center and later the J. J. Pickle Research Campus. It was the first step in launching the University of Texas at Austin on its journey to become one of the leading research universities in America.

LBJ loved the University of Texas, even though he'd graduated from Southwest Texas State Teachers College (now Texas State University) in San Marcos, thirty miles to the south. But his wife, Claudia—Lady Bird—earned two bachelor's degrees (history and journalism) from UT, and the couple shared a strong lifelong bond with the institution. At his commencement address at UT in 1964, the president invoked the university's school spirit song, "The Eyes of Texas": "A few nights ago in Washington, many thousands of people, among them leaders from all parts of this great land, rose from their seats with me as the band played 'The Eyes of Texas Are Upon You.' Such a moment was full of pride for any Texan, but tonight it is not just the Eyes of Texas which watch you—the eyes of the nation, the eyes of millions in faraway lands, the eyes of all who love liberty are upon you. You cannot get away. Do not think you can escape them until you have brought us to the early morn of a nation without rancor and a world without fear."

It was a rousing, powerful speech in which he challenged a new generation of young Texans to be worthy of their heritage "in a booming state, in a bountiful land," and to join him in building a Great Society. "The choice is yours," he told the young graduates. "The power to shape the future is in your hands, the path is clear. It is the path of understanding and the path of unity."

His words really resonated with me. I believed in LBJ's strongest personal aspiration to unite a nation divided by racism and economic disparity. He fought that battle hard for the next four years in office and in the four years beyond that, until his damaged heart could no longer sustain the fight.

MY BARE-BONED SELF

The future author and *Harper's* editor Willie Morris and I arrived at the University of Texas for the fall semester of 1952. We got off the bus in downtown Austin—although he came from Yazoo City, Mississippi, and I came from Corpus Christi, where I'd just graduated from high school at the age of sixteen.

In his superb autobiography *North Toward Home*, published in 1967, Morris observed that our classmates at UT were a different breed than the Ivy League college intellectuals experiencing "a deepening of perceptions, or of learning, or culture." Instead, "for so many of us who converged on Austin, Texas, in the early 1950s, from places like Karnes City or Big Spring or Abilene or Rockdale or Yazoo City, the awakening we were to experience, or to have jolted into us . . . did not mean a mere finishing or deepening, and most emphatically did not imply the victory of one set of ideologies over another, one way of viewing literature or politics over another, but something more basic and simple. This was the acceptance of ideas themselves as something worth living by."

When I went through registration at UT's Gregory Gym, huge fans were blowing furnace-hot air across the tables set up on the basketball court. Texas was in the midst of a major drought, but the boiling August heat didn't hinder my enthusiasm. I was curious and wanted to look around and be there in the middle of it all and experience what was going on.

The first night, I walked across campus and headed south to the Capitol and walked through the rotunda, admiring its terrazzo floor with the seals of the six governments that had flown their flags over Texas, and then I walked downtown and roamed around Congress Avenue until finding my way back to campus. My wandering left quite an impression. It was an awe-inspiring experience for one of the many who converged on Austin in that 1950s generation.

The campus itself was visually enchanting to someone who'd begun his education in a one-room Arkansas schoolhouse. The biblical message "Ye shall know the truth and the truth shall make you free" was chiseled across the façade of the Main Building, and there were lofty inscriptions by famous thinkers painted on the beams of the Hall of Noble Words in the Life Science Library. I was elated that the University of Texas was a place where there were these thoughts, these ideas, this literature, these young minds and wise teachers. Willie Morris was right. I was beginning to realize that ideas and deeper feelings were worth exploring and living by.

Willie and I became friends. When he was the editor of the student newspaper the *Daily Texan,* he wrote a column about my campus activities. I lived in Roberts Hall and he lived next door in Brackenridge Hall, a stone's throw from Waller Creek and the football stadium. Our dorms were interchangeable. As he noted in *North Toward Home*: "Brackenridge Hall was where life was, stripped of its pretenses, where one saw every day the lonely, the pathetic, the hopeless young men—often poor though sometimes not, often ignorant but not always, but never anything if not various. Here a fairly sensitive boy could not avoid a confrontation with his basic and bare-boned self, and see a big state university in its true dimensions."

But my life wasn't in the dorm with those homesick young men. I was on the move around campus, exploring and enjoying it in all of its true dimensions.

WORKING FOR BIRD AND THE MAN

When I was a student, a state representative from Kingsville, Texas, named Ben Glusing gave me a job as a part-time secretary at the Texas state legislature. I didn't know how to type, so I signed up for a typing course at UT's College of Business. The class was primarily composed of women who wanted to become secretaries.

The House chamber was not air-conditioned in those days, and the old place was sweltering. We secretaries had seats on the floor of the chamber, folding chairs next to our representatives. There was a typewriter pool behind the Speaker's podium, and you'd go back there and type letters and bills on manual typewriters. As I sat and observed the proceedings, I became riveted by the legislative process and well versed in the rules of the House. I admired its elegant protocol: "Mr. Speaker!" someone would call out. And then the Speaker of the House would say, "The chair recognizes the honorable representative from the great community of Muleshoe. Home of the oldest wildlife refuge in the State of Texas. Home of the world's largest mule shoe." Etcetera.

One day in 1956, my journalism professor, DeWitt Reddick, said to me, "Neal, I know you're interested in broadcasting."

He was a very gentle man, soft spoken, with piercing eyes behind his glasses, and he'd look at you as if you were the only person in the world. (He later served as dean of the College of Communication.) He steered me toward taking a wide range of courses as I was working on three degrees at the same time—a bachelor of fine arts in radio-television, a bachelor's degree in journalism, and a bachelor of arts in speech.

He said, "Bill Moyers is leaving KTBC Channel 7. He's been there part time, writing and working in the news department. Would you like me to call them and open the door for you?"

I had met Bill Moyers in Marshall, Texas, his hometown and the place where I spent the summer of 1953. In the *Marshall News Messenger* I had read a call for musicians to play at summer band concerts in the gazebo downtown, and I'd signed up as a snare drummer, an instrument I'd played in high school and with UT's Longhorn Band. A young Bill Moyers was the master of ceremonies for the musical events, and that's when I first said hello to him.

I was excited about the possibility of tying my experience at the state legislature to a career in broadcasting. DeWitt Reddick made the phone call and I got the job replacing Bill. KTBC's news director, Paul Bolton (Mr. B), hired me on a provisional basis.

Bill had set a very high bar for writing. Even in those early days, as a college student in his twenties, he was a brilliant, incisive thinker. When I took over his job, everybody was full of praise for him and I knew I had to perform. But Bill's shoes were nearly impossible to fill.

The Johnson family owned KTBC-TV and an AM radio station, and they would later add FM radio. So at the KTBC television station, LBJ's name was omnipresent. When I was finally introduced to him, I was very nervous. I walked into the station one morning and there he was, the powerful Senate majority leader, larger than life, and I was this pimply-faced college kid from the sticks.

Mr. B said, "Neal, I want you to meet Senator Johnson."

"Yes, sir. How are you, sir? It's an honor to meet you, sir."

The normal salutations, but I was awestruck. It was all I could do not to jabber on about seeing him emerging from a helicopter when I was twelve years old.

LBJ gazed down on me and said, "Neal, I want you to know that whenever you shoot any film of me, this is my good side." With a half-joking smile, he showed me which side.

In a *New Yorker* article in 2019, biographer Robert Caro revealed that it was LBJ's mistress Alice Glass who counseled him "always to be photographed from the left side, because that side of his face looked better."

If you examine most of his posed pictures, they're taken from the left side. He had very large ears and a prominent nose, with a memorable face. I recall actor Sean Connery saying, "I attribute my success to having an interesting face." LBJ was the same way.

At that first meeting, I didn't know what to expect, and all I got out of it was to shoot his best side. It was the beginning of my many remarkable interactions with Lyndon Johnson over the next sixteen years, some of them warm and pleasant, some of them not.

Lady Bird Johnson had used her inheritance from her well-to-do East

Texas family to purchase the AM radio station (590 on the dial) in 1943, and she'd expanded her interests by launching a television station in 1952 (KTBC-TV). These wise investments helped fund her husband's political ambitions.

Critics have speculated that Mrs. Johnson was an absentee owner who rarely took an active interest in her stations, but that couldn't be further from the truth. In her biography *Lady Bird*, Jan Jarboe Russell quotes Mrs. Johnson as saying, "[Lyndon] told me I needed to get down there to Austin and learn all about the station—to familiarize myself with the staff, the market, and the accounts. I understood that we couldn't make a success of it and be running the station from Washington, so I went to work full-time." When she arrived in Austin, she found the station in need of cleaning, and she recalled, "I got a bucket, a mop, and a pail and started to work on it."

In person, she was incredibly gracious, genteel, very polite, and she had a way about her. There I was, a small-fry college student, one of her employees working in her television studio, and yet when she talked to me she'd look directly at me, listening thoughtfully and conversing as if I had something valuable to say. Those were her hallmark virtues: personal, kind, attentive. She was a woman of great integrity and charm.

I never called her Lady Bird. Never. That would've been too familiar. It was always Mrs. Johnson. And even today, more than sixty years later, I still refer to her in conversations as Mrs. Johnson.

At that time, KTBC was located in a small space on the ground floor of the elegant Driskill Hotel at Sixth Street and Brazos in downtown Austin. In 1960, KTBC moved four blocks away to its own building at Tenth and Brazos, an old YWCA they converted into a television studio. It had an apartment on the top floor that was used by the Johnson family when they were in town. Mrs. Johnson and their daughters, Lynda and Luci, were often in and out. The Johnsons used it as a place to cook, have meals, and spend the night.

KTBC was a family operation with a friendly atmosphere, Texas-style, less formal than the corporate structure in New York and elsewhere. Lynda and Luci would sometimes bring home-baked cookies to the staff. LBJ, the consummate dealmaker and arm-twister, would have farm-fresh eggs delivered from their ranch, and the employees were asked if they wanted to buy them. We bought them. It seemed like the wise thing to do.

When I began working at KTBC in 1956, it was a CBS affiliate and the only TV station in town. Critics believed that because the powerful Johnson family owned the station, they kept everybody else out of Austin. It was a popular urban myth, but it wasn't true.

When the Johnsons applied to the Federal Communications Commission for a television station in 1952, there wasn't a competing local application because owning a TV station was very expensive and a big investment. It required towers, studios, experienced staff, on-air personalities, sponsors, the whole thing.

NBC and ABC had no station in Austin, so KTBC program director Cactus Pryor negotiated a deal with those two networks to carry some of their programs.

Around 1958, KTBC decided to be like the big boys in New York City and run the news at 11:00 p.m. rather than at 10:00 p.m., like everyone else in our part of the country. Eleven o'clock news was unheard of in the Central Time Zone at the time.

Of course, KTBC didn't have any competition. But the real reason for the change was it gave the station an extra hour of prime-time programming in the 10:00 to 11:00 p.m. time slot, where KTBC could drop in an NBC or ABC show. Cactus maintained that Austin viewers got the best of the TV world because he was picking and choosing the best programs from all three networks. KTBC would play popular series like *Gunsmoke* and *Bonanza* at different times, so the best shows didn't overlap or compete with one another.

I wanted to be a broadcast journalist because that profession put you in the middle of everything. You were at the legislature when lawmakers were debating and passing bills. You were in the center of the action when there was a major new construction in the city, a tragic event, a community celebration. You rushed to cover what was going on. That's the attraction of the news business, and that's why I was delighted to work at KTBC.

Austin in the late 1950s wasn't very impressive. About 156,000 people—a state university, state-government town. There were small businesses, small industry, nothing remarkable about it yet.

My first job at KTBC was to go to the cop shop at 4:30 every morning and read through the overnight police reports, make notes on police activity, then return to the station and write up the stories. They worked them into newscasts all day long. And that was great for me because it didn't interrupt my UT classes. I'd finish up at about 8:00 in the morning and stop by the PK Grill on Seventh Street for a great homemade breakfast of eggs, sausage, and biscuits. It was the kind of lunch counter that rarely exists anymore, where the waitresses called their customers "darling" with a warm and innocent affection that was common in that era all over Texas. My favorite waitress called me "sweet pea."

The first time I ever got on the air was when I called in to Paul Bolton to say I'd found a great story in the police reports. He said, "Get on the phone and let's put it on the air." So I went on the telephone and said, "This is Neal Spelce at the police station" and finished the report. We were using the kind of primitive technology that typified those early days of radio and television.

I found out later that Cactus Pryor, the program director for both KTBC-TV and AM radio, heard that report and said, "I don't want that guy on the air ever again. His voice is horrible."

I was very green, I had an Arkansas accent, and I wasn't schooled in on-air speech.

Nobody had television experience in those days, and to be honest, Paul Bolton didn't have any of the qualities you'd think would be successful on air. He was a crusty codger who'd been an International News Service (INS) correspondent and bureau chief, strictly a print and wire-service man. When KTBC put him on the air, everybody joked about him because he was fumbling around and didn't know he should be looking at the camera. He was terrific at writing the news and an expert in terms of content, but the camera did not love him.

Mr. B was my mentor, but he was a notorious curmudgeon. One day we were sitting back to back, writing stories with the police radio on nearby, and I stopped typing. Without turning around, he asked, "What's wrong?" I said, "I'm trying to figure out a way to end this story." And he said, "When you finish what you have to say, just shut up." So I said okay and ripped the story out of the platen. "Thirty," as we used to say. *Finis.*

In my first months at KTBC, I managed to mess up all the time. On one occasion I was working on the night shift, and as Mr. B was leaving, he said, "LBJ always says, 'Make sure you turn out the lights when you leave.'" That was LBJ's signature frugality, ever the poor country boy saving nickels and dimes, even in his White House years later on.

When I finished up, I turned out the lights and went back to the teletype machines and turned them off, too. I didn't think a thing about it. The next morning, there was no news, no copy, because the teletype machines had been shut down all night. They weren't computers that could store memory.

When Mr. B came into the office in the morning and didn't have any copy waiting for him, I don't know how he managed. But he let me know in no uncertain terms that I'd screwed up. As I recall, he led with "How stupid can you be?" Not "Everyone makes mistakes, son. Take a minute and reflect on what you just did." There was no snowflakery in those days. I got my butt chewed out real good.

Even though I was still wet behind the ears, I wrote stories to accompany the film we put on the air. I was eager to do anything and everything I could. I delivered a radio report here and there, and I was on television a number of times, reporting from the field. At some point, they eased me into the studio and let me start reading the news on camera.

One of the reasons Paul Bolton hired me at KTBC was because I'd worked as a secretary in the legislature. One morning when I was working a little late, still writing stories at 10:00 a.m., Mr. B turned to me and said, "I got a call that James Cox is going to appear at the legislature shortly to make a personal privilege speech."

James E. Cox was a Texas state representative who'd been audiotaped at the Driskill Hotel accepting a $5,000 bribe from the president of the Texas Naturopathic Physicians Association. When the story broke in the *Austin Statesman*, Cox didn't show up for a couple of days at the legislature, so it was a big deal when he decided to address members on the floor of the House.

Mr. B was getting ready for the noon television and radio newscast— we ran both simultaneously—and he said, "Neal, grab a camera and go up to the Capitol and cover that."

I literally ran from Sixth Street and Brazos up Congress Avenue to the Capitol, which was five long blocks away. I arrived out of breath, and while Cox was making his personal privilege speech, I took notes and snapped photos. As an indication of how early it was in the history of television broadcast news, the camera I grabbed was a black-and-white Polaroid, the kind in which you took the picture, pulled the negative out, smeared a gel fixer on it to set the image, like a developer, and waited for the gel to dry.

In the KTBC studio, we'd jerry-rigged a curved panel with a black matte finish, and we would attach those Polaroid photos to the panel, pan the images from one to the next using the studio camera, and use it as the "video" for the story. Eventually, the station bought 16mm cameras and the processing equipment and studio playback equipment for black-and-white 16mm film, which was a historical leap in TV news technology.

Early in my career at KTBC, John Nance Garner was having a nineti-eth birthday party out in Uvalde, Texas, a whole different world on the edge of the Texas Hill Country, 160 miles southwest of Austin and not far from the Mexican border. "Cactus Jack" was a former US Speaker of the House and had served as vice president under FDR. We got the word in advance that former president Harry Truman was going to be there, and I thought, "Wow, a very impressive event." I had always wanted to meet Harry Truman. So I asked to go to Uvalde to cover the story, and in what was typical of that time in the local news business, I drove my own car and paid my own way.

Uvalde native Dolph Briscoe was hosting the party. He was a wealthy rancher and former Texas state representative who would later become governor of the state.

Several national leaders were there to honor Garner, including his fellow Texan Sam Rayburn, who had been Garner's protégé in Congress and was by then the powerful Speaker of the House. Truman was invited because he and Garner had become friends when Garner had presided over the Senate as vice president and Truman was a US senator.

Truman was famous for taking his morning constitutional, an invigo-rating walk in the early hours of daylight. Uvalde is not a big town. We reporters thought, "Let's go out and stand around early in the morning." And sure enough, here came Harry Truman briskly walking along. We ran up to him, but he didn't break stride. I asked him a dumb question, just something to start a conversation: "Mr. President, what kind of vice president was John Nance Garner?" He kept walking and walking, and he finally said, "Well, he's a lot better than that birdbrain we've got now."

His reply was a shocker. I didn't have a comeback, so he filled the void. "If you don't know who I'm talking about," he said, "I'm talking about Richard Nixon."

That was Truman's hallmark. He was straightforward, outspoken, and very open.

Years later, when LBJ took a group of us to visit the Harry S. Truman

I didn't have a personal camera when I first interviewed former President Harry Truman, so years later when LBJ visited Truman in Missouri about his presidential library, I grabbed this shot that showed Truman's exuberant personality. I don't care if it is technically imperfect. It captured the essence of Truman. *Photo by Neal Spelce*

Presidential Library and Museum in Independence, Missouri—while LBJ's own presidential library was under construction in Austin—I took a photograph of Harry Truman that showed him ruddy-faced and vigorous, as we all remember him. Unfortunately, that picture has a blur on one side because my camera cover swung around and got in the frame. But his face had so much character, I didn't mind.

I interviewed Sam Rayburn years later, when he was a visitor at the LBJ Ranch. It was one of those interviews where I got blindsided. I walked over with my microphone and stuck it in front of him and asked him a question. He grabbed the microphone out of my hand, looked into the camera, and started talking. He had a very forceful personality, with a hard look, and I was too intimidated to stop him. He finished his remarks, gave the mic back to me, said thank you, and walked away. My brilliant interview amounted to him making a speech.

As I look back at those times in the late 1950s and early 1960s, it's difficult to assess myself and my colleagues and the quality of our work at KTBC. There was a camaraderie on our staff, a mutual respect. We all liked one another and shared a collective sense of humor. We sometimes tried to crack each other up on the air and make someone laugh on camera.

Jesse Kellam was the general manager of the television and AM radio station and a longtime supporter of LBJ. I don't think Mr. Kellam had a broadcast background. He was a former high school football coach. When I asked him to write a letter of support for my application for a CBS Fellowship at Columbia University, he wrote, "I don't have a son, but if I did, I'd want him to be like Neal."

That amazed me. My gruff old boss thought of me as family.

That was the attitude throughout the station. We were friends working together. Family. I don't know where that came from—from up top or down where I was—but that was the ambience at KTBC. Most of the people I worked with became lifelong friends, staying in touch long after we all went our separate ways. The station seemed to be a reflection of LBJ's informal Texas style. It was a great work environment.

Cactus Pryor was the first face that viewers had ever seen on TV in the Austin area. I was going through the Delta Upsilon fraternity rush at UT in the fall of 1952 when I began watching the Thanksgiving Day Longhorns-Aggies football game on a black-and-white television set. It was the first time I'd ever seen a TV program. Thirty-year-old Cactus was on camera in the studio, introducing the game before they switched to the football field, and little did I know that I would one day work for that young TV personality with a strange first name.

Cactus was the funniest guy I've ever met. At one point, KTBC had an extra fifteen-minute slot to fill around suppertime, and he asked himself, "Well, what are we going to put there?" He created a little show called "Cacti's Fill Time," and he'd do just about anything that popped into his head. There was a hatched door that opened up from the KTBC studio in the Driskill Hotel, and sometimes Cactus would wheel the camera out onto the sidewalk and leave it on, capturing the scene in all its raw street splendor.

He also introduced a segment called "Toupee or Not Toupee?" He would try on different hairpieces and say into the TV camera, "Call and tell us. Do you like this one, or do you like this one?" He would straighten out the hairpiece. "How does it look to you?"

Television was primitive in those days, with little money to spend on gimmicks and gadgets, so Cactus used his fertile imagination to engage people. He was a genuine talent.

His wonderful sense of theater came from his father, "Skinny" Pryor, who owned the Cactus movie theater in downtown Austin, and that's how Richard S Pryor Jr. got his nickname.

Cactus grew up inside that theater, absorbing movies—especially Westerns, which he loved—along with serials, cartoons, newsreels, whatever appeared on the screen. It was the early 1930s, and all across the nation, movie theaters were becoming open, friendly, and safe environments for a generation of children.

Cactus told me that his father was very popular because kids would come to the theater and say, "Mr. Pryor, I don't have any money for the show." And Skinny would say, "Okay, you can work for it. Go get me a glass of water." When the kid returned with a glass of water, Skinny would say, "You earned your ticket. Go on in."

Cactus was a boy soprano, performing in groups and sometimes solo. He got his start on stage as a young singer, and at the same time he was learning his entertainment chops by watching what Hollywood was projecting on his father's movie screen. When Cactus's voice changed and eventually developed into that great mellow baritone he used for radio and television, his evolution was complete.

At the University of Texas, his focus was naturally communications, which was primarily radio at the time. But World War II soon broke out, and he dropped out of UT to join the Army Air Corps.

Cactus was more than a standup comic telling one-liners. He knew how comedy works, and he wrote jokes and great speeches for others. One time when we scheduled a roast at the Headliners Club, Governor Preston Smith called Cactus and said, "I understand you're gonna roast me pretty good."

"That's right, Governor, no holds barred," Cactus said.

"Well then would you write me something to say in response?" asked the governor.

Cactus wrote the governor's comeback responses and gave him the best lines, making him look like a comedy genius and Cactus the butt of the jokes. Listeners said, "Hey, the governor got the best of Cactus tonight." Which was exactly what Cactus wanted to hear.

H. L. Mencken once wrote, "As I look back over a misspent life, I find myself more and more convinced that I had more fun doing news reporting than in any other enterprise. It is really the life of kings."

Austin American-Statesman reporter Ben Wear described us journalists as "an irreverent and clever breed," noting that "reporters don't have to punch a clock, we get to follow our curiosity almost anywhere and we have license to ask impertinent questions of the powerful. Quite often what we do makes a real difference in the civic sphere. We get to know, often on an intimate basis that can approach friendship, some truly impressive and dedicated people. Reporters are really beholden to almost no institution or creed, other than our own guiding ethical principles."

I was part of the KTBC family from 1956 to 1971. Those were my formative years, both professionally and as a proud and active participant in the growing Austin community. Our sleepy college town was becoming one of the most vibrant and fascinating cities in the nation, and I was there with a pen and notepad and very often a camera, covering every moment of that amazing transformation.

TALKING HEAD

I had been working at KTBC for two years when I was asked to broadcast the eleven o'clock news. I was only twenty-two years old. On the first night I was definitely nervous about going on the air, even though I'd been involved in all aspects of the radio and television news operation, absorbing as much as I possibly could and spending extra time doing extra things around the station.

When the hour arrived, I was sitting behind the news desk and staring into the camera. I knew my job was to communicate in a very straightforward way to only one person in the audience, but that's a challenge when the producer is saying in your ear, "Stand by, we're getting ready to go here," and you're talking about something totally different to the television viewers and trying to maintain your believability. It's an out-of-the-ordinary experience and you've got to make it look ordinary. You've got to sit there and convince the viewer that everything is okay while the producer is shouting, "Oh my god! We can't find the clip! We've lost the tape! Neal, keep talking."

Sure, I was nervous. Someone who's not nervous in that situation has no feelings. But I discovered this truth about myself: I may feel nervous when I'm speaking on television, but it doesn't come across. It's only an internal feeling.

I don't remember making mistakes that first night, but I probably stumbled over a few words. I wasn't like the character in the movie *Broadcast News* who went on the air with sweat pouring off him. My hands weren't shaking and my mouth wasn't dry. I enjoyed it. Anchoring the news was somewhat of a high, and I discovered that it gave me an adrenaline rush. I took to being on the air, in front of cameras, and I never looked back.

A friend of mine once said, "Neal, you have this demeanor about you that's always positive, whether you're on camera or not. When you were a talking head, you projected confidence and that positive manner. Did you ever get emotional? Have you ever lost your temper in the studio?"

In all my years at KTBC, I didn't shout at anyone or lose my temper,

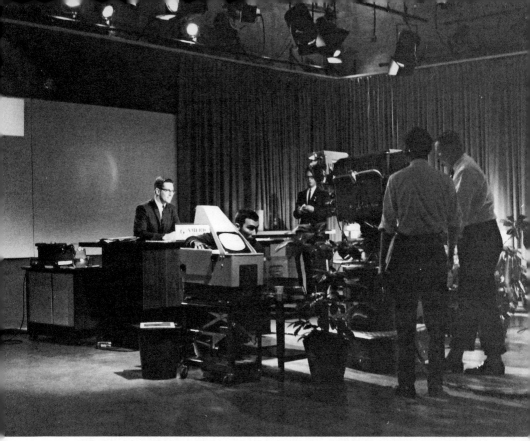

Talk about the early days of TV—an overhead projector provided handwritten graphics and there was no teleprompter on Election Night 1962. *Photo courtesy Neal Spelce*

but from time to time I did get concerned and somewhat upset. However, I'm a believer in laughter. I love jokes and comedy. So when things weren't going well, I always tried to smile and find humor in the chaos and frustration. Humor gives me great happiness and usually provides a way out of a bad situation.

I've never cried on camera, although there were moments that deserved a tear. I've felt what Walter Cronkite was feeling when he announced the death of President Kennedy. But for me it was a matter of self-control, knowing that I had a job to do and I was going to do it. I usually caught myself, took a breath, and continued. Conversely, I'll cry at a movie or in some touching family circumstance. But I've never shed a tear on camera.

During my anchor years, I would put on my anchor uniform (recognizable suit and tie) and go to the state legislature and spend the day observing and absorbing what they were discussing and voting on. Not that I reported every day from the Capitol, but I sat at the press table and asked questions at the appropriate times, eager to understand everything taking place at the Texas state seat of power.

Our little market in Austin had higher ratings for news than the network stations in the larger San Antonio, because San Antonio news-viewing was divided between three stations. Of course, KTBC continued to be criticized roundly for being a monopoly. Viewers wanted more choices, and they cussed LBJ for keeping all the competition out of the city.

But we had the genius of Cactus Pryor picking really good programs. For example, we were carrying CBS's Douglas Edwards on the evening news, but when *The Huntley-Brinkley Report* came along on NBC, it started winning all the ratings and awards. It was the first time a network featured two anchors, with Chet Huntley in New York and David Brinkley in Washington. They would talk back and forth on the air, and it was entertaining as well as informative. Cactus dropped CBS news and began carrying NBC news, and that caused a problem at CBS, which didn't want to lose its dominant position in the Central Texas market. But Cactus and the local folks prevailed, and it turned out to be a really good move for our ratings.

That was before Walter Cronkite at CBS. He was a former University of Texas student, and when he emerged as a featured anchor, we switched back to CBS.

When I became the news director at KTBC-TV in 1960, I came up with the idea of establishing a consortium of Texas news directors that would share stories of statewide interest to our particular markets. Our group was composed of Dan Rather at KHOU in Houston, Eddie Barker at KRLD in Dallas, and Al Anderson at WOAI in San Antonio. The four of us were in continuous need of information and big stories from the three other Texas cities. Not just car wrecks and beauty pageants, but substantive reports.

Our group created the very first statewide newscast at very little cost. We would put our local stories on the TWIX, which was a transcription service, and say, "Here in Austin I've got the governor's conference. I've got the state agency planning the Texas lottery." Al would say, "I've got a story on cleaning up the River Walk." Dan would say, "We've got a report on the grass dying in the Astrodome." Then we news directors would get on the phone to one another with our lists: this one from Houston, this one from Dallas, and two of these from San Antonio.

We'd make copies of our black-and-white film at no cost to our partners, put the film in grapefruit sacks, and run them out to the now defunct Trans Texas Airways at the airport every day and send them off. When the plane arrived with film for us, we'd send someone out to pick it up. Today we have satellites and the Internet, and we can feed a story instantaneously. Everyone receives information at the speed of light. But not in those days.

Our consortium used a primitive and time-consuming method, but even so, we were ahead of our time. We cooperated and shared information in a very competitive business. We confided in one another. We discussed which stories were important to our listeners and which ones were not. And in the process, the four of us—Dan Rather, Eddie Barker, Al Anderson, and myself—developed relationships that made our jobs easier, more successful, and more enjoyable. I really liked those guys.

Dan Being Dan

Decades after it happened, Dan Rather told this story at a Halloween party at our house in Austin. It was also his birthday. Lady Bird Johnson was there, dressed as a witch with a pointed hat, and Liz Carpenter—Mrs. Johnson's friend and former press secretary—was with her, dressed as a yellow-dog Democrat, wearing yellow chiffon and a dog nose.

Dan said that when he was a young reporter at a radio station in Houston, he got word that LBJ was going to announce his bid for president while he was at the Johnson ranch. Dan asked his bosses if he could go to the ranch and cover the announcement, and they said, "No, the wire services and the networks will cover it. Don't worry about it."

Dan being Dan, he decided to go anyway and hitchhiked from Houston to the LBJ Ranch, which was 225 miles away. As a young, wet-nosed reporter, he went wandering around the ranch, snooping out the story. But there was no announcement and no press conference, just some low-level function. He asked someone on staff, "Is there a phone in the house?"

He walked into the ranch house to the room where LBJ had set up his office. Dan was the only one there. He picked up the phone and called collect to the radio station in Houston, telling them, "He's *not* announcing for president yet. But if you'll roll tape, I'll go ahead and give you a report from right here at the ranch."

He was talking on the phone, reporting: "This is Dan Rather live at the

LBJ Ranch. We were anticipating that Senator Lyndon Johnson would be announcing that he's running . . ." And then he felt a large hand on his shoulder that spun him around. It was LBJ, his huge physique looming over him. The senator said, "I don't know who the hell you are, son, but you get out of here *right now.*"

Dan was kicked off the ranch. It wouldn't be the last time he had a confrontation with a powerful authority figure and was thrown out of somewhere.

He had to hitchhike back to Houston, so he set out walking down that long road that leads from the ranch house to the highway. When he heard a car behind him, he turned and saw that it was Mrs. Johnson behind the wheel. She pulled up beside him, rolled down the window, and they exchanged pleasantries. Then she said, "Hop in, young man. You can come on back. Don't worry about Lyndon."

Lady Bird had smoothed it over. Dan's point was that for the rest of LBJ's career, Mrs. Johnson was there smoothing things over.

She was a refined East Texas woman with impeccable southern manners. I was around her a lot, especially during the presidential library dedication and in the years after her husband's death, and I never heard her raise her voice. She was the same person in private that you saw in public, always deeply involved, and sometimes very concerned about what was going on around her. It was hard to find anybody who didn't like her. During the White House years, there were those who made fun of her cultured southern accent and old-fashioned decorum, but she was beloved by so many. The admiration and respect for her grew even stronger as she spent the rest of her life teaching us to appreciate and preserve the beauty of nature and to become responsible stewards of our natural surroundings.

THE 1960 PRESIDENTIAL CAMPAIGN

When LBJ ran against John F. Kennedy for the Democratic nomination in 1960, there was an obvious contrast in age and style. JFK was youth personified—that was his image—and LBJ countered with his seasoned experience. His campaign slogan was "A Leader to Lead the Nation," and he used that famous profile photo (the correct side) with a little gray in the temples. He worked that to his advantage, insisting that every now and then you needed someone with a touch of gray in their hair, a sign of maturity. His approach was "Kennedy is a young senator, but I'm the Senate majority leader."

KTBC covered the 1960 primary from the Texas perspective, especially when LBJ was having a function in Austin. There was an aura about The Man. Trailing after him with cameras, we knew we were a part of history being made.

Our station was a very interested observer of the Democratic Convention in Los Angeles, when LBJ was selected as vice president. I wasn't there; I watched it on television. We knew the players on the Texas side. His trusted aide and the future governor of Texas, John Connally, was a key supporter and a leader in LBJ's effort for the nomination.

LBJ and JFK hadn't been enemies, but they were combatable. (Bobby Kennedy despised LBJ until the day Bobby died.) To butcher an Ann Richards analogy, JFK was born on third base, and LBJ was born in the dugout. There was an enormous difference in their personalities, upbringing, culture, and geography. And yet they knew they had to come together to map a strategy for the Democratic campaign against Richard Nixon and Henry Cabot Lodge.

After he was selected as the VP running mate at the July convention, LBJ took the Texas Capitol press corps to the Kennedy compound in Hyannis Port, Massachusetts, and I was fortunate to be invited. The White House press corps was also there covering the discussions. The two running mates considered the occasion an opportunity to get to know each other better in a casual setting and in a different light.

The press joined JFK to laugh at LBJ's lighthearted remarks as they kicked off the campaign at the Kennedy family compound in Hyannis Port, Massachusetts, July 30, 1960. *Photo by Neal Spelce*

Pierre Salinger herded the press at Hyannis Port for the two senators, just as he did later as JFK's White House press secretary. *Photo by Neal Spelce*

Two future first ladies, Lady Bird Johnson and Jackie Kennedy, charmed the press corps in Hyannis Port. Jackie Kennedy's radiance may have been due to her pregnancy with John Kennedy Jr. *Photo by Neal Spelce*

"Neal, you want to get a picture with us?" LBJ gestured toward JFK. "Well, sure." "Vern, come over here and take a picture," LBJ said to Vern Sanford, the executive director of the Texas Press Association. This iconic picture of me with two US presidents is one that I truly cherish. *Photo by Vern Sanford*

When I arrived, the Kennedys were throwing a football on a grassy lawn leading down to the waters of Nantucket Sound. It struck me as a summer home where everybody was on permanent vacation. The presidential candidate and the vice presidential candidate were wandering around the lawn, and the press was observing their every move.

The public scrutiny didn't seem to bother the Kennedys. They didn't appear to be posturing; they were being themselves, wearing sneakers, khakis, and open-neck shirts. Their press conferences were informal, unlike those in previous administrations and today, where everything is well scripted. When JFK approached the press corps to make a statement, he didn't wear a tie or a jacket, per tradition, usually just a golf shirt. He was open and direct about their plans: "Lyndon is going to work the South, and here are a few other things we've decided on."

On one occasion, Jackie Kennedy very graciously came outside to say hello to the press. What a beautiful lady! She was pregnant with John Jr. at the time, and she was positively glowing. Like everyone else in the country, I was impressed with her. She wasn't trying to make headlines; she was simply an elegant and charming hostess greeting her guests. She understood the importance of good relations with the media.

There was a special moment for me when I was standing with both JFK and LBJ on the porch at the compound, and LBJ asked, "Neal, you want to get a picture with us?"

"Well, sure."

Vern Sanford, who was the Texas Press Association's executive director, was there with his camera. "Vern, come over here and take a picture," LBJ said.

Sixty years later, it's hard to believe, but I actually appeared in a photograph with LBJ and JFK. It's an absolute treasure—the young Neal Spelce standing between two monumental figures in twentieth-century American history who would eventually serve as presidents of the United States. And there I am, shaking Jack Kennedy's hand and looking into the eyes of Lyndon Johnson.

Back at KTBC, everyone saw the photo and a joke went around the station: "Neal, you certainly know who your boss is, don't you?"

I also have a photo of me standing with LBJ and President Richard Nixon at the dedication of the LBJ Presidential Library, and another one of me between former presidents George W. Bush and George H. W.

Bush after the three of us had been together on a small bass boat at a lake in East Texas. Those pictures are absolute gems. Getting photos between pairs of United States presidents is being in the right place at the right time.

JOHN CONNALLY'S EYEPATCH

John Connally tried to talk LBJ out of becoming the vice presidential running mate when John Kennedy offered it. There were bruised feelings, but LBJ accepted the position, and he even convinced Kennedy to appoint Connally as secretary of the navy after the election.

Connally had been LBJ's aide and campaign manager, and they had a close friendship that transcended their political leanings. John Connally was a conservative Democrat, while Lyndon Johnson was a moderate who swung his support back and forth between the liberal and conservative factions in the state's Democratic Party. Those factions fought it out in the party's primary elections, which were the only elections that counted in those days because the Republicans were such a small minority in Texas.

In the early 1960s, John Connally had ambitions to run for governor in Texas, but he hadn't held public office and was virtually unknown to the public. Serving as secretary of the navy gave him some exposure.

The powers that be at the University of Texas were certainly aware that their alumnus Secretary John Connally was a leader on the rise with political aspirations. In the fall of 1961, the UT Ex-Students' Association (also known as the Texas Exes) honored Connally as the sole recipient of the university's Distinguished Alumnus Award (DAA). Their elegant annual ceremony usually celebrated three or four honorees.

UT doesn't give out honorary degrees, and the alumni association's DAA is the closest recognition of that kind. By selecting only John Connally that year, the choice seemed both prescient and audacious. Everyone wondered if the selection committee had had their arms twisted, or had simply foreseen the future with great clarity.

When Connally flew into Austin's Robert Mueller Municipal Airport for the DAA ceremony, UT's Naval ROTC Honor Guard was waiting on the tarmac to salute him in their white dress uniforms with bayonets fixed to their rifles. KTBC had stationed its cameraman behind the Honor Guard, filming Connally as he stepped off the plane and walked down the line of young cadets, inspecting the troops. The protocol called for them to motion with their rifles, one at a time, in a salute to the secretary of the navy, and then pull back as he passed by. However, when Connally walked in front of one cadet, his bayonet flashed up and jabbed the secretary on the orbital bone right under the eyebrow. Blood started gushing, and if the blade had struck an inch lower, Connally would've lost an eye.

Everyone raced toward him, and our camera caught the Honor Guard disrupting as well. With blood pouring down his handsome face, Connally was rushed to the ER. Fortunately for everyone, it turned out to be a superficial cut and looked worse than it was.

There was discussion about canceling the Distinguished Alumnus banquet, but Big John said, "No, no, let's not cancel it. I'm okay. But I've got to wear an eyepatch because it's messy and doesn't look pretty. There are stitches. So find me an old pirate eyepatch for this eye and I'll make my speech."

The banquet was a black-tie event held in the columned area outside what was then called the Crystal Ballroom at the Driskill Hotel in downtown Austin. The illustrious guests were all there, waiting in anticipation, the women in their finery, the men in tuxedos. They were all aware of what had happened to the future governor. When John Connally was escorted into the banquet, he did a double-take of the audience and burst into laughter. Everyone was wearing black eyepatches. It broke the ice, and there was a thunderous applause.

CBS FELLOWSHIP AT COLUMBIA UNIVERSITY

B y 1960, I'd been working at the CBS affiliate KTBC for four years, and I decided to apply for a CBS Fellowship. The CBS Foundation selected nine people every year to participate in a fellowship program at Columbia University, which involved taking graduate courses and interacting with other young news junkies dedicated to broadcast journalism. It was patterned after the Nieman Fellowships at Harvard. A distinguished group of judges, including Edward R. Murrow, Fred Friendly, and the dean of Columbia's School of Journalism, chose three from CBS News, three from the CBS affiliates, and three from educational television.

I submitted my application and made the cut, and they paid my way to New York City to be interviewed by the committee. I was as nervous as a preacher in a strip club. One of the questions on the application was, "Why do you want to do this?" and my answer was something along the lines of "Texas is getting ready for a revolution, and I want to be prepared professionally to cover it." I declared that there were dramatic changes taking place in the state's social fabric, its demographics, and its political leaning.

At the interview they said, "Tell us about this revolution down in Texas," and I wondered, "Did I use the wrong word?" But I'd covered the Texas legislature for KTBC and I was very tuned in to current affairs.

When I returned to Austin, I received a telegram that said, "Congratulations, you've been selected as a fellow." The fellowship stipend covered room, board, and expenses for a married couple to exist in New York City for a year.

The CBS Fellowship program was a transformative experience. I was there from the fall of 1960 until the summer of 1961, an incredible year to be in New York, the epicenter of world events, during that historic presidential race between Richard Nixon and John F. Kennedy. It was a time of change, not only in my life, but across the globe. There was a sense that we were entering a more modern era focused on the future and not the past, an era of hope, adventure, and a renewed American spirit.

In a UT radio-television class, I'd met an attractive young woman named Sheila Allen from Edinburg, Texas, and we'd been married for two years when we drove up to New York together, looking like Beverly Hillbillies in a Ford Fairlane packed to the roof. We didn't own any furniture. When we arrived in the city, we saw a sign for rent—a little studio apartment on East Forty-Ninth, a wonderful location between Third and Lexington on a crosstown thoroughfare and around the corner from CBS headquarters. I said to Sheila, "Let's walk in and see what happens."

Naïve? I couldn't even spell the word at that time, but I was the personification of it. I said to the leasing agent, "We'd like to rent the place. I'm here on a CBS Fellowship." And he said, "We'll have to get back to you." I said, "No, we need something right now. We don't even have a place to stay tonight." He said, "You have to be approved by the co-op's board of directors, young man. What references do you have here in New York City?"

And that's when working for the Johnson-owned KTBC paid off.

I said, "Would the majority leader of the United States Senate be a good recommendation?"

The leasing agent said, "Do you mean Senator Lyndon Johnson? You can get a recommendation from him?"

I said, "May I use your phone?"

I called the senator's office and his staff said, "Neal, to whom should we address this letter?"

I said, "Is there a way you can send it right now?"

LBJ's office sent a telegram to the leasing agent, and that was that.

It turned out to be a third-floor studio apartment that was owned by an older man—a designer of Broadway theaters, an architect—whose family had moved him out because he was getting to an age when he needed assistance. There was no bedroom, just a one-unit living room, dining room combination and a pull-down Murphy bed. We could open a window and reach out and touch the bricks of the adjacent building.

When winter came and snow covered the streets, the traffic disappeared and there was a peaceful quiet that fell over the city. One day, after nineteen inches of snow, I bundled up, took my camera, and wandered out to capture the serenity of urban life under its mantle of snow. I photographed two old codgers sitting at a table in Central Park, scraping aside the snow so they could set down their chess board and play.

Sheila and I were living in the heart of New York City, the most exciting city in the world, and we were young and everything seemed exhilarating and possible.

The fellowship program let students choose their curriculum, and I selected graduate studies in government and economics. The distinguished historian Henry Graff was the professor assigned to us, and he called himself our shepherd. He'd assign a book to read once a month and then bring in the author to discuss it with us.

Our country was in the midst of the Cold War, and that tense global situation dominated most of our meetings. Government professor Zbigniew Brzezinski, the future national security adviser for President Jimmy Carter, spoke about his book on Soviet totalitarianism. Former ambassador George Kennan outlined his foreign policy study regarding the USSR and the West. After the discussions, we'd have a lavish dinner at the Columbia faculty club, with wine flowing freely and heady conversations.

Columbia University was a totally different educational experience from the University of Texas. I don't know what I'd expected, but an Ivy League university afforded more intellectual opportunities and firsthand sources, more direct exposure to ideas and current events, and a deeper well of culture and the arts. One of the courses created for the CBS Fellows was team-taught by a Nobel Prize winner in physics, Polykarp Kusch, and a highly acclaimed biologist. The two of them discussed science and its impact on society. That sort of scholarly discourse was invaluable, even though I had no background in physics or biology, except for an advanced freshman biology course that I nearly flunked at UT.

The fellows considered me the "LBJ expert" because of my association with him in Austin. There had been a lot of Texans on LBJ's campaign staff when he was running for president earlier in the year, people he knew and trusted. In October, I received a call from one of them who said, "Neal, The Man wants to see you." The caller said they were in town at the Roosevelt Hotel and asked me to join them.

When I walked into the hotel's presidential suite, where LBJ was staying, there was a battery of campaign staffers at work, typewriters clicking away and people on the phone. I looked around and didn't see him. An aide rolled his eyes and said, "He's back there in the bedroom. Go on in."

I was taken aback to find LBJ lying on the bed, getting an enema while giving orders to the staff members who'd gathered around him. The odor, the sounds! I nearly lost my lunch. But that was LBJ. His attitude was, "I can't stop because I need an enema. Let's keep moving and

Soviet Foreign Minister Andrei Gromyko flustered me when he pointed at me and said something in Russian while I was taking his picture at the United Nations. Someone pointed out that Gromyko was telling me that the cover on my little Argus C3 camera was blocking the lens. I corrected it and took this picture. *Photo by Neal Spelce*

working." The rumors were true that he sometimes conducted meetings on the toilet, with the bathroom door open.

My conversation with him wasn't anything earthshaking. "Neal, good to see you. How are you doing at Columbia? How is CBS treating you?" He hadn't called me in for any special reason. He just wanted to touch base and make sure I was doing well in New York City.

While I was a fellow, I asked CBS for credentials to cover the United Nations. What could have been more exciting than international politics in 1960, a year when Fidel Castro's revolution had taken over Cuba, U-2 pilot Francis Gary Powers had been shot down over the Soviet Union, and Soviet leader Nikita Khrushchev was banging his shoe in the UN General Assembly? I went to that legendary shoe-banging session in October with my little Argus C3 35mm camera. Dozens of professional photographers were there with cameras hanging around their necks and long lenses, and it was fascinating to be in the middle of all that commotion. I called in a story or two on the telephone to KTBC in Austin about what was happening at the UN.

As I was walking around, I noticed Andrei Gromyko, the Soviet minister of foreign affairs, talking to someone in front of a very colorful mural that rose two or three stories high. I thought, "I gotta get this picture." So I went over with my camera and turned it for a vertical shot, with the mural in the background, and when the camera flashed, Gromyko pointed at me and said something in Russian. I had no idea what he'd said and started backing away, concerned that I'd violated protocol. A Japanese photographer, with as many cameras as his arms and legs could carry, said to me, "I know what Gromyko just said. When you were taking your shot, your lens cover fell over the lens, so you didn't get the picture. The foreign minister was saying, 'You need to take another picture, young man.'"

I smiled and took another picture of Andrei Gromyko. He didn't mind; in fact, he was directing me on how to frame the image, and it was a great photograph because of the mural and the UN setting.

Wandering the floor during that same session, I also saw Eleanor Roosevelt sitting in her seat as the US ambassador to the UN, and I walked over and graciously asked, "Madam Ambassador, do you mind if I take your picture?" She smiled and agreed. She was such a strong and intelligent woman in her own right, and I was awestruck in her presence.

While wandering the floor prior to the start of the UN General Session, I spotted Eleanor Roosevelt, the US ambassador to the UN, reading her newspaper. After getting her permission, I snapped this photo of the former first lady. *Photo by Neal Spelce*

Former presidential candidate Adlai Stevenson also was in attendance as a US envoy to this history-making United Nations session, which featured Soviet Prime Minister Nikita Khrushchev banging his shoe on the desk and Cuba's President Fidel Castro, who had recently assumed power. I couldn't get close to them because of security concerns. *Photo by Neal Spelce*

UN Secretary General Dag Hammarskjold presided over the momentous and controversial 1960 session. A few months later, in 1961, he was killed in a plane crash. *Photo by Neal Spelce*

Still thoroughly naïve but determined, I asked CBS if I could cover the Kennedy-Nixon race for the presidency. On election night in November 1960, I was a flunky at a desk in a pool of coworkers as election returns were coming into CBS headquarters, doing whatever they asked me to do. I was assigned tasks like, "Can you call Arkansas and find out how much longer they're going to take for the vote count?" They asked me to call Texas, and I reached my friend Dan Rather at KHOU-TV in Houston. He said, "Neal, I heard you're up there. Congratulations! How do you like the program?"

I said, "So far, so good, Dan. New York is amazing. You should come up here when you get a chance."

Dan said, "I applied for a CBS Fellowship but didn't make the cut. Maybe I'll try again next year."

The CBS network came calling on Dan Rather a year later, following his amazing on-the-scene coverage of Hurricane Carla when it ravaged the Gulf Coast of Texas in September 1961. They recognized Dan's extraordinary talent and brought him to New York for a while, then promoted him to bureau chief in New Orleans. On the day President Kennedy was assassinated in Dallas, Dan had been assigned to lead the CBS team covering the president's trip.

CBS held an annual banquet at the Waldorf Astoria, where they brought in their affiliates to schmooze with all the folks working at the network's headquarters. Many of the stars from CBS's various television series mixed with news reporters, interns, and financial supporters. At the banquet in the fall of 1960, a representative from KTBC Austin couldn't attend, so I was given his seat. Once again, I was an eager replacement player. Toward the end of the meal, the lights went down and I thought, "Is the power going out in the hotel?" Waiters swooped in bringing Baked Alaska Flambé, and it was quite a dramatic treat for this small-town Arkansas boy.

The guy sitting next to me was an actor named Clint Eastwood, who played Rowdy Yates on the TV program *Rawhide*. It was a command performance for him, and I don't think he enjoyed being there in a tuxedo, putting up with a young news reporter fawning over him and telling him that *Rawhide* was a timeless work of art.

It was that kind of year for me in New York. It felt as if I were in the beating heart of the universe, and nothing would ever be the same again.

CAMELOT, 1961

Sheila and I attended the JFK inauguration in January 1961. It was an astonishing experience, and added to my excitement was the fact that I knew the man in the long topcoat who was seated directly behind the inauguration podium and would soon be serving as vice president of the United States.

It was bitterly cold and snowing in New York when we left for the nation's capital, and for the first time in my life I put snow chains on my tires. But when we reached the freeway, there was no snow on the road and suddenly—bang, bang, bang, bang—the bare pavement had smashed the tire chains and they'd come loose and were banging against the wheels. Somehow we survived that ordeal without a blowout.

Hotels in Washington, DC, were booked up, so we rented a room in the home of a lovely couple. We didn't attend any inaugural balls, and we didn't have VIP seating or press seating at the swearing-in ceremony itself. President John F. Kennedy delivered perhaps the most memorable inaugural address of my lifetime—the "Ask not what your country can do for you" speech. Sheila and I were caught up in the patriotism of that supremely democratic transfer of presidential power and the Kennedy family glamour and all the pageantry of that historic moment in January 1961. We were young and filled with joy and optimism, and I've never been prouder to be an American.

"I DON'T KNOW HOW LYNDON DOES IT"

On that trip with Vice President Johnson in May 1961—after witnessing napalm for the first time and racing after LBJ into a South Vietnamese village—our entourage traveled to Thailand, which was more of a ceremonial visit. We stayed in a beautiful hotel in Bangkok, and we were entertained by traditional Thai dancers. Because the city had a complex network of canals, it was known as "the Venice of the East," and we toured the place on boats.

We then flew to India, where LBJ met with Prime Minister Jawaharlal Nehru, who was serving as the first prime minister of that country since its independence from Great Britain in 1947. All reports indicated that the meeting was pleasant and uneventful.

Afterward, we visited the Taj Mahal. I don't know if it was because LBJ requested it, or if the Indians wanted to show off that stunning architecture, one of the Seven Wonders of the Modern World. In the Indian sun, the light gleamed off the ivory-white marble and the reflecting pools leading to the shrine itself. Built in 1643 as a tomb for the emperor's favorite wife, it had become an enormously popular destination for tourists from all over the world.

We had removed our shoes and were roaming around inside those beautiful chambers with their intricate carvings and inlaid gemstones when LBJ said, "It really is magnificent inside and out. I wonder how the acoustics are in here?" He let loose a cowboy yell—*Yee-haw!*—that echoed through the vaulted space. It broke the rules of decorum, and of course that became the story: LBJ goes hog-wild Texan at the Taj Mahal. You can take the boy out of the country . . .

He was given a replica of the Taj Mahal, and he said, "Neal, come over here and take a picture with me." In the photo, I'm standing with LBJ and his replica of the Taj Mahal with the actual palace in the background. The replica is in the LBJ Library.

After India, we flew to Pakistan. Those two countries had been at odds with each other since they'd become independent nations and free of British rule in 1947. At the time of our visit, there had been a history of

After letting loose a cowboy yell inside India's sacred shrine, LBJ asked me to pose with him alongside ivory-carved replicas of the Taj Mahal. *Photo courtesy Neal Spelce*

border skirmishes and disputes, a war over who controlled Kashmir, and unrest between Hindus and Muslims in both countries.

Pakistan president Ayub Khan had been educated in Great Britain at the Royal Military Academy, Sandhurst, and had fought in World War II as a colonel in the British Indian Army. He spoke the Queen's English and several other languages. He'd become president through a military coup three years before our arrival. A barrel-chested, imposing man, large and balding, Ayub Khan was the kind of strong leader that the tall and imposing LBJ admired.

For LBJ's visit, President Khan had arranged a welcoming banquet outdoors under tents. The press corps was invited. There was a bar where the alcohol was flowing freely, which was highly unusual for a Muslim celebration. It was a magnificent feast, and I'd never seen anything so extravagant. As usual I was sampling the food and enjoying myself im-

In Agra, India, on the way to the Taj Mahal, this was the musical "welcoming committee" greeting LBJ. *Photo by Neal Spelce*

After LBJ's first meeting with India's Prime Minister Jawaharlal Nehru, I heard him insult Nehru to another world leader. *Photo by Neal Spelce*

mensely, but I'd lost track of time until I looked around and noticed that the press bus had gone without me.

There were only a few of us left. LBJ was sitting beside Ayub Khan on pillows and a Persian rug at the end of a low table, nursing a scotch and soda on ice while the Pakistan president was smoking a cigar. Just two good old boys sitting around and having a fine time together. LBJ glanced at me, smiled, and said, "Neal, come on over here," like an uncle inviting his nephew to join a poker game.

I walked over and sat down on the carpet at the feet of the two men resting higher up on overstuffed pillows. There were only three of us, but I knew my place. I wasn't really a part of their conversation, only a fly on the wall, but I was listening closely and fascinated by the British and Texas accents trading back and forth. At one point, Ayub Khan asked, "So Lyndon, what did you think of Nehru?"

LBJ didn't hesitate: "I think the little sumbitch is queer."

That turned my head. I expected Ayub Khan to laugh, but he took the comment in stride, almost as if he agreed. Then he said, "Well, Lyndon, do you think you can work with him?"

LBJ replied, "I'll have my hand on his knee and up that skirt of his in no time."

In Karachi, our motorcade rolled slowly through streets filled with flag-waving admirers, but I suspected that the cheering crowds had been staged by military and government officials. At one point, LBJ stopped his limo and jumped out. He'd seen a man with a camel and wanted to meet him. As the vice president was shaking Bashir Ahmad's hand and asking about his animal through an interpreter, I took a great photo of the camel and LBJ and the scruffy camel driver. He was smiling and attentive and having great fun conversing with the towering American dignitary. LBJ concluded the interaction by saying, "Sure good to meet you. You come and see us sometime, okay?" And then he stooped back into the limo.

Headlines: LBJ invites camel driver to USA.

As it turned out, in the weeks ahead, the media pressure began to build. "When are you bringing the camel driver to the United States, Mr. Vice President?"

LBJ always knew the difference between a hamburger patty and a cow patty. He said to his staff, "Let's go ahead and do that."

A few months later, Bashir Ahmad arrived at the Johnson ranch. LBJ

LBJ stepped out of his motorcade to shake hands with a camel driver in Pakistan. When he said, "Y'all come see me some time," the headlines trumpeted "LBJ Invites Camel Driver to US." *Photo by Neal Spelce*

used the opportunity to show him—and the rest of the world—how his dam projects had irrigated the dry countryside in Central Texas and created the Highland Lakes, and how the dam system now controlled the water supply for drinking, irrigation, electrical power, recreation, and flood prevention. LBJ's message: "I noticed in India and Pakistan that there wasn't electricity in a lot of the villages, and I want to demonstrate how we addressed that challenge in rural Texas."

LBJ phoned Henry Ford II, who was one of the vice president's supporters, and persuaded Ford to donate a pickup truck to the camel driver. They shipped the truck to Pakistan, so when his camel died, the driver would have transportation to help with his work.

President Kennedy's response to Bashir Ahmad's visit: "I don't know

On a visit to the LBJ Ranch, Pakistani President Ayub Khan gave LBJ a fancy silver-inlaid saddle. *Photo by Neal Spelce*

how Lyndon does it. If I had done that, there would have been camel dung all over the White House lawn."

President Ayub Khan also made a trip to the ranch later that year and gave LBJ a fancy saddle inlaid with silver. The two leaders continued to get along famously. It was a case of personal diplomacy working out for the benefit of both countries.

After Pakistan and the camel driver, we traveled to the island of Taiwan, and LBJ met with Generalissimo Chiang Kai-shek, the former dictator of China whom the Communist Mao Zedong had defeated in the Chinese civil war. Chiang had fled to Taiwan, where he'd established a government in exile and served as its president. The Communists in the People's Republic of China were upset that the American vice president was meeting with their enemy in Taipei, but the United States recognized the Taiwan government and would remain its ally for several more years.

My life had been fairly parochial before that whirlwind trip with LBJ. To travel to those global hot spots at the age of twenty-five gave me a great perspective from a world affairs standpoint for the rest of my career. It

Generalissimo Chiang Kai-shek hosted LBJ on Taiwan island, where Chiang had fled the Communist government of China. This US acknowledgment could not have made the Beijing government happy. *Photo by Neal Spelce*

was an amazing opportunity to be part of a national news team that was briefed by the State Department on every aspect of a country's culture, politics, and military status. I had experienced a tiny morsel of what the vice president of the United States had experienced, and it certainly was an eye-opening adventure. Once again, my association with LBJ was a life-transforming experience.

On the way back to the States, we stopped in Athens. It wasn't part of the official trip, but an opportunity for R&R and sightseeing.

Athens was one of those places that has stuck with me forever. A CBS reporter stationed there gave me a local's tour of the ancient ruins, and that evening she took me to a small nightclub where Edith Piaf was singing in person. Can you imagine? They called her "the little sparrow"— she was a small lady, frail from alcohol and painkillers—but her voice was incredibly haunting and beautiful. That voice! Oh my God, that voice. I sat there drinking ouzo, a licorice-tasting aperitif I'd never tried before, listening to her mesmerizing vocals. It felt almost like a spiritual awakening. Or maybe I had had a little too much ouzo.

I had tried to buy a little souvenir from each place we visited on that remarkable tour. In Vietnam, I'd bought a small lacquered platter, a decorative piece that sat on a tripod. In Hong Kong, I'd ordered a bolt of dark silk for Sheila, and shoes for myself at Lee Kee, the famous custom shoemaker, choosing the leather from their many samples. What I acquired in Athens was something I couldn't carry home in a suitcase—a love for Edith Piaf. For years afterward, I could hear her song "Non je ne regrette rien" marching valiantly through my head. I can still hear it and remember her fragile presence onstage. If I need a reminder of that special moment in time, the rare taste of ouzo will bring it all back.

LBJ ASCENDING, 1961–1963

O nce LBJ became vice president, his Secret Service detail was in and out of the KTBC building in Austin all the time. We had some fun with them. I owned one of those retractable pointers that professors use, and I would get on the elevator with the agent assigned to elevator duty and pull out the retractable pointer like a walkie-talkie and speak into it—"Secret Service on the elevator, stand by"—and collapse the pointer and put it away. Their heads would jerk around. When I went into the lobby: "In lobby now. Secret Service clearly visible." I would do that every time there was a new agent, and I was lucky they didn't throw me to the floor.

I had been to the LBJ Ranch for small events before he became vice president, but it was when he served as VP that the ranch became a folksy, comfortable gathering place for world leaders and a familiar geographical reference in the public mind, like Hyannis Port and Warm Springs, Georgia. And of course, when he was president, the ranch became known as the Little White House.

LBJ loved hamburgers made at the Night Hawk, a beloved institution among Austin's most popular restaurants. The original place was located at the south end of the Congress Avenue Bridge and had been in business since 1932. Harry Akin was the owner and later elected as mayor of Austin, and he was an early supporter of LBJ. Every time the Johnsons hired a new cook, LBJ would phone Harry Akin and tell him, "Harry, I have someone I want to send down there. I want you to teach him how to make those burgers like you make them."

LBJ's favorite was the Frisco Burger, with its Thousand Island–like special sauce on a buttered and toasted bun. After the cook was trained, LBJ would sit in his suite above the KTBC studio and eat Frisco Burgers the way they made them at the Night Hawk.

Harry confided to me that LBJ was the one who told him to integrate the Night Hawk. He said, "You've got to lead on this, Harry. We've got to serve Negroes."

Harry had already been hiring minorities to work in his kitchen and

LBJ hosted many world leaders at picnic tables for barbecue at the LBJ Ranch. *Photo by Neal Spelce*

as wait staff for many years, but serving African American diners was a bolder step during those volatile times. When he decided to integrate his restaurants, there was no muss, no fuss. He just did it. I don't remember anyone making a peep.

During that same period, in the spring of 1960, African American students from UT and the historically black Huston-Tillotson College had begun to conduct sit-ins at the lunch counters downtown on Congress Avenue at Woolworth's, the Kress five-and-dime store, and other variety stores and department stores. In Austin, there were demonstrations on both sides of the integration issue, but by May of that year, thirty-two lunch counters and restaurants in Austin had voluntarily desegregated. It was a relatively quick and peaceful transition.

LBJ really did surprise people. As a southerner, he was able to push for social progress and accomplish many things that were not expected of him. Observers assumed that a northeastern liberal like JFK would lead the charge on progressive social issues, but it took a liberal southern

LBJ Ranch events usually featured colorful props to create a festive atmosphere. *Photo by Neal Spelce*

Democrat to get things done. He achieved significant success because he'd come up through the Senate and knew how to twist arms. Literally! I'd seen him do it. He would lean over you with that large physical frame and tell you exactly what you needed to do or say.

With Lyndon Johnson serving as vice president and later as president, Austin was becoming more visible in the national consciousness. Whenever world leaders arrived, they'd have to land at Bergstrom Air Force Base (now Austin-Bergstrom International Airport) outside Austin and then be driven or choppered out to the ranch in Stonewall, Texas, which is sixty miles away. The ranch had a small runway that could handle two-engine planes, but not the larger ones. Whenever LBJ or someone else was due to land, the Secret Service would rush out to the landing strip and chase the deer away so there would be no mishap while the plane was touching down.

In time, Austin became an extension of the ranch itself, not only because of the proximity, but also because the White House press corps would stay in Austin when there was a newsworthy event at the ranch. They usually stayed in the Driskill Hotel downtown, and besides their coverage of LBJ, they soon they began writing sidebars about the charming college town.

Previous presidents didn't have a colorful ranch. LBJ owned cattle and horses and an expanse of land along the Pedernales River. (The proper Texas pronunciation of that river is *PURR-de-NAH-liss.*) He provided deer hunting and exotic game. By Texas standards it was little more than a gentleman's ranch, but he had a ranch foreman to make it official—and the barbecue was fantastic.

LBJ had great fun with his visitors. He enjoyed entertaining them. I could see him get a twinkle in his eye whenever he was about to pull a prank on the tinhorns. He loved to drive around his ranch and check on his cattle, and on a few occasions I went along for the ride. He owned a small German-made Amphicar convertible, lagoon blue in color, that could float and maneuver on water. But he didn't tell his guests it was an amphibious vehicle. They'd get in the car and he'd say, "Let's go look at the ranch. I'll show you my cattle. I've got this bull out here you gotta see."

The Pedernales River flows through the ranch property and runs over a little dam, and although passengers can't see this from a car, the water is streaming over the top of a road. LBJ would drive along, talking about his property and pointing out its woodsy features to the visitors, and then he'd suddenly head straight into the moving water. They didn't know he was driving on a little strip of road. At other times, he'd shout that the brakes had failed and he'd steer the car splashing into a small lake. While the terrified passengers were catching their breath, he would laugh and guide the amphibious car toward dry land.

LBJ also owned a convertible Lincoln Continental with two coach doors in the rear, the kind of doors that open in the opposite direction of standard vehicles, and he would take his visitors around in the Lincoln because it could hold more people.

On a couple of occasions, I heard him get pretty vulgar. One day he told me, "I was driving around the pasture and discovered it's a great place for screwing. There was this couple out there, and her legs were up."

He would talk about his big old bull and its balls hanging down and how proud he was of that animal. One Secret Service officer's nickname for LBJ was Bull Nuts.

True to his reputation, LBJ enjoyed off-color jokes and salty language.

THE KENNEDYS IN TEXAS

Before going to Dallas, the Kennedy entourage had traveled to San Antonio, Houston, and Fort Worth, campaigning for his 1964 reelection bid. After lunch in Dallas on November 22, they were scheduled to fly to Austin, and our station was preparing for major news coverage of their landing at nearby Bergstrom Air Force Base. A gala event in the Municipal Auditorium was planned for that night, where many dignitaries and political leaders would gather to meet the president and his lovely wife.

I had become KTBC's news director by that time, and I was in charge of our coverage. As a small-market TV station, we had limited resources, so we were trying to figure out where to place our cameras, where to station reporters, a slew of logistics. I made the decision that nothing important happens in a motorcade, so let's put a camera out at Bergstrom when they land and then we'll pick them up again when they arrive downtown. In those days, there were no satellite feeds to make our coverage easier. All we knew was that Jackie Kennedy was going to the Commodore Perry Hotel to freshen up and change, and JFK would be meeting with donors in the same hotel, then on to the banquet at the auditorium.

And yes, you read that correctly. Neal Spelce decided that *nothing important happens in a motorcade.* History has been unkind to that judgment.

I was having lunch with Austin police chief Bob Miles at the Driskill Hotel, touching base with him about the flurry of events surrounding the Kennedys' appearance in Austin and the functions scheduled for the ranch. The Johnsons had planned to have a barbecue beside the river, and the word was that LBJ was going to take President Kennedy deer hunting. My colleagues had joked that Lyndon would probably hobble a deer with a rope, so they wouldn't have to chase the animal too far. The chief and I were laughing at that scenario when a patrolman came running in and said, "There's been a shooting in Dallas at the presidential motorcade."

Chief Miles and I jumped up and left our food, and I sprinted the

President John F. Kennedy never arrived for a banquet at the Austin Municipal Auditorium on November 22, 1963. *Photo by Bill Malone, Austin History Center, Austin Public Library*

four blocks to the television studio while he headed to the police station. The first reports said that President Kennedy was seriously wounded but not yet declared dead. The CBS network news leaped into the coverage, and when they didn't have something to report, they played funeral dirge music as we waited in horror and suspense. And then came that famous moment when Walter Cronkite removed his glasses, looked at the clock for the exact time—1:00 p.m. Central Standard Time—and choked up as he announced that President John F. Kennedy had died. Many observers have called it the moment when America lost its innocence.

We reporters and staff members were all waiting for word in the newsroom, and we had the same reaction as Walter Cronkite. But we were the only television news broadcaster in Austin, and we were well aware of our responsibilities to local viewers. Our mantra was always *What does this mean for Austin?* I took a camera crew to the auditorium, where workers were setting up for the big banquet. The tables were all nicely arranged and everything was ready for the Kennedys. When we got there, the wait staff was crying; people on the street were crying; and we interviewed many of them.

Although we KTBC reporters were in shock and mourning for the loss of our president, a key concern was that Texas governor John Connally had also been shot and was seriously wounded. CBS News was covering the national tragedy, and we felt it was our duty to cover the assassination's impact on Texas. After all, Nellie and John Connally had been in the car with the Kennedys, and the Johnsons had been in a trailing car. Connally was our governor, and thousands of Austin government employees were directly or indirectly affected by his condition.

At KTBC, we had two major news sources: CBS News and United Press International (UPI). Our teletype machine was ringing nonstop—*ding ding ding*—and we were reading everything that came across the wire and watching TV continuously for hours and hours. We were absorbing information, chasing down leads, and generating our own stories. We wanted viewers to dial Channel 7 for updates about Governor Connally. For the next several days, we broke into the CBS national coverage to inform our viewers how he was recovering.

Julian Read was the press aide to Governor Connally, and Julian was in charge of the Texas press corps, which had merged with the White House press corps when they were in Dallas that day. Julian had been riding on the press bus in the motorcade, and he'd watched the JFK limousine turn onto Houston Street shortly before he heard the gunshots. We knew that Julian was in Dallas, so we contacted him as soon as we could get through. We also connected with George Dillman, a Connally volunteer who'd helped set up an office in Parkland Hospital near the governor's room to handle the business of state and to coordinate information about his condition.

At that point, there were many serious questions that troubled our city and our state. First and foremost, was Lieutenant Governor Preston Smith taking over, or was Connally able to carry out his duties? For twenty-four hours after the governor was shot, it was uncertain if he would survive.

Governor Connally was surrounded by a very capable team—aides Howard Rose, George Christian, Larry Temple, John Mobley, Mike Myers, and Julian Read. Because of their capable, take-charge leadership, it wasn't necessary for the lieutenant governor to assume power. The Connally staff impressed LBJ during those first weeks following the tragedy, and after he was in the White House, President Johnson tapped Larry

Julian Read, aide to Texas governor John Connally, briefed the press on Nellie Connally's account of the shooting that killed JFK and seriously wounded her husband in the presidential limousine. Read was only a few vehicles back in the motorcade when the shots were fired. Fort Worth Star-Telegram Collection, *Special Collections, The University of Texas at Arlington Libraries*

Temple as his general counsel and George Christian as his White House press secretary, both with the full support of Governor Connally.

When the Secret Service was interviewing people to vet them for the White House counsel job, they contacted me about Larry Temple. It's standard procedure. For security clearances, they interview everybody they can. But to my surprise and displeasure, the Secret Service agent revealed information about Larry that he shouldn't have disclosed. It was nothing negative. But I thought, "He shouldn't be telling me this. He ought to be keeping his findings private." It struck me as inappropriate, so I made a phone call after he left, and that agent was reassigned.

In one of our earliest stories after the assassination, our news crew went to the Johnson ranch to show the preparations that had been underway and what had been scheduled to take place there with the Ken-

LBJ press secretary George Christian and I shared many laughs and stories during our decades of close friendship. *Photo courtesy Headliners Club*

nedys. Cactus Pryor was in charge of the program, and the ranch staff had been extremely busy getting ready for the event. Cactus told a story about Zephyr Wright, the cook at the ranch, who was really upset about the tragedy and said, "Who's going to eat the pie I baked for President Kennedy?"

Small, poignant things like that popped into people's minds. The assassination was traumatizing. It was huge. The Kennedy presidency had been an enchanting, storybook presidency for so many Americans. People were still using the word "Camelot."

As a reporter, you have to remove yourself from the overwhelming emotions surrounding an event like that and report on the event itself. At journalism school, I'd been taught that you didn't make yourself part of the story. In this case, I was able to avoid doing that, although I was deeply disturbed by what had happened in Dallas and my emotions were raw. But a reporter had a job to do. So you sucked it up and pulled yourself together and did it. You put your own feelings aside for as long as it took. I don't know that it was a conscious thing. When you went home at night, the chaos and frustrating search for the truth sometimes caught up with you and caved in on you, despite the comfort of loved ones. But then you got up the next morning and went after it again.

In television, you're the eyes and ears for the people who are watching you on a screen, and you've got to tell them what's going on. That's ingrained in being a reporter. It's part of your psyche and how you go about your work. You need to establish the facts and be as clear-headed as you can be, no matter what the circumstances or your personal feelings and biases. You practice that almost daily in the news business. Even for mundane stories—Who's speaking at the Rotary Club luncheon? What's on the agenda of today's city council meeting? What happened in police arrests overnight and what's in the coroner's report?—you have to listen carefully. You show respect for every story, even the boring ones, because at some point you'll have to decide what's newsworthy and what's not.

When the assassination occurred, Retired Admiral Bob Inman was serving on the national security staff stationed at the White House, and he told me later that when they received word of the events in Dallas, they scrambled to find out if there was an international conspiracy. Cuba? Russia? He said, "We determined within a few hours that there was no direct connection that we could see at that time."

Conspiracy theories began spreading immediately. People were wondering who was involved and why. How could that have happened in the United States of America? Was there more than one shooter? What led him to do that? Even today, whenever you hear about a mass shooting or major tragedy, all of these questions pop up instantaneously, just as they did back in 1963.

In the first few hours after the assassination, when LBJ was rushed to Love Field and Air Force One, preparing to return to Washington, he said, "I'm not leaving here without President Kennedy's body." And then he added, "Get me Bill Moyers. Bring him up here."

When LBJ took the presidential oath of office aboard Air Force One in Dallas following JFK's assassination, Bill Moyers (in the background wearing glasses) is the only one pictured who is still alive as of this writing. Bill was hastily flown from Austin—as it turns out, breaking a state law—to take the flight to Washington as a new member of LBJ's White House staff. *LBJ Library photo by Cecil Stoughton*

Bill Moyers was—and continues to be—very articulate and a man of eloquent words. LBJ was both fascinated by and dependent on Bill, and he wanted him close by that day. But Moyers was in Austin, having lunch with Ben Barnes, a state representative and future Speaker of the Texas House of Representatives and lieutenant governor of Texas, and a law had to be broken to transport Moyers to Dallas.

The Texas Department of Public Safety (DPS) had its own airplanes, so Barnes called the director of DPS to put Bill Moyers on a plane and fly him to Love Field immediately. It was against the law to use a state plane for that purpose, but they did it anyway.

In the iconic photographs of LBJ being sworn into office aboard Air Force One, with Jackie beside him in her pink outfit, Bill Moyers is standing far in the background, wearing glasses. At this writing, he's the only person still alive from those photographs.

Liz Carpenter, Mrs. Johnson's press secretary and staff director, was also on the plane and played a key role, although she didn't appear in the photographs. When Air Force One was nearing Andrews Air Force Base (now Joint Base Andrews) near Washington, DC, returning with President Kennedy's body, LBJ asked Liz to write a statement for him to read when the plane landed.

Liz was a journalist and speechwriter, and she wrote those historic fifty-eight words on a 3x5 index card, and then typed them on a manual typewriter. These were the first official words delivered by the newly sworn-in president, Lyndon Baines Johnson: "This is a sad time for all people. We have suffered a loss that cannot be weighed. For me, it is a deep personal tragedy. I know that the world shares the sorrow that Mrs. Kennedy and her family bear. I will do my best. That is all I can do. I ask for your help and God's."

That card is in the LBJ Library, and visitors can see his handwriting in pencil where he went through and made a change or two. In deference to the Kennedy family—and because his Texas momma had taught him good manners—Lyndon Johnson waited until they removed JFK's body from the plane before he stepped out and read that statement to the world.

THE ZAPRUDER FILM

Dan Rather was in Dallas on November 22, 1963, and he was given a look at the disturbing 8mm Zapruder film that showed President Kennedy being struck by gunshots. Dan was the reporter who first described the film to the world, a vivid word picture almost frame by frame. He described the trauma to the president's head, John Connally slumping over, and Jackie Kennedy climbing toward the back of the convertible to reach Secret Service agent Clint Hill. Through Dan Rather's description, the nation was able to visualize those fateful moments several days before thirty frames of the Zapruder film were published in *Life* magazine.

At the time, many people wondered how Dan had such quick access to the film, which Abraham Zapruder had given to a Secret Service officer for processing. I know the answer: through good shoe-leather reporting by Dan and his CBS team, he actually reviewed the film in Zapruder's home.

As I mentioned earlier in the book, Eddie Barker, Dan Rather, and I had formed a small consortium of Texas TV news directors, and we knew one another very well. When I went to Dallas after the assassination to report on Governor Connally's condition, I checked in with Eddie. He said, "Neal, do you want to see the Zapruder film?" To this day, I don't know how he got his hands on a copy of the film. But I said, "Hell yeah, I do."

Eddie and I were alone in the KRLD newsroom, just the two of us, when I watched those final tragic seconds of President Kennedy's life, including frame 313 and the fatal head shot. I was absolutely shocked by what I witnessed. I'd never seen anything like the president's violent death. The brutality, the rawness, the terrible finality. I'd met President Kennedy at Hyannis Port, and there was a photograph of me shaking his hand. We'd had a pleasant conversation. I couldn't believe that the witty, dapper president I'd liked so much had been killed in such a ruthless and distressing way.

The public wouldn't be shown the upsetting frame 313 until 1975, twelve years after I'd seen it. That image stayed with me for those dozen years, and it has stayed with me ever since. Like everyone else, I've wondered what the world would've been like if John Kennedy hadn't been assassinated that day in Dallas.

A CONTROVERSIAL PRESIDENT

After the assassination, President Johnson took office under difficult circumstances. All the Kennedy loyalists who were still serving in the federal government had lost their beloved leader. They revered JFK, and suddenly LBJ was in charge, a crass Texan they'd never liked or respected. Especially Bobby Kennedy, the president's brother and attorney general. There was an irreconcilable tension between him and Lyndon Johnson.

LBJ asked many of the cabinet members to stay on and carry forward JFK's legacy, and they did, to a great extent. But that still didn't mollify the personal feelings. Fortunately for the new president, those feelings weren't shared by every member of the Kennedy family. LBJ enjoyed a very good lifelong relationship with Senator Ted Kennedy, and for years, Mrs. Johnson and Jackie Kennedy spent private evenings together—just the two of them—during summers at Martha's Vineyard.

I covered the 1964 Democratic National Convention in Atlantic City, when LBJ was nominated for president, a foregone conclusion. There was the usual hoopla—the music, the banners, the delegates in silly costumes and funny hats, a cacophony of Americana and pure political theater. The only major controversy was a credentials dispute over the seating of a predominately black delegation from Mississippi that challenged the legality of the state's all-white, segregationist delegation. The delegation dispute outraged Lyndon Johnson. He had desperately wanted unity and a conflict-free convention. In the end, LBJ sided with the all-white delegation from Mississippi in a futile attempt to placate the all-white delegations from the other Deep South states. The controversy, however, planted seeds that sprouted in 1965 as the Voting Rights Act.

I was nosing around and somehow I obtained a copy of the campaign song that was going to be unveiled later in the convention. It was "Hello, Lyndon," a spoof on Carol Channing's popular "Hello, Dolly," which she'd perfected in a new Broadway musical of the same title.

When I phoned in my report to KTBC, I said, "I have a copy of the campaign song. It's not public yet, but I can tell you it goes something like this." And I sang, "Well hell-ooo, Lyndon," trying to mimic Carol Channing. They ran it on the air. It was silly, of course, but as a reporter you try to capture the flavor of such things. I thought I did a passable imitation of Carol Channing's voice, but to my disappointment, I didn't receive any offers to become her understudy.

Despite solid opposition in the Deep South, LBJ won reelection by one of the biggest landslides in American history.

For many, the passage of time has made it easier to examine LBJ's record. The personal feelings toward him have become less insistent over the decades. The people in the northeastern centers of power didn't like this Texan with his drawl and crude behavior. He just didn't feel right to them. And the southern segregationists despised his support of civil rights. But critics and historians sit back now, without hearing or seeing the man on a TV screen, and they acknowledge the tremendous social and political change he accomplished.

LBJ frequently told the story of a Wall Street banker who emerged from the subway and stopped at a newsstand every day. (An audio recording of this story is available in his presidential library archives.) The banker always tossed his money beside the stack of papers, picked up the *New York Times*, glanced at the front page, then returned the paper without opening it. One day, the newsstand operator asked the banker why he paid for the paper every day but only glanced at the front page. The banker replied that he was only interested in the obituaries. The newsstand operator pointed out that the obits were on the inside of the paper. The Wall Street banker said, "When the bastard I'm interested in dies, it'll be on the front page."

LBJ made it clear that he was the butt of that joke as he told the story with a wide grin.

After spending several years knowing and covering Lyndon Johnson, I ultimately realized he was a very sensitive man. He cared what people said and thought about him. But he was stubborn and dedicated to his principles, and he plowed straight ahead and tried his damnedest to get his opponents and those who didn't agree with him to find common ground. His favorite quotation was from Isaiah 1:18 in the Bible: "Come now, and let us reason together." And in his better moments, that was the way he conducted his presidency.

JAKE PICKLE: MEAT-AND-POTATOES GUY

I began covering J. J. "Jake" Pickle in the late 1950s, when I was a reporter for KTBC and he was chairman of what was officially called the State Democratic Executive Committee (SDEC). I watched him at work for his party, and later as a candidate, and I admired him. Why? He was a pragmatic public servant who adamantly supported his constituents and his university. Over time, I got to know him personally and began to like him very much. Who didn't like Jake Pickle? (Okay, I can name a few. After all, he was a politician.)

Born in 1913 in the small West Texas town of Roscoe and raised in Big Spring, he attended UT Austin as a championship swimmer. (I never understood how a great swimmer could hail from dry, dusty West Texas.)

He and John Connally became friends at UT, each serving as student body president, and when they returned from combat in World War II, they founded the KVET AM radio station (the "VET" because they were veterans) with other veteran business partners in Austin.

Jake admired Lyndon Johnson and considered him a mentor, and he worked for LBJ's campaigns in the 1940s. They became friends and domino partners on the campaign trail, and when LBJ was elected president, he often invited Jake to come play dominoes in the White House.

Jake used to joke that during the early campaigns, he was LBJ's hat catcher. When Candidate Johnson stepped off a helicopter and made a stump speech, declaring, "I want your vote! Send me to Washington! Thanks for coming out! Yeeee-hah!" and threw his hat into the crowd, it was Jake's job to fetch that hat and bring it back. He once told me, "I had a few scuffles over the hat."

In the first seventy years of the twentieth century, very few Republicans were elected to office in Texas, and observers joked that the GOP could hold its conventions in a phone booth. The state was dominated by the Democratic Party, and whoever won the Democratic primary would win the general election.

But the Texas Dems had two contentious divisions, conservative and progressive. (Some wags would've said conservative and less conservative.) Governors Allan Shivers and John Connally represented the more conservative side, and the progressives were represented by leaders like Senator Ralph Yarborough and Frankie Randolph, cofounder of the *Texas Observer*.

For most of the 1950s, Jake Pickle was a partner in the advertising firm of Syers, Pickle and Winn. It was responsible for producing a pro-Shivers, anti-Yarborough television ad in 1954. So when Jake was selected to head the SDEC, he was labeled as a member of the Shivers-Connally conservative camp.

While raising money for the SDEC, Jake encountered opposition from liberals and labor unions whose slogan was "Dollars for Democrats, But Not a Nickel for Pickle." They didn't want to contribute financial support to what they perceived as the dominating conservative wing of the party, and they set up their own separate account.

But Jake was a political anomaly. He was a longtime supporter of LBJ, who transcended those divisions within the Texas Democratic Party, which meant that in reality, Jake Pickle straddled the line with a foot on each side.

Jake wasn't a big-time lawyer or a wealthy oil man; he was a party aficionado. He wasn't a visionary; he was a workhorse. He wasn't an out-front sort of guy. But in 1963, he decided to run for office in a special election for LBJ's former Tenth Congressional District seat. Homer Thornberry had succeeded LBJ but had resigned the position when he was appointed as a US district court judge.

Jake's Republican opponent was conservative Jim Dobbs, a former minister who bought billboard ads that said, "Let's Beat Lyndon's Boy, Jake." Visually, the ads looked like this:

Let's Beat—
L—Lyndon's
B—Boy
J—Jake

So it also read, "Let's Beat LBJ." In essence, Dobbs was campaigning against Lyndon Johnson and linking Jake to the vice president. The Dobbs campaign rented a billboard for the message right outside the KTBC-TV studio, which, of course, was owned by the Johnson family. You could throw a rock from the station's door and hit that billboard. They were trying to rub it in the noses of the LBJ family.

Jake was running in that special election in November 1963 when John

Former Texas governor Allan Shivers represented the more conservative wing of the Texas Democratic Party. In spite of disagreeing with LBJ on many political issues, he was often a guest at LBJ Ranch events. *Photo by Neal Spelce*

F. Kennedy was assassinated in Dallas. I was on the air all day covering the president's death and the serious condition of Governor Connally, and as I left the TV station around midnight that Friday night, wiped out physically and mentally, the first thing I noticed was that the Dobbs billboard ad had been taken down. Someone had removed it that day. His campaign staff must've realized it was inappropriate under the circumstances. The nation needed to rally around the new president, Lyndon Baines Johnson, who was thrust into the monumental job of holding our traumatized country together. After those shots were fired in Dallas, all of the Dobbs billboards came down, and Jake Pickle won the special election in December.

One of Jake's most important—and very first—votes in 1964 was on the Civil Rights Act. LBJ called him personally and said, "Jake, I need your vote. I've got to have it on this civil rights package."

Jake told me, "That was totally against everything my district stood for at the time. But I voted for it. First of all, I believed in it. I think the country needed it. And my president asked me to do it." He was one of only eight southern representatives to vote for the landmark Civil Rights Act of 1964.

Jake wasn't doctrinaire. He always had a practical sense about him: Let's do what we have to do and get things done. If we have to compromise, we'll compromise.

As a television reporter in the 1960s, I was around him a lot because we covered his campaigns and his votes. Back in those days, the news media mingled with politicians and state leaders. We'd gather at the Headliners Club in Austin, a popular spot, and some elected official would say, "Neal, come on over here and have a drink." The same thing took place in Washington, with Sam Rayburn, Everett Dirksen, and LBJ swapping jokes and having a drink together, even though they might be on opposite sides on a particular bill. Friendships were separate from political views.

We in the media knew that generation of politicians and their idiosyncrasies and occasional indiscretions. History has shown that there were "gentlemen's agreements" back then, for better or worse, between the media and elected officials, and we didn't report improprieties nearly as much as reporters do today. Certain types of personal behavior were treated as off limits by the press. "Oh, well, that's so and so. That's the way he is." But if it didn't impact the job he was doing in office, we left it alone.

I've never agreed with any politician 100 percent of the time. Some congressional representatives go to Washington and get caught up in the glamour and bright camera lights of the Washington scene. But for those who focus on getting the work done, it can be difficult to decide what to spend time on—issues that affect the entire nation, or issues for your own district, such as fighting for a bridge or a hospital. In my view, Jake Pickle was the best combination of both: a political leader who took care of his constituents back home and was an active voice in important national issues.

If someone in his district raised a question or wanted something done, they got a response the same day. He did whatever he could to help the citizens of Central Texas, often in support of the region's economic development and high-tech emergence. As a loyal graduate, he called the University of Texas at Austin "my university" and the Longhorns "my team." To honor the congressman for his decades of securing major financial support for research projects at UT Austin, the university renamed its pioneering Balcones Research Center as the J. J. Pickle Research Campus in 1994.

Jake helped me on one very important issue that still has major repercussions for Central Texas today. When I became chair of the Austin Chamber of Commerce in 1980, the executive director was Vic Mathias, who asked me, "Do you have anything special that you'd like to accomplish during your term? What would you like to work on?" I maintained that to improve the Austin economy, "We need to have our airport designated as an international port of entry."

In those days, you couldn't fly internationally to or from Austin's small Robert Mueller Airport. There was a popular joke at the time: If you die and go to hell, you'll still have to change planes in Dallas.

It was bad for Austin's businesses. They couldn't ship goods internationally or receive products and parts from other countries. They had to go to San Antonio, Houston, or Dallas to pick up the parts or to ship their products out. And it was difficult for leisure travelers as well.

When we checked into it, there were a lot of airports ahead of Austin for consideration as international ports of entry. So we called Jake Pickle and he jumped on it, and by the time my term at the chamber of com-

Congressman Jake Pickle was instrumental in helping meet my goal as Chamber of Commerce president in 1980 by securing international port of entry designation for Austin's airport. *Photo courtesy Headliners Club*

merce was over at the end of that year, we were able to announce that Austin had just received the designation. It was a major coup for our city, and it wouldn't have happened without Jake Pickle's influence and power of persuasion.

In the national arena, Jake was well known for his efforts in tax reform, in broadening student loans in higher education, and in increasing federal funding for research in science and engineering. As chairman of the Social Security Subcommittee of the House Committee on Ways and Means, he fought to improve Social Security benefits and to preserve that massive federal program and keep it from being weakened.

Jake had a great sense of humor, and everywhere he went, he would shake hands and hand out small plastic pickles that squeaked when you squeezed them. They were made by George Nalle at an Austin-based company called Nalle Plastics, which also made pickle-shaped buttons that simply said "Jake" on them.

The ultimate good sport, Jake attended his share of parades in small towns, like the Luling Watermelon Thump or a Christmas parade in Bastrop, and he'd ride in convertibles or sit on floats and throw plastic pickles to the kids.

In physical appearance, Jake wasn't Robert Redford or tall handsome John Connally with his movie star looks. Frankly, Jake was kind of dumpy. Short, unimposing, a meat-and-potatoes guy. When he spoke, he'd nervously rub the back of his head, which meant he was animated and completely engaged in what he was saying.

Jake sometimes gave the impression of not being the sharpest knife in the drawer, and the unaware mistakenly thought of him as a country bumpkin. But he always knew the issues in detail, and he won voters because he was open and gregarious and very much *of* the people and *for* the people.

Jake returned to Austin on weekends to answer phone calls and meet with constituents, and the nonstop Braniff flight from Washington to Austin was nicknamed the Pickle Express. He would walk down the aisle and shake every hand on the flight. He barely ever sat down in his seat.

Back in Austin, he'd go to lunch at the Headliners Club and work the entire room, shaking hands and visiting with the local movers and shakers. He knew most of them by name.

He'd sometimes approach strangers eating in restaurants and say, "Hi, I'm Jake Pickle. I'm your congressman. How you doing? What business are you in? What are your concerns? Can I help you in any way?"

He genuinely enjoyed meeting his constituents. And he usually had an aide following behind him to handle the details. "Paul, let's follow up on that," Jake would say. "Can you get a phone number from these folks?" The family would leave the restaurant saying, "Wow, my congressman's going to help us." And he did.

Jake's friendly, hand-squeezing public persona wasn't a front or a political gag. It was genuine. He'd learned that affable, man-of-the-people style by watching his old mentor and domino partner, Lyndon Johnson—the master of shirtsleeve diplomacy. Although less charismatic than LBJ, Jake had his own approach to leadership that suited him very

As a member of Congress, Jake Pickle, center, next to Hillary Clinton, campaigned for candidate Bill Clinton in August 1992. *Photo by Larry Murphy, UT Office of Public Affairs Records, Briscoe Center for American History, the University of Texas at Austin*

well as he served his Central Texas district with great distinction for more than thirty years.

Loyalty over a Bowl of Chili

Loyalty was crucially important to LBJ, but that loyalty was sometimes tested. Three of LBJ's staunchest loyalists were Congressman Jake Pickle, who'd been elected to LBJ's old congressional seat in Central Texas; Austin attorney Ed Clark; and George Christian, who would eventually serve as White House press secretary.

It helped if an LBJ loyalist had a sense of humor. George Christian certainly did, and he told a story to a group of us at a meeting of the Headliners Foundation Board of Directors in 2002 that still brings a smile to my face.

When LBJ was campaigning throughout Texas with Ed Clark and

Jake Pickle, he suggested that the three of them stop for a bowl of chili in Giddings, a small town fifty-five miles east of Austin. LBJ loved spicy food, especially the kind of chili that will make your eyes water and sweat pop out on your brow as you grab for a cold beer to ease the burn. On that occasion, LBJ loved his bowl of red-hot chili so much he ordered another round for the three of them.

According to George Christian, Ed Clark had struggled with the first bowl. Clark spoke in a high, squeaky voice with a bit of a lisp and a drawl from his small-town East Texas upbringing. He said, "Lyndon, I have traveled the dusty roads of Texas for you. I have danced with ugly women for you. I have shed tears over the faces of dead men I didn't know for you. But Lyndon, I'll be damned if I'll eat another bowl of that chili!"

Ed Clark survived this show of "disloyalty" and ended up serving as the ambassador to Australia during LBJ's presidency.

THE HEADLINERS CLUB: "NOT WHO, BUT WHAT"

L iquor by the drink was against the law in Texas for most of the twentieth century. You couldn't walk into a restaurant or bar and order a martini or a margarita. It was a frustration to business leaders, out-of-state travelers, most politicians, and non-Baptists from El Paso to Orange.

So in the early 1950s, three Austin leaders—Charlie Green, the editor of the *Austin Statesman*; Paul Bolton, the news director at KTBC-TV; and prominent Austin attorney Everett Looney—decided to form a private club, which was the only kind of establishment where an adult could order a mixed beverage. They named it the Headliners Club.

Soon after the club was chartered in August 1954, the "general membership committee" sent out a memo that read, "The Headliners Club will be an expanded downtown press club. Voting members will include the headliners in press, radio, television, business and professional groups, government officials, educators, etc. We figure such a club will become the crossroads of discussion as concerns our city, county, state, nation. We may even take in the world."

Women were not accepted into the club at first. The ostensible reason was that there weren't many female reporters or elected officials at the time. But that would eventually change.

The Headliners Club had two hundred founding members but no physical watering hole until early 1955, when remodeling of the Driskill Hotel annex was completed. A grand opening gala took place in April of that year in the Driskill ballroom, and Hollywood celebrities Greer Garson, Dana Andrews, and director Mervyn LeRoy joined the festivities.

I was inducted as a member of the club in the early 1960s, when I was still in my twenties, and I served as president in 1965. In those early days, Charlie Green just tapped people he liked on the shoulder and invited them to join. I tell the joke that I was so young I lied to Charlie about my age so I could drink legally.

The Headliners Club gave this young Austin newsman the opportunity to rub shoulders with the city's and state's movers and shakers and

Cactus Pryor and I surprised and embarrassed NBC-TV anchor Chet Huntley during a roast by playing a video of him that we secretly taped. Austin American-Statesman *photo courtesy Headliners Club*

opinion-makers. I was becoming a "headliner" because of my public exposure as a TV anchor, and there were times when the club was the best place to find a news source or an expert in any given field. Or just someone wise and experienced who could inform me about the history of a famous local oak tree, what the engineers were working on at that research center on the northern outskirts of town, or what was the secret ingredient in a Frisco Burger at the Night Hawk restaurant.

Every respectable club has a fancy Latin motto, and the Headliners' is "Non Quis, Sed Quid," which translates as "Not Who, But What." It makes clear that wealth and family name don't matter, but rather, what you've accomplished in life. I appreciated that. It meant that a young man raised by a single mother in small-town Arkansas could be accepted into the company of successful individuals if he'd made something of himself and earned their respect.

The popular Headliners Club eventually outgrew the Driskill annex and in 1966 moved to the spacious top floor of the Westgate Building, a high-rise just west of the Capitol, accommodating the legislators, state officials, and Capitol press corps a block away. But the city of Austin was growing rapidly and so was Headliners membership, and eight years later, the club moved again to its permanent place on the twenty-first floor of the American Bank Tower at West Sixth Street and Lavaca.

Membership has its privileges. I defy the adult-beverage aficionados of Austin to find a better old-fashioned than the ones served at the Headliners Club. And it's said that the velvet hammer drink was invented there.

Celebrity roasts were gold mines at the Headliners Club, such as this one with Academy Award-winning actor Gregory Peck, Governor John Connally, and MC extraordinaire Cactus Pryor. *Photo courtesy Headliners Club*

TV anchor Dan Rather, sportscaster Verne Lundquist, and I created a live satirical newscast for the Headliners Club's 60th anniversary gala on November 1, 2015. *Photo courtesy Headliners Club*

There's an old joke about the bank of urinals in the men's room at the club. The urinals face a wide glass wall that provides a great view of the city, and some wags have suggested that it was constructed that way so the members can look out and piss on Austin. That rumor became so prevalent that on several occasions, male club members were pressured into showing the urinals to curious wives and female friends. I myself succumbed to that request one day. I made sure the men's room was completely vacant before escorting my future wife, Connie, to see the magnificent view.

THE WHITE HOUSE ON THE PEDERNALES

Most presidents have elegant, candle-lit state dinners in the White House with fine china and polished silver and crystal goblets, accompanied by lovely string music and woodwinds. That's all well and good, and President and Mrs. Johnson certainly did have formal state dinners like that at the White House. But it was something special if a political leader was invited to the ranch. That honor was reserved for only the most important dignitaries.

The ranch barbecues were legendary. They were always a very big production, and LBJ would lay it on heavy. Even the national flags representing foreign visitors would fly over the ranch grounds.

Liz Carpenter was one of the funniest people I've ever met, and she organized those events at the ranch. The festivities took place outdoors, along the banks of the Pedernales River and its long grassy slopes. The stream was controlled by a dam, the water always flowing calmly past the party site. Whenever needed, large tents were erected to shelter guests against the rain or scorching hot sunshine.

For entertainment on one occasion, Liz hired a guy from the Hill Country who raised dogs, sheep, and monkeys. He would put small saddles on the dogs and set monkeys on the saddles, dressed up in cowboy outfits with hats, and then those dog-monkey combos would run around and herd the sheep. To the casual observer, it looked like the cowboy monkeys were riding high and doing their job as sheep wranglers, but in reality they were hanging on for dear life. Only in Texas. The spectacle was both hilarious and bizarre.

On another occasion, Liz brought in actors and horses from an outdoor musical extravaganza called *Texas* that was being staged for tourists in Palo Duro Canyon, south of Amarillo. The cast danced and sang for the ranch guests, and it was like watching a Broadway play in your backyard.

The Johnsons had a favorite caterer, pitmaster Walter Jetton out of Fort Worth, the acclaimed "King of Barbecue," and Walter would do it up right. He would add the extra touches—benches, red tablecloths, and

Mexico's President and Mrs. Gustavo Díaz Ordaz were typical of world leaders hosted by President and Mrs. Lyndon Johnson at the LBJ Ranch. *Photo by Neal Spelce*

red cowboy bandanas for the guests so they would get into the Texas spirit. Walter would have a fire going with a calf roasting on a spit, but you didn't eat that, it was there for show.

After the 1964 Democratic National Convention, there was a big gathering at the ranch, and it was reminiscent of the campaign-planning meetings at Hyannis Port four years earlier, when JFK and LBJ were chosen as the Democratic ticket. The ranch was mobbed with reporters—the White House press corps, the Capitol press corps from Austin, the networks and wire services. Everyone was there to cover the kickoff of the campaign.

LBJ had chosen Senator Hubert Humphrey of Minnesota as his vice presidential running mate. Humphrey was known as "the Happy Warrior" because of his charm and sense of humor. He was a great sport and easy to laugh. Khakis were what LBJ always wore around the ranch, so he

LBJ's daughters Lynda (left) and Luci acted as genial co-hosts at various LBJ Ranch events. *Photos by Neal Spelce*

Fort Worth's Walter Jetton, LBJ's favorite barbecue caterer, did it up right "with all the fixin's" for ranch guests. *Photo by Neal Spelce*

VP nominee Hubert Humphrey, looking uncomfortable in LBJ's favorite ranch garb of kha-kis and Stetson hats, joined LBJ on horseback to greet reporters at the ranch following their party's nomination in 1964. *Photo by Neal Spelce*

decided to dress up Humphrey as an LBJ twin—khaki pants and khaki jacket with a tie, boots, and LBJ's trademark Stetson 6X Open Road fur felt cowboy hat.

I don't know if Humphrey had ever been on a horse before. He looked awkward riding and waving his hat beside a seasoned Texas horseman, and I'm sure the future vice president realized he looked ridiculous, like Michael Dukakis trying to appear manly and fearless with his head stick-ing out of an armored tank. But Humphrey went along with the stunt with his usual grace and humor, and he won admirers for being a team player. He was a loyal devotee to LBJ, and if they'd tossed him into the Pedernales wearing that outfit, he would've been happy to oblige.

It's strange to recall that our nation had no vice president for the four-teen months between the assassination of President Kennedy and Lyn-don Johnson's inauguration as president in January 1965. (The Twenty-Fifth Amendment to the Constitution, adopted in 1967, establishes clear procedures for presidential succession.)

LBJ invited the first two chancellors of West Germany, Konrad Ad-enauer and Ludwig Erhard, to the ranch, because he wanted them to appreciate and enjoy the deep German heritage in the Hill Country and

An aide wiped spilled barbecue sauce off West German Chancellor Ludwig Erhard's suit at a ranch meeting with LBJ. *Photo by Neal Spelce*

Central Texas. (I snapped a photograph of Chancellor Erhard with barbecue sauce on his suit.) On separate occasions, LBJ took them to Fredericksburg, only a twenty-minute drive from the ranch, a town that was founded by German immigrants in 1846 and named after Prince Frederick of Prussia.

In the old market square there's an octagonal-shaped structure called the Vereins Kirche (Society Church), a replica of the earliest church in Fredericksburg. To everyone's surprise, the world-renowned pianist Van Cliburn was waiting inside for the chancellor and LBJ's entourage. Van Cliburn was a Texan and the first American to win Moscow's International Tchaikovsky Piano Competition. When the group walked into the Vereins Kirche, they found the pianist sitting in tux and tails at a grand piano. When he flipped back his tails to begin the performance, the German guests saw he was sitting on a bale of hay. It was that extra little

Texas classical pianist Van Cliburn performed his award-winning Tchaikovsky's Piano Concerto no. 1 for ranch guests gathered in nearby Fredericksburg, using a hay bale as his piano bench. *Photo by Neal Spelce*

touch that said, "You're in Texas, *meine Freunde.*" And then with his usual dignity, grace, and physical energy, Van Cliburn played Tchaikovsky's Piano Concerto no. 1, the masterpiece that had made him the toast of Moscow and the Russian people in 1958.

On one occasion when I was out at the ranch with a television camera crew for a minor function, I noticed Jim Wright, the US Speaker of the House from Fort Worth and a close ally of LBJ, swimming in the pool. Wright was a man of great ambition, and he was thinking about running for the US Senate. I said to the crew, "Let's go talk to him about his upcoming campaign."

We wandered over and I said, "Mr. Speaker, do you mind if we interrupt your swim? Can you step out of the pool? Let's talk about your race for the Senate."

"Sure, Neal, don't mind at all." He recognized free publicity when he saw it walking toward him.

He climbed out soaking wet and stood at the edge of the pool. It was a straightforward interview. "Mr. Speaker, how's your race going for the US Senate?"

He began to pontificate. *We've got a lot of support. We're doing this, we're doing that.*

His swimsuit had dropped down so you could see his navel, and the camera cropped the picture just below that, so it looked like I was interviewing a naked Jim Wright. I couldn't see what was in the camera, and of course Speaker Wright couldn't either.

"Thank you, Mr. Speaker," I said, wrapping up.

"You bet, Neal. Glad to do it."

When we processed the film back at the studio, it was hilarious. We ran it on the air, and we explained that the interview was poolside, but he could have been skinny dipping for all the viewers knew. Jim Wright had a good sense of humor, and he laughed about being "nekkid" on TV.

LBJ went to the ranch frequently, and because the White House press corps followed him wherever he went, he would hold news conferences out there. At one news conference, I was part of the press corps inside the house, in his office, and he was leaning on his desk as reporters asked questions. I felt something in my hand and realized that George Reedy, who was LBJ's press secretary, had slipped me a piece of paper. I looked at George and he nodded. I read the note quickly and saw it was a question

JFK press aides Andrew Hatcher and Pierre Salinger conferring before an outdoor press conference at the LBJ Ranch. *Photo by Neal Spelce*

Secretary of State Dean Rusk was one of many JFK cabinet members to remain in the LBJ administration. *Photo by Neal Spelce*

LBJ conducted a press conference in his LBJ Ranch office where I agreed to ask a planted
question and was embarrassed when it became obvious. *Photo by Neal Spelce*

for the president, but I had no earthly idea what the subject was about. It
was some esoteric foreign policy issue, an arcane topic.

Press secretaries plant questions all the time for a president, usually
something he wants to talk about, and this was one of those questions.
I dutifully read the question, stumbling over the phrases, knowing full
well I didn't understand the issue. It was very obvious I was reading
something I knew nothing about. The press corps started laughing, and

so did LBJ. He made a funny comment—"Pretty good, Neal. You did that so well"—and then answered the question. I was embarrassed, but that kind of thing happens to reporters. It never happened to me again, because LBJ and his press secretary learned their lesson that slipping me a question to ask was not a good idea.

The White House press corps understood the ground rules at the ranch. They'd have a news conference, ask all their questions, get their work done, and then a social hour would follow. In those days, many politicians socialized with the media, unlike today, when there's a vast chasm between the two groups. One afternoon, we reporters were wandering around the ranch with LBJ, adult beverages in hand and talking, and I said, "Mr. President, I was meaning to ask you at the news conference . . ." and asked him a question. He glared at me and said, "Neal, you know the rules. You're not supposed to ask questions outside of the news conference. I don't want you to do that ever again."

The United Press reporter immediately ran off, got on the telephone, and called in a story that said, "Today, LBJ criticized a reporter who works at the TV station that his family owns."

It cleared the wire worldwide, and when I returned to the KTBC newsroom, my colleagues had already ripped it off the wire. Someone had drawn a black *in memoriam* border around the story and tacked it on the bulletin board. My colleagues clapped me on the back, one by one, and said, "Glad to have known you, Spelce."

I had broken the ground rules, but I would live to cover another day.

BOTH SIDES JOURNALISM

When Barry Goldwater was running against LBJ in 1964, the Republican presidential nominee booked a campaign stop in Austin, in the heart of LBJ country. Goldwater was a pilot, and he flew his own plane, a fairly large DC-3. We reporters headed out to the old Mueller airport in East Austin, and when Goldwater rolled to a stop on the landing strip, we were out there with our cameras. His supporters were there, too. He pushed open the pilot window and stuck his head out and waved to the crowd. "I'm glad to be here," he said. "When I took off from Phoenix, they asked me if I'd ever been to Austin and if I knew where it was. I said, 'No, I've never been to Austin, but I'm gonna fly east and when I get to a fairly good-sized city with only one TV tower, I'm going to land.'"

Folks were amazed that I put that on the air because it was "critical of LBJ's family ownership of the KTBC-TV station." But I said, "It was a great quote."

In all the years I was working at KTBC as a reporter and then as news director—making decisions about what stories to air and what not to air—never once did LBJ or the Johnson family give orders to cover this and not that. There were newsworthy events at the LBJ Ranch, and we'd go out there with reporters from all over the nation to cover a prime minister or some other visiting dignitary. That was news. But we were never told "you must come."

In one case, Walter Jenkins, one of LBJ's trusted aides, was arrested for a sexual liaison in a men's room in Washington, DC, and it was a serious scandal. Mrs. Johnson was very supportive of Jenkins, but in spite of her objection, President Johnson accepted the aide's resignation.

I ran with the Jenkins story on the air, and the next day I received a call from *Time* magazine. "Spelce, we're just checking around the country to find out how this Walter Jenkins story was covered. How did you cover it in Austin?"

"We led with it at ten o'clock last night."

The caller said, "You did?"

"It was the top news story of the day," I said, "so we led with it."

They were trying to find out if KTBC had buried the story because it was negative toward LBJ and his family. Our coverage was indicative of how we handled the news at KTBC, even when it wasn't advantageous to our owner.

That objectivity had been instilled in me by the University of Texas School of Journalism and by Paul Bolton. He was a stickler for getting a story accurate before putting it on the air. Get it *first*, if at all possible, but get it *right*, and let people draw their own conclusions based upon what you report. Don't hide it, don't dodge it. If it's out there, it's out there, and it's your job as a reporter—as someone who's conveying important information—to present the facts. The topic doesn't matter. You want the viewers to say, "Wow, I didn't know about that."

Today, there are so many ways for individuals to get news. With the Internet and twenty-four-hour cable news, viewers can go anywhere and find whatever they want to find, with whatever stripe they may want to put on it. But back in the 1950s and 1960s, KTBC was the sole source for television news in Austin and we had a serious obligation to cover it accurately and make sure the facts were correct. I always tell folks, "Don't rely on a single source. Whenever you're looking for news, broaden your scope. If you want to watch a left-leaning channel, watch a right-leaning channel as well, so you can balance your judgments and make up your own mind."

In today's world, that attitude is considered quaint and out of step with current realities. Sometimes I sound like a Pollyanna, even to myself, but that's the way I roll.

In my view, polarization is a problem in our society. Most people watch or read to reinforce their own worldviews. And although they're passionately engaged, they're missing something if they don't explore various websites and check other programs and read this blog or that article. I love to go to the online aggregator sites that represent different viewpoints and report on a variety of subjects. I encourage people to get a more complete picture, so whatever their position may be, it's either reinforced or questioned. It's important to challenge our assumptions and biases.

Now in my seventh decade as a reporter, I'm often asked, "What do you think about that story that broke today, Neal?" I usually respond, "I was fascinated by it." Not believing the story, necessarily, but fascinated by the news itself. After so many years in the business, I've found a way of standing back and looking at things philosophically.

I'm intrigued by what the left does and what the right does and how everybody reacts to that. I don't get caught up in "I'm taking his side, and the other side be damned." I think it goes back to that journalistic training. You're trained to walk into a situation, whatever it may be—a city council meeting, a public hearing on rising water bills, a school shooting—and analyze what's going on, what's newsworthy, what's most important to your audience. And then you write the story. You don't get caught up in "Don't quote this person, but quote this person." The pursuit of balance and objectivity has carried me forward throughout my long career.

News analysts are everywhere now, but they're not really that new. I can remember back in the early days when Eric Sevareid would come on CBS as an analyst and commentator. Dan Rather told me one time, "I envision what happens in Eric Sevareid's life. I can see him waking up, putting on his robe, padding to the front door in his slippers, and picking up several newspapers and reading through them. And then he gets on the phone and says, 'I think I'll talk about this today,' and calls that person and they go have lunch, usually with a martini. And then Eric comes to the office and sits down and writes his piece and records it and goes home. What a life!"

Dan was out there getting punched in the gut, stalked, and shot at, but there's Sevareid having a martini at lunch.

To be fair to Eric Sevareid, he'd covered the fall of Paris to the Germans in World War II and later parachuted into Burma from a crashing airplane, so he deserved those martinis, because he'd earned his status as a commentator. I watched his analysis over the years, and I'm not sure he ever took a hard right or hard left position. He'd say, "Here is this and here is this, too, and there's going to be a big battle over this, and we'll have to watch and wait and see."

A turning point in polarization may have come with the popular "Point-Counterpoint" segment of *60 Minutes*, which aired from 1975 to 1979, a weekly debate between liberal Shana Alexander and conservative James J. Kilpatrick. It was famously satirized on *Saturday Night Live*, with comedian Dan Aykroyd (Kilpatrick) often replying to Jane Curtin (Alexander), "Jane, you ignorant slut." I'm not sure if it was the humorous satire or the "Point-Counterpoint" segment itself, but that formula exploded all over country, a harbinger of the future.

Today there are entire teams of folks out there analyzing, pontificating, and arguing "I'm right, you're wrong." It's sometimes entertaining, but usually produces more heat than light.

After I left daily television, I was often brought back to analyze the voter returns during election night coverage. One evening during a statewide race, I was sitting on the set with the anchor and co-anchor, and I had my yellow pad and pencil in front of me. As election returns came in, it was my job to announce that at 7:00 p.m., this candidate was ahead, and at 8:00 p.m., South Texas had not been counted yet and voting in Houston was heavy. That kind of thing. It's what computers do now, but all I had was a yellow pad and a number two pencil.

The anchor sitting next to me wasn't the brightest bulb on the porch, and when I said, "We'd better keep an eye on this. The margin is narrowing, and it looks like the other candidate may win," he said, "Really, Neal? He's been behind all night long. How can you say something like that?" And I very calmly and quietly said, "Because of the trendline and votes that are still uncounted. South Texas is normally going to go in this direction, and they're not in yet—and that could put this candidate over the top."

That's the kind of pad-and-pencil analysis I did back in the day, and that's the way I like to watch election returns now. But the computers are so far ahead of everybody, they calculate results down to the minute and report, "We can now declare a winner in the congressional district northeast of Dallas." Not to mention, "Hey, California and the West Coast, the election is already over and we've declared a winner. Your vote is superfluous."

The Donald Trump election of 2016 is a great example of how analysis can go awry. All the ratings and data showed that Hillary Clinton was going to win. I'd been watching a lot of television coverage, and I stayed up to speed on what was happening. Two or three days before the election, I made the comment, "Trump can win this." I mentioned that to a pollster who was polling for Trump and the Republicans, and he said, "There's just no way." But I insisted, "I don't think the polls are right."

I'm not claiming credit for predicting Trump's victory, but when I was seeing such large, passionate crowds at his rallies, I tried to figure out, "Who the heck are these folks who are so angry and engaged?" And I realized that those folks were not being polled because they were "anti-media" and "anti-polling"—"I'm not going to talk." Nobody looked at their numbers. But sitting back in my armchair and watching news coverage week after week, I could see what was taking shape. So when I made that "bold prediction," I was dismissed, but it came to pass.

It's the job of the reporter to analyze what's happening with a cold eye to the truth. Polling has become essential, for better or worse, to that highly competitive media world that has emerged over the past thirty years. Unfortunately, the polls sometimes drive public opinion instead of the other way around. I have examined polls, and even conducted polls when I ran my PR firm, and I know that you can direct the results by how you phrase the questions.

When John Connally was running for governor of Texas for the first time in 1962, he was not well known and he was running against a sitting governor, Price Daniel, who was pretty doggone popular. One of Connally's tactics was to encourage his supporters to vote early. It was a unique idea at that time, and reminiscent of what candidates do today. His campaign would contact the *Austin American-Statesman* and other newspapers and say, "I understand there are big crowds at the polling places right now, voting early. You ought to send a reporter out there and find out what's going on."

Of course, it was a set-up. The reporters would ask the early voters, "Who are you voting for?" and the response was usually, "I'm voting for John Connally."

Governor Price Daniel's response was, "My voters can go vote tomorrow."

But the overall effect was it looked like an enthusiastic groundswell for this unknown candidate named John Connally. The press was being manipulated by his campaign. It wasn't the first time that a political campaign had outmaneuvered an opponent, and it certainly wouldn't be the last.

COMPETITION REARS ITS HEAD

In 1965, the Kingsberry family and a group called the Southwest Republic Corporation—its members active in Republican politics—established the first television station in Austin that challenged the Johnson family's market monopoly. The new station was KHFI-TV (UHF Channel 42), and it later switched to Channel 36 and then 24. The group had the financial wherewithal to challenge KTBC, and they hired as general manager the former sports director at KTBC, Dan Love, and brought in a small staff.

ABC and NBC would not take the leap to partner with Channel 42 at first because it was so new and had no audience. The network position was, "Why would we want to give up our audience on KTBC Channel 7?"

KHFI-TV got the leftovers of NBC and ABC, with no CBS at all, so it had a rough time in its early days. But it was a groundbreaking first step and an investment born out of the idea that someone had to compete against the LBJ domination of the Central Texas airways.

One of the members of the Southwest Republic Corporation was Rod Kennedy, who co-owned the KHFI-FM radio station already up and running. Rod would soon launch the popular Chequered Flag music club at Fifteenth and Lavaca in Austin, and in 1972 he started the internationally acclaimed Kerrville Folk Festival.

On campus in the 1950s, Rod and I both ran for the College of Fine Arts student assembly. I was a gung-ho young fraternity guy, and he was a veteran of the Korean War. His campaign picture showed him in his Marine fatigues with a rifle. There were two positions in the assembly, and he and I were both elected.

When cable television first came on the scene in the 1960s, potential companies had to gain city council approval because the channels had to use city utility lines to string their cable. So in order to get the cable franchise, you had to negotiate with the city for permission and pay to run your cable lines on city utility poles. It would've been difficult, if not impossible, for a private company to string its own poles at that time because of private property ownerships.

There was a loud public debate over cable issues. The Johnson family rightly surmised that "if cable is coming here, it's going to reach a lot of folks and we want to be a part of that."

At the time, the Johnsons were represented by UT graduate and highly decorated World War II veteran Frank Denius. They partnered with a Little Rock outfit whose ownership included Arkansas senator Bill Fulbright, the chairman of the Senate Foreign Relations Committee and a fellow Democrat and close friend of LBJ's. The two teams joined forces to form the Capital Cable Company and applied for Austin city approval.

Other companies applied as well. I recall that at one point, the Joseph family, owners of drive-in movie theaters in Austin, hired John Cofer, a large, imposing figure and outstanding local attorney, to represent them. I was covering city hall at that time for KTBC, and John Cofer stood up and said, "I don't understand why cable should be regulated. It's just like a slant oil well. As a cable owner, you put the stick up in the air and you steal signals and you put them on your cable channel."

Slant drilling was a big scandal back in those days. It involved slanting your drill under your neighbor's property, taking oil from their land.

In the beginning, cable was controversial because viewers had to pay for it. On-the-air programs were free, "so why am I going to buy cable when I get free TV stations?" Viewers eventually realized that cable gave them many more attractive options, with movies, in-depth news coverage, a greater variety of sports events, and original programming.

By 1971, there were three different TV stations in Austin, and they were all locally owned. Today, the three major network affiliate stations are owned by outside corporations. I understand the financial aspects of ownership, and it makes economic sense, but outside owners can be clueless about local events and local culture, especially in a place as culturally rich and complex as Austin, Texas.

KTBC, and the other local affiliates that eventually came on the air, were heavily involved in covering local news and events, and we concentrated on local sources that were necessary in helping us say, "This is what's going on in our town. This is what's happening in our community." You don't get that as much now. Some of the more responsible corporate-owned stations do dive into local stories and should be congratulated for that. But the temptation is always, "Let's carry more national news. It's easier for us to access and package. We don't want to get our hands dirty or break a sweat in that Texas heat."

TOWER TRAGEDY

Another shot! The sniper fired three quick, successive shots. Apparently in the length of time it takes to cock the weapon and then . . . Another shot! He just fired another shot and this time . . . Another shot! That's the fifth shot now in about twenty or thirty seconds. He's still situated below the University of Texas clock on the south side. The clock now shows 12:32. And he's coolly and calmly sitting up there firing away . . . generally in our direction.
—Neal Spelce, KTBC on-air report

On August 1, 1966, I was thirty years old and had worked my way up from cub reporter to the news director at KTBC. It was a pretty routine Monday at the station, hotter than hell outside, deep in the heart of a Texas summer. We were going about our regular chores. I did a radiocast every day at noon, and then I'd do the television newscast at six o'clock in the evening.

The newsroom was always chaotic. The teletype ran nonstop, clackety clackety clackety clack, the police radio transmitted voices speaking back and forth, the on-the-air programs were fed into the room. A casual visitor would think, "My gosh, what a commotion." But it all worked. You listened to everything out of one ear as information came into your head, and you became attuned to newsworthy things popping up.

In the midst of all that sound, I heard a dispatcher on the police scanner instructing an Austin Police Department unit to respond to a report about shots being fired at the Tower. My first thought was that he was referring to Tower Drugs north of the University of Texas campus, a drugstore where you might expect a robbery incident.

I turned to Phil Miller, our sports announcer, who was heading to lunch. "Phil, can you go check out that report?" I asked, and he said he would drive over to the campus and have a look around.

In 1966, Austin was not a big city, and the university was often the center of activity. If you didn't work at UT or go to school there, you probably knew somebody who was associated with the institution. It dominated Austin, along with the Texas State Capitol only a mile away.

Completed in 1937, with 28 floors and a symbolic Greek temple at the very top, the University of Texas Tower rises 307 feet above the campus and originally housed the central library's book stacks. Just below the clocks, there's a narrow observation deck that wraps around all four sides of the building with a panoramic view of the city—the pastures and prairies to the east of Austin and the hills to the west. For three decades, the Tower had been the most iconic symbol of the university itself. The clock chimes signaled the time, its carillon bells played every weekday at noon, and its white lights turned burnt orange (the school color) after sports victories and major academic achievements. The Tower could be seen from miles around, and it brought a sense of pride to everyone in the Texas Longhorn family and to anyone who respected what "a university of the first class" meant to our state.

Within minutes after Phil Miller left the station, more reports were coming in on the police radio. "We have another report of a shot fired." And they kept saying "the Tower."

We carried the CBS radio national newscast for a couple of minutes every day at noon, the top of the hour, and then returned to do the local news. That day I went in first, before the national news, and issued a bulletin: "Good afternoon. This is Neal Spelce. We have a report of a shooting at the University of Texas. We'll get you those details right after CBS."

At that point, we knew it was a serious situation and that multiple gunshots had been fired. We had no idea about the scope of the incident, but we knew it wasn't people mistaking a firecracker for a gunshot. The police radio activity confirmed what was taking place.

Joe Roddy was the KTBC radio news director and a former manager for Gordon McLendon's radio stations. Joe and I sometimes overlapped in our work. I did some radio news and he did some TV news, because we really were an integrated news department. I said, "Joe, you want to head over to UT and see what's going on?"

He took one of the three mobile units we called Red Rovers and rushed to the campus, then reported back to me: "Ambulances are running everywhere up here. I'm going to the hospital to cover it there."

That left nobody at the scene except Phil Miller, who didn't have a way to communicate except by using a landline telephone. There were no cellphones in 1966, of course, and no easy way to report live situations.

Realizing that we had to have someone at the scene besides Phil, I dashed outside wearing a suit and tie, jumped into another Red Rover

I did my entire live broadcast of the UT Tower shooting on a "push-to-talk" microphone tethered to the KTBC mobile unit. *Photo by Joe Lee*

station wagon, and started driving toward campus. By then, Phil was in the middle of the action and had reported the overall picture: gunshots being fired, pedestrians dodging bullets, students ducking and running for cover, bodies on the ground. We didn't yet have any idea of fatalities.

There was a two-way radio in Red Rover, a push-to-talk microphone device attached to one of those curly cords that you could stretch out, the same device that taxis used. I contacted the studio and said, "Put me on the air," and boom, I was live. It was 12:20 p.m. when I began broadcasting from the car at Tenth Street and Brazos, just a few blocks south of campus. "Here we are, driving north toward the campus area, where shots are being fired," I said, drawing within range of the sniper's bullets. I kept talking into that microphone, virtually nonstop, my hand aching from holding down the button until my broadcast ended an hour and forty minutes later.

The heat was pervasive at noon on that summer day in Texas. It felt like one hundred degrees. When I reached the university campus, I rolled down the window so I could catch all that was going on. I was overwhelmed by the cacophony of sound. Sirens were screaming, people were screaming: "Look out! Watch out! Get down! He's shooting! Get out of the way! Somebody help that person!" I could hear the gunshots and the very human sounds of panic and fear.

I had enormous love and respect for the University of Texas. As a UT graduate in the 1950s who'd played in the Longhorn Band and had served in student government, my blood ran burnt orange. I had met my wife at the university. UT had transformed my life, giving me a sense of purpose and guiding me toward a career in journalism.

It's a large and beautiful campus, and I was familiar with almost every inch of it. I parked Red Rover below the South Mall at the Littlefield Fountain, the university's most prominent sculpture, its streams of water spraying into a granite pool with large bronze mythic figures arranged in a tableau intended to honor University of Texas students who died in World War I. I had clear sight of the Tower five hundred yards away, but the sunshine was brutal and sweat was burning my eyes as I tried to broadcast what I was witnessing.

A number of things were going through my head: first and foremost, to caution people to stay away from an obviously dangerous situation. There was no way that the police could cordon off the entire area. Students and professors could walk onto the campus from dozens of directions, heading to and from classes or just meandering through the open walking areas.

Red Rover was a bright red Pontiac station wagon with the large white letters KTBC painted on the door. It was a huge, conspicuous target. I hunkered down outside the driver's door and spoke into the radio mic, saying these exact words, which were recorded by our studio at the time: "This is Neal Spelce in Red Rover on the University of Texas campus. This is a warning to the citizens of Austin. Stay away from the university area. Traffic is now converging on this area, and there is a sniper on the University Tower firing at will. Several persons have been injured. We have no reports on whether there are any fatalities, but we do know a boy riding a bicycle has been shot and seriously wounded. There has been a report of a policeman that has been shot."

At that moment, the sniper fired over my head and hit Roy Dell Schmidt, an electrician for the City of Austin, who'd stood up from his crouched position behind a Chevrolet on University Avenue just south of me, nearly six hundred yards from the Tower. The young man was dead on arrival at Brackenridge Hospital.

There was a sudden haze of incredulity floating over the university area. No one could believe what was happening. People were ambling on the Guadalupe Street "Drag" that runs along the west side of campus, asking, "What's going on?" They couldn't fathom it, and they became targets.

As I said over the air, "There's no report as to who this man may be, or what he's doing up there, or what prompted this apparent madness. But the man is located on the University Tower observation deck, below the clock—which now shows 12:25—and he's shooting."

A young UT staffer named Charlotte Darehshori looked out of her office window and saw two young men dropping to the ground on the Main Mall. She raced outside to help them, then heard the bullets hitting all around her and realized she was under fire herself. UPI photographer Tom Lankes captured one of the most iconic photos of that day—Charlotte crouched behind the concrete base of a flagpole on the Mall, pulling her legs underneath her. It was a small hiding space, and she knew if she stuck her head out at the wrong time, it would be all over. She remained in that position for an hour and a half, resting her head against the blistering hot concrete, able to hear the ongoing tragedy surrounding her. A doctoral student named D. Maitland Huffman lay wounded beside a hedge several yards away, and when he began moving and asking for her help, she advised him, "Just keep still."

To get closer to the Tower and the Main Mall, where bodies were lying in the sun and pools of blood were visible, I drove around to the Inner Campus Drive and stopped near the statue of Woodrow Wilson (now removed), using the statue's base and a limestone wall to shield myself from the sniper's scope. I was at the southeast corner of the Main Mall, only a hundred yards from the Tower. The action was too close for comfort, as I described over the airwaves: "He's shooting our direction. We just saw a puff of smoke. He fired again. It's a battle now. It's a battle between the sniper and the police. It started out as a one-sided affair—the man picking off targets from a good distance away. He knocked a boy off a bicycle. He shot windows out of the Texas Union."

I continued: "It's an unbelievable sight. The serene University of Texas campus, bathed in very hot sunlight, a temperature approaching one hundred degrees now, and apparently a madman located on top of the University Tower firing and shooting at any movable target that he can see. The sight is reminiscent of some sort of war, a small-scale war, without uniforms except those of the police."

I stayed inside Red Rover, tethered by that microphone, but several times I opened the door and leaned out to get a clearer picture of what was happening. I was sweating profusely, wearing that tie like a noose around my neck in the August heat, but strangely enough, my heart wasn't pounding and I felt no fear. Using my power of concentration, I forced myself into a laser-like focus on the task at hand. Everything else disappeared from my mind. I knew it was my job to describe to the world what was going on, to warn everyone in the listening area, and to interview folks when I had a safe opportunity. "What did you see and hear? What do you know about the situation?" I interviewed a young law student named Leland Ammons, and this was our conversation, recorded verbatim:

Spelce: We have a man here just came from the base of the Tower. . . .
    Leland, what is your position here?
Ammons: I'm a law student.
Spelce: A law student. What have you seen?
Ammons: I was coming back from the law school and they . . .
Spelce: You better duck down a little bit here.
Ammons: This guy opened up over there, evidently sometime around
    five minutes till noon, I don't know how much sooner. He wounded
    a young policeman . . . beside me. I was pretty close, down by the
    Batts Hall, and the one ambulance driver told me he carried in five
    people. So, and there's two or three laying out that evidently cannot be
    reached at the moment.
Spelce: You were standing beside the policeman when he was shot?
Ammons: Yes.
Spelce: Do you know the policeman's name?
Ammons: No, I don't.

[It was APD Officer Billy Speed, who later died from his wound.]

Spelce: Was there just one shot fired?

Ammons: Well, he opened fire on us, and when he saw the policeman with his shotgun converging, and he evidently is a quite accurate shot, because . . . placing his shots right on target. The policeman was walking. He shot him through the supports near the statue of Jefferson Davis there on the Mall.

Spelce: Where was the policeman hit?

Ammons: The policeman was hit in the shoulder. We couldn't tell whether it was a ricochet. We did all we could for him. . . . He was still conscious when they carried him off in the ambulance. We don't know, it may be a superficial wound.

Spelce: The shots came near you at the time, though?

Ammons: Oh yeah, there were shots all around. We could hear the shots hitting the concrete around us before we could hear the reports coming from the Tower.

Spelce: There's still firing up there now. We've heard several reports while we've been talking to Leland Ammons. . . .

Spelce: What else did you see as you came through the campus? Did you see any other injured persons?

Ammons: Well, one detective was coming up. I cautioned him to get under cover, and he saw another person on the Mall get shot. There are several people laying out on the Mall at this time. . . . People that were there before I got there said that three of them may be shot, and the others may just be laying there.

A short time later, I added, "There was another officer that was positioned in a nearby building. He stuck his head out and drew fire. And the window splattered not six inches from where he was standing."

KTBC had begun feeding my broadcast to other news networks and outlets all across the North American continent. The world was listening in on my live reports. And as Gary Lavergne observes in *A Sniper in the Tower*, there was one person in particular who was listening: "Everywhere in Austin people huddled near radios and televisions to witness the unfolding drama. Even Charles Whitman [the sniper] tuned his fourteen-transistor Channel Master radio, with the volume as high as possible, to KTBC to listen to Neal Spelce's vivid descriptions. [Whitman] had to have been pleased with what he heard."

By that time, I wasn't the only reporter on the scene, as I announced: "We've got KTBC reporters ringing the campus. Newsman John Thawley has just now run across through the university area, hiding behind automobiles to get a closer look out. He ran dangerously through the line of fire, but there were no shots fired."

I interviewed Gordon Wilkison, a reporter and photographer for KTBC, who "just came back to the mobile unit [Red Rover] from shooting film and says the man is still directly below the clock on the south side of the University of Texas Tower on the observation deck. Wilk, do you have anything else?"

Gordon said, "Shoulder and arms are in full view, and you can see him raising his rifle."

We continued our dialogue: "Gordon Wilkison is watching the man through a telephoto lens on his camera. Getting the shots and watching, and sees the person there. Gordon, is it possible to describe the person? What color shirt is he wearing?"

Gordon said, "Light."

I confirmed that it was a light shirt, asking, "You can't tell about his hair, whether he's a dark-haired person or not? Is he wearing glasses? Is he light or fair-skinned?" Then: "From this distance, Gordon Wilkison reports fair-skinned."

The studio for the local public television station KLRN (later KLRU) was in a building on the east side of the Tower, and some staff members focused an old monster studio camera on that side of the observation deck, with limited range, showing at least one of the sniper's smoky discharges. It was a fairly static image and the only live shot of the Tower to appear on TV. KTBC-TV showed that KLRN visual with my live audio broadcast as the voiceover.

My colleague Phil Miller was pinned down in a drugstore on the Drag by the gunfire, but once he was on the move again, he was in danger. At one point he jumped behind a tree as a bullet struck it. He was also near Officer Billy Speed—the same officer Leland Ammons had told me about—when Speed was shot underneath the Jefferson Davis statue (now removed) at the southwest corner of the Main Mall, about thirty yards from the Woodrow Wilson statue. As Phil worked his way around campus, he kept wondering, "Why me? He doesn't know me. Why is he shooting at me?"

When Phil caught up with me, I interviewed him live: "It's a bizarre scene. It's a rare sight. A campus that earlier today was filled with the normal students, shirtsleeves, going to their summer school classes in the morning. And now there are students in their shirtsleeves lying prostrate on the ground, in the grass, on the sidewalks, dead, or seriously wounded, unable to move, and no help able to get to them."

I felt it was necessary to record every moment, every gunshot, not only to inform the public, but to help the police reconstruct the scene of the crimes at a later time: "Another shot. The sniper fired three quick, successive shots. Apparently in the length of time it takes to cock the weapon and then . . . Another shot. He just fired another shot and this time . . . Another shot. That's the fifth shot now in about twenty or thirty seconds. He's still situated below the University of Texas clock on the south side. The clock now shows 12:32. And he's coolly and calmly sitting up there firing away. Quick shots fired, and police are returning the gunfire."

I elaborated on what I called "a tricky situation": "The balustrades of the University Tower are such that he was able to sit back and just lean up, just exposing a small portion of his body, lay his rifle over the edge and fire. The shots were fired again, with large puffs of smoke preceding the sound. The distance, I'd say, from where we're broadcasting, is about a block."

I knew it was important to locate the sniper's range of targets: "Another shot was just fired. A heavy report. This one seemed to be aimed a little over to our right, more toward the east. He first was firing, in this last series of shots, generally in our direction. And now the fire has turned over and is heading more toward the southeast."

At that time there was no EMS in Austin. Funeral homes had ambulances, and when there was a car wreck or major accident, rival funeral homes would rush to beat the others to the site and claim patients. So the funeral homes knew how to scramble, and they were scrambling toward the bloody scene on campus. Once they understood the large number of victims impacted and the magnitude of the situation became clear, they began to improvise, bringing hearses and whatever vehicles they had on hand, because the casualties were mounting. As I reported into my microphone: "More ambulances are screaming up and down the University Drag, and the ambulances are apparently carrying those persons whom we had reported as lying on the sidewalk, shot in front of the Varsity Theater, and other buildings along the Drag."

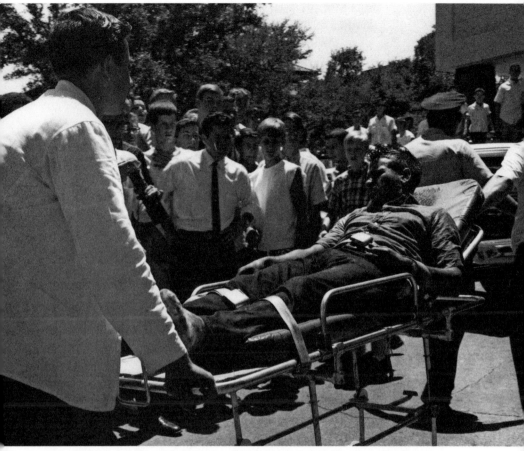

One of the many victims of the UT Tower shooting was taken for treatment after the sniper was shot and killed. *Photo by Frank Armstrong, UT Texas Student Publications Photographs, Briscoe Center for American History, the University of Texas at Austin*

By then, Joe Roddy was stationed at Brackenridge Hospital. In a *Dallas Morning News* interview years later, Joe recalled, "It seemed like the ambulances were coming in every few seconds. I remember all the stretchers they had. There were two or three dozen just piled up, waiting." Ambulances were parking wherever they could in the street outside the ER.

Robert Heard, an Associated Press (AP) reporter and Korean War veteran, was shot in the shoulder as he was running across the street near Mary E. Gearing Hall (Home Economics) on the north side of the Tower. It knocked him down and he rolled over, searching for cover, and witnesses in the nearby Biological Sciences building rushed out and dragged him behind a car. When Heard and his rescue group looked up at the Tower, they saw Whitman peering down at them with binoculars, assessing the injury he'd caused and hunting for more victims.

At one point, I thought there might be two shooters up on the Tower. As I observed, "It's like a battle scene. . . . There's another shot, and another shot. There are two different kinds of shots. Apparently police are returning the fire now. Which means there's a danger of ricocheting bullets off the University Tower. But we heard two different reports. One, a heavy-caliber-sounding weapon, which apparently was a rifle. And then another, lighter caliber sound, which could be police returning fire."

And a short time later: "He's moving now. We can see him moving. He's bending over and crouching, and moving around toward the west side of the building. Another fire, another shot. Another shot. Two shots in quick succession. There may be two people on the University Tower. There may be two people up there. One shot immediately came below the clock on the south side, and then another shot below the clock on the west side. I don't know that there are two people, but the shots came in quick succession. Almost too quick for a man to run from one clock to the other, and to fire."

I found out later that the police had had the same reaction about two possible shooters. Whitman had apparently lashed a rifle into one of the low rainspouts on the observation deck, and he would run over and pull the trigger, shooting randomly and trying to cause confusion. So it looked as if the gunfire was coming from two places at once.

There were no helicopters available to the Austin Police Department, but they received a phone call from a small airstrip in Pflugerville, a community eighteen miles north of the city, volunteering to fly a police sharpshooter over the Tower to take out the sniper. A part-time deputy sheriff named Jim Boutwell piloted a small two-seat Champion Citabria with APD sharpshooter Lieutenant Marion Lee on board, and they flew over and circled the Tower. From that vantage point, they were able to get a better look, and they broadcast back to the police station, "There's only one guy up here." Lieutenant Lee tried to get a bead on the sniper, but the day's rising heat was causing an updraft and bucking turbulence at that altitude, and there was no safe shot. Whitman, however, saw them and fired two shots that passed all the way through the fabric-covered plane, nearly downing them. The Citabria was too easy a target, so they got the hell out of there.

Down below, near the Main Mall plaza, my adrenaline was pumping like crazy, but I kept broadcasting, constantly asking myself, "Okay, where do we go next? What do we say next?" It was quite a challenge to describe the terror. There was nothing like this in anybody's experience, an event of such enormity. What in our collective memory would've led anyone to believe that a sniper could be shooting a high-caliber rifle from the top of the University of Texas Tower? In the heat of the moment, I couldn't recall a mass shooting of that scale in American history. We had no perspective at all. And I continued to ask myself, "How is this going to end?"

The Austin Police Department didn't have adequate weapons with the range to accurately reach the observation deck of the Tower. They had shotguns, pistols, and Remington 35 rifles, which were not designed for long-range targets. That was it.

Several ordinary citizens had heard my reports on the radio and decided to help. Texans being Texans, they came from their homes carrying deer rifles with scope sites and started shooting back at the sniper. It had an immediate effect. Whitman did less damage from that point on, because he was being pinned down effectively and becoming worried about his own life. The observation deck was fortified by stone balustrades that had served as his cover, but now there were bullets firing up at him and exploding against the walls and ledges, puffing limestone dust all around him.

One of my concerns as a reporter on the ground was that there was no police command post set up on campus to coordinate the many officers converging on the scene. It was a serious problem. The police leadership didn't say, "Let's divide up. Martinez, you go in this entrance; McCoy, you go over here. Head up to the observation deck. We're sending backup." None of that happened. The officers had their walkie-talkies, but it was a seat-of-the-pants reaction by trained individuals who said, "I've got to stop this." The police officers who went to the top of the Tower and ultimately killed Charles Whitman took their own chances without being ordered to do so.

The truth is, we didn't have an organized plan at the news station, either. There was no Plan A or Plan B for an event of that kind. Our reporter John Thawley grabbed a little handheld camera and rushed to campus on his own. I didn't send him out. A couple of times he set his camera down, ran out into the open, and pulled a victim to safety.

KTBC reporter Charles Ward was also a National Guardsman, and he strapped on his helmet and rushed into action with cameraman Gary Pickle (nephew of Congressman Jake Pickle), who carried the heavy gear of a 16mm sound-on-film camera on his shoulder. At some point, Charles and Gary were stationed at a window in Batts Hall, near the Main Mall, and Gary captured the most famous black-and-white footage of rifle blasts from the Tower. Afterward, law enforcement credited our film staff for helping them visualize the situation, and several news agencies applauded our station for jumping into immediate danger and capturing what was taking place at the University of Texas that day.

In all that chaos, there was no rescue system to save wounded victims. Bodies were lying in the hot sun on the Main Mall and the Drag, and several phenomenal students took it upon themselves to run out into the open range of fire and carry gunshot victims to safety. You never know how you're going to respond in a time of crisis like that until it happens. Some people freeze in fear; others rise above it all and do things they never thought they could do.

A student named Claire Wilson was the first person Whitman shot. She was eight months pregnant, and the bullet killed her unborn baby. Her boyfriend, Tom Eckman, was shot dead and fell beside her. She lay there on her back on the hot concrete of the Main Mall in the sweltering heat, with a distended belly, while bullets were flying and people were yelling and sirens were wailing in the distance.

One of the most incredible acts of heroism was when an art student named Rita Murphey Jones—who would later change her name to Rita Starpattern and become an Austin feminist icon—ran out into the wide open space of the killing zone to lie down next to Claire. Rita started talking to the wounded young woman, attempting to give comfort and settle her down. Claire was moaning, and Rita feared that the sniper would notice and shoot her again.

"Claire, where are you from?" Rita asked, trying to take the young woman's mind off her pain, trying to keep her alive mentally and emotionally while she was lying next to her dead boyfriend in all that heat and confusion. "What classes are you taking?" Rita asked her.

Years later, Claire would recall, "When she came out, it really was wonderful because for one thing it made me not feel alone. And another thing it gave me, you know, I could keep talking and not just drift off, and she kept me talking the whole time."

Rita had put her own life in mortal danger, because if Whitman saw her moving or talking, or if he looked down his scope and noticed there was a third person there, that would have been the end of both Rita and Claire.

Two other students, John Fox (now better known as Artly Snuff) and James Love, were playing chess at their co-op when they heard about the sniper on a radio report. They went running to the campus out of curiosity and ended up huddled with the group below the Jefferson Davis statue. Eventually Fox and Love gathered their courage and raced out to the Main Mall to rescue Claire Wilson. Seeing the young men rushing to help, Rita jumped up and ran toward the Woodrow Wilson statue to hide from the sniper's rifle scope.

Fox grabbed Claire's ankles and Love grabbed her wrists, and they carried her to the safety of a waiting ambulance, saving her life. But while he was out in the line of fire, lifting Claire Wilson, Fox felt an icy fear that he described as a spot the size of a grape between his shoulder blades, where he was certain he was going to catch a bullet. He says he sometimes feels that grape-sized spot even today when he thinks about that Monday in August 1966.

At the same time that Fox and Love were carrying Claire off the Mall plaza, a young Vietnam veteran named Brehan Ellison grappled with the lifeless body of Claire's boyfriend, Tom, eventually bearing him to cover behind the wall near the Jefferson Davis statue. When KTBC reporter Charles Ward interviewed Ellison moments later, the rescuer's T-shirt was bloodstained:

Ward: One of those who is out of breath now after running out onto the Mall rescuing those who have been shot is Brehan Ellison, of Austin, who's been in Vietnam. He's been back for two years. Brehan, how many have you gone out to rescue?
Ellison: Today two.
Ward: What did you have to do?
Ellison: Run hard and keep low.
Ward: How many have you seen that are dead today?
Ellison: Just one. I hope not any more.

But there were more. Many more. When the shooting was over, the sniper had killed fourteen people (including Claire Wilson's unborn child) on the UT campus and wounded thirty-one others. His reign of terror lasted ninety-six minutes.

APD officer Ramiro (Ray) Martinez was off-duty until 3:00 p.m. that day, and he was at home fixing lunch when he heard a news report about shootings at the Tower. He checked in with police headquarters and a lieutenant said, "Report to campus and direct traffic." When Officer Martinez reached the university area, he saw that there was no traffic to direct. He heard my words on the radio—"Another shot. He just fired another shot and this time . . . Another shot"—and he realized it was his duty to go take out the sniper on the observation deck.

Police officers Ray Martinez, Houston McCoy, Jerry Day, Phillip Conner, and several other law enforcement officers entered the university grounds in different ways, but with the same purpose. They risked their lives dodging gunfire and eventually entered the Main Building on the ground floor. The details of their heroic actions to locate and kill Charles Whitman on the observation deck have been well documented in Lavergne's *A Sniper in the Tower* and Keith Maitland's outstanding 2016 documentary film *Tower*.

A burly military veteran named Allen Crum was a floor manager at the University Co-op on the Drag and had hurried across the street to help a boy who'd been shot on a bicycle as he rode down Guadalupe. When Crum realized there was a sniper, he made his way unarmed toward the Tower, slipping in and out of buildings, uncertain what he'd do when he reached the Main Building. But once inside, he encountered a Texas Department of Public Safety trooper with two weapons, and the trooper handed Crum a rifle.

The Tower elevators don't go all the way to the top floor. You have to get out on the twenty-sixth floor and climb two flights of stairs to the reception room, which opens onto the observation deck.

Officer Ray Martinez arrived at the elevators a few minutes behind the others and rode up to the twenty-sixth floor by himself. He'd seen the carnage and wondered if there was more than one sniper. "It's just me with my handgun," he thought, "and snipers up there with high-powered rifles and who knows what else." He didn't know that Whitman had brought a footlocker full of weapons and was well stocked with food and water.

As a Catholic, Martinez made an act of contrition, which begins, "O my God, I am heartily sorry for having offended Thee," while withdrawing his handgun, prepared to fire it. When the elevator door opened on the twenty-sixth floor, he stood facing a pistol and a rifle. Officer Jerry Day was pointing his pistol at him, and civilian Allen Crum was pointing the rifle. It was a brief standoff, Day and Crum on the alert to anyone coming out of the elevator.

While Day checked the offices on the twenty-sixth floor, Martinez and Crum raised their weapons and cautiously mounted the stairs to the twenty-seventh floor. They could hear shots from above on the deck and bullets hitting outdoor walls from the deer rifles and ground fire below.

Ray Martinez was a young patrolman, not a veteran sergeant or lieutenant, not someone who was used to being in charge. But a police officer knows you have to take charge wherever you go, so he did. He said to Crum, "I'm going up to get the shooter." Crum responded, "You're not going by yourself. I'm coming with you. We'll do it military-service style. I'll cover you and you'll cover me."

A few steps higher, they found a lake of blood on the stairs, and there were two dead bodies lying on the first landing, a teenaged boy and his aunt. They were members of the Gabour family from Texarkana, who were vacationing in Austin and had decided to take in the magnificent view from the Tower. Martinez then discovered the boy's wounded mother drowning in her own blood and turned her over to prevent her from choking to death.

Higher up the stairs, there was another wounded victim, Mike Gabour, eighteen years old and a cadet at the US Air Force Academy. He managed to tell Martinez and Crum there was only one shooter.

As I reflect back on that day, I still don't know what's in the psyche of a person who says, "I'm going to murder as many people as I can." Whitman's killing spree had been well planned. Before going to campus, he'd stabbed his wife and his mother to death, in separate Austin locations, and left a note saying of his wife, "I love her dearly . . . I don't want her to have to face the embarrassment my actions would surely cause her."

When he entered the Main Building, Whitman was wearing coveralls and pushing a dolly bearing that footlocker, pretending to be a UT maintenance worker doing his job.

Just before Martinez and Crum jammed their way through the blocked door into the reception area on the twenty-eighth floor, Crum asked the young cop, "Are we playing for keeps?" Martinez said, "You're damn right we are." Crum said, "Well, I guess you better deputize me." Martinez looked at him and said, "Consider yourself deputized."

Allen Crum was interviewed by weatherman Jack Balzerson on the KTBC news special later that evening, and Crum described the next few moments, including discovering the body of receptionist Edna Townsley: "We got to the top of the stairs and this man [Whitman] had barricaded the staircase [door] with a desk and a chair and a waste can. And we figured he was either in there, or out on the walkaround ledge. So we very cautiously pushed the desk out and we saw blood on the floor. And we realized someone had been killed up there, or badly wounded. We found a lady up behind the couch. Then [Jerry] Day joined us again, and we began to work our way out on the [observation deck]."

There's only one door to the deck itself, and it's on the south side, facing the Texas State Capitol a mile away. There are windows facing east and west, but the space is relatively small. Whitman had also barricaded that one glass-paneled door with the dolly wedged against it from the outside, and Martinez kicked and rattled and banged the door, making a lot of noise until the dolly fell and the door opened onto the deck. By that time, Officers Houston McCoy and Phillip Conner had also arrived in the reception room.

It was one of those incredibly tense situations when police officers don't know what they're getting ready to face. Martinez swung open the door with the others behind him and stuck his head out, glancing west and east, worried that the dolly noise might have alerted the sniper. But the young officer saw that the south deck was clear, and he hurried over to the southeast corner and peeped around the wall, discovering that the east side was also clear.

Recalling that scene decades later in an interview with Spectrum News, Ray Martinez said, "It was kind of hairy because every time I looked, I didn't know what to expect. Thank the good Lord there was nothing. So I came back, got Crum out, and I said, 'Now I want you to point the rifle over here to the west wall, southwest wall, and if he comes around the corner, shoot him because I am going around to look for him.'"

Deer rifle bullets were striking the wall above them, spraying limestone dust, and Martinez turned around and saw Houston McCoy enter the deck with a twelve-gauge shotgun. "He was a tall boy and standing straight up," Martinez said, "and I motioned to him to get down, get down, because I didn't want to shout. I didn't want anybody to hear me, and he didn't get my signals. But a couple of bullets hit above his head and he knew what I was indicating, so he got his head down."

Martinez crouched down and duckwalked north along the east deck with McCoy following him with the shotgun. Crum and Officer Day were covering the southwest corner, and Officer Conner remained inside the reception room to guard the west window.

One of the challenges with the observation deck is that there's a protrusion about midway on each wall, and you can't see the far corner until you get past the protrusion. Martinez and McCoy were cautiously moving toward the northeast corner, and when they cleared the protrusion, they could see that the shooter wasn't there. That meant they knew exactly where he was—the northwest corner—and they knew that once they peered around the corner ahead, they would find him.

At that instant, Allen Crum discharged his rifle and the round hit the wall above Jerry Day. Martinez and McCoy heard the shot, but they didn't know who had fired it. Whitman had heard the shot, too. He was sitting down, facing south, and he aimed his M1 carbine in that direction, ready to kill whoever was coming around that corner.

Martinez and McCoy slipped around the northeast corner, saw Whitman looking the other way, and opened fire on him. The crouching Martinez hit him with the first round from his handgun, and Whitman stood up to face them and squeezed off an errant round. But Martinez kept advancing toward him, emptying his six-shooter, and McCoy blasted Whitman with two rounds of buckshot. As Whitman's body was jerking and going down, Martinez reached up and grabbed McCoy's shotgun and raced toward the sniper, shooting him one final time and then shouting, "I got him, I got him."

Years later, Martinez recalled, "I dropped the shotgun because my knees and my legs just kind of deserted me. They were like pure rubber." He was in shock.

While McCoy searched Whitman's body for identification, Martinez ran down the west side of the observation deck to where Day, Crum, and Conner were holding their positions. The hero was almost shot to death by his fellow officers. But the team quickly located another officer with a walkie-talkie and reported to headquarters that the sniper was dead.

There's been a long debate about which shot killed Charles Whitman. As far as I'm concerned, that's neither here nor there. Two very brave

Austin police officers—Ray Martinez and Houston McCoy—both put an end to the sniper and stopped the massacre.

The most sobering part of the drama for me personally was that when the officers fired the fatal rounds that silenced the first mass school-shooter in American history, Whitman's radio was still on at full volume, playing my live broadcast. He had indeed been listening to my nonstop reporting. Perhaps that's why he didn't seek out Red Rover as a target. Was he a narcissist who wanted to keep hearing what I was saying about him? Did he want a reporter's account validating his accuracy, the human damage, the extent of his destruction?

Many times over the years, I've asked myself if I'd known he was listening to me, would I have said anything to him? In a one-way transmission like radio, I probably couldn't have talked him down—not like someone on a telephone line, speaking directly to him one on one. Even so, what would I have said to a mass murderer over the radio? Could I have risen to the moment?

Charles Whitman died at 1:24 p.m. Soon more police officers arrived on the observation deck, and they were gathered around Whitman's body when they heard my announcement on the killer's radio: "This is Neal Spelce with a bulletin from the KTBC radio newsroom. The sniper is dead."

Our reporter Phil Miller was standing by an APD officer when his police radio picked up the report that the sniper had been killed, and the radio even revealed his identity based on an ID they found on his body. The public didn't know the name until Phil wrote it down, ran over to me near the Woodrow Wilson statue, and put the piece of paper in my hand.

Shots were still being fired up at the Tower by citizens with deer rifles, even though Allen Crum was bravely waving a white towel from the observation deck, signaling for a ceasefire. People on the ground thought it was the sniper surrendering. But the shooting didn't stop until I announced over the airwaves, "The sniper—apparently tentatively identified as Charles J. Whitman, twenty-five years old, from Needsville—is dead."

The town is Needville, Texas, but Phil wrote it down with an "s" in the name. Needville is in Fort Bend County, about forty miles southwest of Houston, and it was the hometown of Kathy Whitman, the wife whose body had not yet been found at their rented home in South Austin.

It was an era of the pocket-sized transistor radio. In 1966, students carried them around like we do with cellphones, some with their own leather cases. They'd listen to music and news bulletins on AM stations—not even FM at that point—usually Top 40 rock 'n' roll. That day, everyone was glued to their transistors all over campus, all over town, listening to my broadcast. When I announced that the sniper was dead, word spread quickly.

What happened next was both amazing and eerie. I stood outside Red Rover's open door and described the people flooding out of every campus building and from behind bushes and walls and cars, gravitating to the Mall below the Tower, where the façade of the Main Building bore the inscription, "Ye shall know the truth and the truth shall make you free." They were like zombies, walking slowly, speechless and numb. Nobody said anything. Today, after traumatic events like that, you see people hugging and comforting one another. August 1, 1966, wasn't that way. I think it was because everyone was in shock. I could hear a few sobs, and there were glassy eyes, but what I remember most was the silence. Seeing the crowd grow larger and larger on the plaza in front of the Main Building, I had a terrifying thought: "I hope my information was correct and he's not up there right now, training his scope on this mass of people down here."

Officer Ray Martinez was bloody, exhausted, and shaken, but it was the Gabour family's blood and not his own. He wasn't injured physically, but the stress had caught up with him. *I just killed a guy. I just stopped the carnage.* It was overwhelming. Another police officer accompanied him down the elevator and helped him into a squad car. Back at the station he had the dry heaves while writing his report. He called his wife to assure her he was okay, then he drove to his brother Gilbert's home and they drank an entire bottle of gin.

Police officers and ambulance attendants brought the bodies of the Gabour family and Edna Townsley down the Tower elevators on gurneys and wrapped in sheets. A quiet crowd had gathered at the doors of the Main Building, watching the solemn procession of the victims being carried away. What could anyone say? The bystanders would never forget that day for as long as they lived.

They brought Whitman's blanket-covered body down to the courtyard at the north entrance of the building, intentionally avoiding the crush of onlookers at the south and west sides. As Gary Lavergne wrote in *A Sniper in the Tower*, "Much of the crowd wanted a glimpse of the body of the sniper. Concerns about the reaction of the crowds were valid. Many civilians with guns were part of the crowd." An ambulance quickly took Whitman's body to Cook Funeral Home.

During the shooting, University of Texas chancellor Harry Ransom had been trapped in his office in the Main Building under the Tower. Afterward, he emerged and read a statement into our KTBC microphones, expressing "deep concern and sympathy for the family of those persons who lost their lives and for those who were injured and their relatives." He praised "the heroism and selflessness of students, law enforcement officers, and staff, who attempted, often successfully, to rescue those hurt and in danger."

And like the rest of the world, which would witness on television the remarkable courage of so many UT students, he was overwhelmed with admiration: "I must add informally that . . . I have never seen, nor have I ever imagined anything like it. Youngsters in white shirts who saw these things happen came out from buildings, at great length, and they rescued or took care of persons who were hit. It's incredible, and it's very heart-lifting. But in a moment of very deep sadness."

TOWER COVERAGE

T hrough my on-air reporting for KTBC radio, the story broke nationally, and the UPI and AP wire services, which had bureau offices in the State Capitol only a mile away, began reporting on the Tower shootings very quickly. CBS Radio had been taping my audio broadcast and playing it on newscasts. All the TV stations wanted sound *and* pictures, but there were no visuals yet, because our cameramen hadn't yet processed their film. In those days before satellite transmissions, the media couldn't just order up a transmission and receive an immediate response.

After Whitman's death, we kept broadcasting live for another half hour. At 2:00 p.m., I said, "That's it from the University of Texas. This is Neal Spelce, signing off," and we hit CBS News at the top of the hour. The network played portions of my broadcast. That's how I knew the story was spanning out big-time.

Veteran newsman Paul Bolton was hired by the Johnsons as news editor of KTBC radio in 1944, and in the early 1950s he became director of the news staff for both the radio station and the new KTBC television station. Mr. B had hired me as a reporter when I was a University of Texas journalism student in 1956, and when he retired in the early 1960s, I was tapped to replace him as the news director and anchor for television.

Although semi-retired, Mr. B would come into the newsroom every morning for his folksy, signature radio show, fifteen minutes at 7:30. At that time, Austin was more like Mayberry than New York City, and Mr. B's program was charming and popular. One of his best segments was about lost dogs. When callers phoned in to say, "I lost my dog," he'd say, "Tell me what it looks like and where you last saw it." He would always conclude the program with a nice human-interest touch.

Hearing about the sniper at UT, Paul Bolton rushed back to the station and began to type quick thirty-second feeds using his fast two-finger style, and he put them in front of staffers who fed them out over the telephone to the radio stations nationwide that were contacting us for a report.

At one point, Joe Roddy called the newsroom from the hospital and said, "It's a madhouse here at Brackenridge Hospital. At least seventeen persons are here undergoing treatment. We have had unconfirmed reports that two persons have died. We have a list of the names."

As news director, I made the decision: "Let's go ahead and put the list on the air."

That was against protocol, then and now. You don't announce the names of victims without first notifying the next of kin. It's common decency. But this was such a major story that impacted so many people in the relatively small town of Austin. Joe had been handed the list at the ER, and when he started reading the names over the phone, he mispronounced some of them because he'd scribbled the list.

The next voice you heard on the radio was Paul Bolton's. He said, "Joe, hold it a minute," his voice quavering. "This is Paul over at the newsroom. Everyone is interested in that list of names. I think you have my grandson [on the list]. Go over that list of names again, please."

His namesake grandson was Paul Bolton Sonntag, and he'd been shot and killed alongside his girlfriend, Claudia Rutt, on the Drag near the University Co-op. The two of them were recent Austin High School graduates leaving soon for different colleges out of town, and they had planned to do some shopping together at the Co-op. One of their classmates has said they were shopping for engagement rings.

When Joe finished reading that list again, Paul Bolton said, "Is that it?" And then Jay Hodgson, the host of KTBC's children's program, said, "We've got it, Joe. Thank you."

Jay took Mr. B home. It was a horrible day for everyone, but especially devastating for those who'd lost loved ones. I learned firsthand why it's necessary to withhold names pending notification of next of kin. That was an awful thing for Paul Bolton to experience.

I was never criticized for releasing the names of victims on the air, but I knew in my own mind that it was ill-advised. Over the years, I have teared up when I've talked about that decision and Paul Bolton's reaction, because I now have grandchildren myself, and I think of how upsetting it would be to hear about their deaths over the radio or on TV. The policy to withhold names for a period of time is a very wise one.

That afternoon in the KTBC newsroom, we started putting together our 6:00 p.m. newscast and also a 10:30 p.m. news special wrapping up everything that had happened that day. We were an affiliate of CBS, but we also carried programming from ABC and NBC, and we started receiving urgent phone calls from them for coverage of the story.

CBS in New York called first and said, "Neal, we need you to do a feed on the Walter Cronkite newscast starting at 5:30 this evening. Can you do it?"

"Yes sir, we'll make it happen."

Within minutes, NBC and ABC called and said, "We'd like to have a feed from you." I told them I'd promised CBS News, suggesting they try them, and they said, "No, we need a feed from you."

A second television station had gone on the air by that time in Austin, an NBC affiliate, but they had a small staff without the resources we had at KTBC. We were the only news source that had what the networks were looking for. Throughout those ninety-six minutes of terror, we were virtually exclusive in our coverage.

I said to the networks, "Look, I can feed you once, at the same time, so why don't all three of you take it?"

The networks were vocal in their objections. They all wanted to be first. They did not play well with others.

I finally said to them, "I'm trying to accommodate you as much as I can, because it's the biggest story in the country right now. But I've got a newscast to put together myself. Right after feeding you, I'm going to be on the air at six o'clock with the local news, and I've also got an hour-long special coming up later this evening."

Their next question was, "Okay, what can we expect?"

I said, "Let's do this. You start off at 5:30, and then thirty seconds later you throw it to me, and I'll feed you the report." They said, "Okay, that works. We'll lead in with the sniper story and then say, 'For the details, we go now to Austin, Texas. Here's Neal Spelce.'"

A skeptical bunch, the networks persisted with, "So tell us what you're going to say." I said, "I'm going to narrate the film." They said, "What's the film going to show?" I said, "I don't have any idea. We haven't processed the film yet." They said, "After you see the film, would you call us back and tell us?" I said, "No sir, I won't have time. The first time it's fed to you is the first time I will see it. We're that tight."

Imagine what was going on in the major newsrooms in New York—the brain center of the broadcast world—the three big-time networks

The KTBC-TV news staff, which rallied to cover the UT Tower shooting, posed outside the studio flanked by the Pontiac mobile units used to cover the deadly rampage. Front row, left to right, Neal Spelce, Paul Bolton, and Joe Roddy. *Photo courtesy Neal Spelce*

pleading with this thirty-year-old kid down in Austin, Texas, for my co-operation. I have to admit I was enjoying it.

They said, "Can you send us a script of what you're going to say?" I said, "No sir, I'm going to be ad-libbing. I don't have time to write a script."

They continued to protest, and I said, "I was there. I saw it. I'll talk about what happened, and you take the feed." I knew what the networks were thinking: "We're throwing our professional reputations over to *this* guy?"

KTBC-TV cameramen had captured the puffs of smoke from the observation deck, the chaos of students and others running for cover, the courageous rescues, and 99 percent of the iconic imagery that everyone remembers from the Tower tragedy on August 1, 1966. It's the footage that's been shown for more than fifty years. But the film wasn't edited until the last minute, our staff hustling to put it on the air. In the end, I was very proud of how our team pulled everything together.

My report at 5:30 came off without a hitch. I sat at the news desk, looking at the film for the first time and talking about it live, which is second nature when you're on television. I was simply narrating what I saw and what I recalled.

In our special program at 10:30 that night, we delved deeper into many other aspects of the tragedy:

We did a report on Whitman's killing of his mother and his wife.

Searching for insight into the sniper's personality and behavior, Verne Lundquist—our local sportscaster and future nationally acclaimed sports broadcaster—conducted an interview with A. J. Vincik, the Boy Scout master who'd worked with Whitman as his volunteer assistant.

Joe Roddy reported from Brackenridge Hospital on what the emergency room was like during the deluge of gunshot victims, and about who the victims were and how they were being cared for. Brackenridge was a huge hospital, and the staff performed amazingly well, the only emergency room involved at that time.

Governor John Connally was on an economic development tour in South America, and we reported that he was returning to Austin and ready to form a commission to investigate the shootings. He'd been a sniper victim himself, just three years earlier, when he was riding in the same car with President Kennedy.

All of that reporting aired the first night, only ten hours after the shootings began on campus. Those stories needed further development, and over the next several days, we followed up on them and chased down other stories. At the same time, we also accommodated the networks and local TV stations from around the country, answering their questions and giving them access to what we had.

We created profiles of as many victims as we could.

I started asking hard questions to the Austin Police Department. For example, "Why didn't you have rifles with scope sights so you could shoot back?" They said, "That's just not part of our arsenal." I thought, "Oh boy, rinky-dink APD."

I called around to major police departments in cities with tall buildings, and they all said, "No, we don't have weapons and training like that, either." They hadn't anticipated the need.

So I was able to report that the Austin Police Department wasn't out of the ordinary. No matter where this kind of shooting took place, the same problems would exist. Any large city in America could face the same situation. No one had specially trained, specially armed police squadrons to eliminate a sniper.

Los Angeles was the first to say, "We'd better address this. What if somebody went to the top of our city hall and started shooting like Whitman?" As a result of the Tower shootings in August 1966, newly created SWAT teams increased nationwide. Police departments across the country were determined to be prepared with proper weapons, trained sharpshooters, and strategic plans to respond to similar crises.

The other positive result was the development of university policies and crisis centers. The University of Texas didn't have a plan for helping so many students cope with this kind of tragedy, so the administration decided to set up a center to offer what we now call grief and trauma counseling.

On the night of the shootings, news crews started arriving from television stations near and far. Crews from San Antonio showed up first because of their proximity. The KTBC newsroom was flooded with phone calls from radio stations around the country and worldwide, asking us for a feed. Some radio stations wanted to have what was called an *actuality*—a report from the scene—inserted in the middle of their newscasts. We were so busy we had to call all hands on deck to come in and help out. Cactus Pryor fed a number of stations, and so did Jay Hodgson, who was better known as Uncle Jay on our children's program.

I had seen the unedited Zapruder film of the shooting of President Kennedy shortly after his assassination, and I was well aware that Abraham Zapruder had sold his film for a lot of money to *Life* magazine, granting them the copyright for reproduction. I considered the Tower footage to be similar—a major news event in American history. But as a journalist, my attitude was different. I decided we should share our footage with other news sources. In fact, we made prints of the 16mm black-and-white film footage on our print machines and disseminated them to media outlets free of charge.

The Tower tragedy was a major story that was pervasive for weeks. It was almost around-the-clock reporting. The staff and I would wrap it up at night and go home and sleep for a few hours and come right back and keep working on it. There were other stories I'm sure we missed during that period, but the incident had major ramifications and impacted so many people in Austin and in the University of Texas family.

One of the unique aspects of the shootings was that most of it took place outdoors, in the open, with rifle blasts captured on camera and victims filmed where they'd fallen. Tragedies like Columbine, Virginia Tech, and Sandy Hook happened primarily indoors or away from cameras. It wasn't until the Las Vegas shootings from a hotel window in 2017, fifty-one years after the Tower, that violence played out in such a public and visible way as it had on the UT campus. Because of its visual record on film, the Tower event has remained distinctive in the long and horrific chronicle of mass shootings in our country.

Journalism: "The First Rough Draft of History"

The film editor at KTBC during that era was a great guy named David N. Smith, and he stayed on at the TV station until his retirement, long after I'd moved on. He called me one day in the 1970s and said, "Neal, I've been told I've got to get rid of all this old film down here to make room for expansion. Would you like the sniper stuff?" I said, "Hell yes, I would!"

That's how I became the sole repository for all the KTBC film shot on August 1, 1966. I retrieved the entire original archive of footage from David—black and white, unedited, including film that had been cut up into bits and pieces. All of it. And over the years, I've let the public have access to it without charge. My position has continued to be, "If you need it and can use it, you're welcome to it." I consider its availability to be important to the preservation and interpretation of a significant moment in American history.

The complete footage has been digitized at the Texas Archive of the Moving Image (TAMI), which was established in 2002 by University of Texas film archivist and professor Caroline Frick to preserve rare and unusual film. TAMI has digitized everything, including images and scenes that were never used on television.

In fact, while reviewing the film with TAMI, I saw something I'd never seen before. There was footage of several people running at the corner of Guadalupe and Twenty-Fourth Street, where the Varsity Theater was located, and as the camera was panning them, the rear runner was hit by a bullet. He jerked around for a fraction of a second before the camera's focus moved elsewhere. It was chilling to watch. I was able to freeze-frame the moment when that victim was struck by the sniper. I suspect that many future researchers will discover details like that in the TAMI archive that will add to our understanding of those tragic ninety-six minutes. To give access to researchers who would like to examine the actual 16mm film footage itself and related materials, I donated the originals to UT's Dolph Briscoe Center for American History.

For our broadcast coverage that day, KTBC received the nation's top award for radio news reporting from the National Society of Professional Journalists at its annual meeting in San Francisco. We also received the highest award for TV coverage in the United States from the National Headliners Club at its ceremony in Atlantic City. To gain that kind of recognition—to be acknowledged by our peers for conducting the best broadcast reporting in the nation that year—meant a great deal to me and to my colleagues at KTBC.

At those two ceremonies, I was elated by how many radio and television journalists came over to greet me and express their admiration and praise, asking detailed questions about my work under gunfire on that very hot day in August 1966. Some asked, "Were you able to implement your disaster plan?" I said, "What disaster plan?"

We had no plan for something like that. But my belief was that if you had good people doing good work, those people would always rise to the occasion, showing courage and grace under pressure. We had a strong, determined staff, and so many of them raced into harm's way in spite of the danger and mayhem. I couldn't have been prouder to be their colleague and friend. They were true professionals, all of them dedicated to their work, willing to risk everything to cover the massacre as it played out in real time.

TOWER AFTERMATH

I have talked to Ray Martinez on several occasions over the past fifty-plus years. I've interviewed him and appeared with him on panels. I've met his wife, and I knew his brother, civic leader Gilbert Martinez, in a totally different context. (I didn't know for a long time that Gilbert and Ray were brothers.) Ray has always been professional and matter-of-fact, without emotion, about his role in taking out the sniper in the Tower. His viewpoint is, "I had a job to do. I did what I was trained to do." He has always dismissed the controversy over whose bullets—the shotgun or the pistol—actually killed Charles Whitman. Ray knows what he did and was satisfied with his role, and he didn't think it mattered who fired the terminating shot.

Police Chief Bob Miles held a news conference after the shootings, and he lined up Ray, Houston McCoy, Jerry Day, and Allen Crum with him in front of the cameras. But Chief Miles wouldn't let any of them speak or answer questions from the media. I asked Ray about that later, and his response was, "The chief said, 'Let me handle this,' and when the chief says something, you do it."

I got the feeling that he resented not being able to respond to questions and tell his story, but once again he avoided controversy. Ray was a good soldier.

I tried reaching out to Houston McCoy for interviews several times over the years, but he was a hard man to find. There was a hanger-on who presented himself to me several times as Houston's power of attorney, but he wasn't a lawyer. The hanger-on had insinuated himself into the McCoy family, and he pretended to speak for Houston.

Houston did give a good interview to NBC when it produced an hour-long special on the Tower several years after the incident. But by then, Houston had admitted publicly that he'd become an alcoholic and that his health had gone downhill. Even though he was lucid and articulate in the NBC interview, he had a haggard look. *Fragile* might be the best word to describe his condition. His point of view was, "Look, I was up on the observation deck too and shot Whitman," and yet Ray Martinez received more credit and was more highly praised for being the one who stuck his neck out, literally, and led the assault.

Martinez and McCoy were a contrast in personalities. One of the most obvious differences was that Ray was friendly and accessible while Houston seemed standoffish and defensive. McCoy left the Austin PD two years after the Tower shootings and faded from public life. He died in 2012.

Martinez went on to the Texas Department of Public Safety and became a Texas Ranger, the elite corps of state troopers. When he retired from law enforcement, he was elected justice of the peace in New Braunfels, Comal County, Texas. And he wrote a book entitled *They Call Me Ranger Ray*, which included his memories of the sniper incident and his activities as a Texas Ranger.

One thing that did disturb Martinez was MGM's made-for-TV movie *The Deadly Tower*, starring Kurt Russell as Charles Whitman. It aired on NBC in 1975, only nine years after the event. Martinez read the script and refused to be involved or allow them to use his name unless they addressed a number of inaccuracies. They didn't.

The producers contacted me as well and asked if I would be available to re-create my role. I said, "Send me a script. I need to see it first." After reading it, I said no. They'd taken the basic event and exaggerated and sensationalized what had actually happened. They'd made Ray Martinez the focal point and constructed a false narrative about him being discriminated against by the Austin Police Department because he was Hispanic, giving the story racial overtones that didn't exist.

Although I refused to be involved as a character in the film, the producers contacted me at my PR firm and said, "We need to get permission to shoot on the University of Texas campus. Can you set that up for us?"

Lorene Rogers was the UT president at the time, and I briefed her on the script, telling her, "This is what it's gonna be." I went with the producers to the meeting with President Rogers and we sat around a big table in the elegant, book-lined Stark Library in the Main Building. She was very gracious and listened to them politely, but in the end decided no, I'm not going to give you permission. As she said in a statement to the student newspaper, the *Daily Texan*, "I do not want to bring back bad memories that are still vivid in the minds of many of our students, their families, and the people of Austin. It would just be opening up old wounds, and I did not want the university to be a part of it."

Artist's rendering of my Tower shooting broadcast from the award-winning documentary *Tower* in 2016. *Photo courtesy* Tower *documentary producer Keith Maitland*

The producers needed a tall tower, though, and they filmed it at the State Capitol Building in Baton Rouge, Louisiana. They used fake Austin police badges and APD insignia on the cars and shot those scenes in a city more than four hundred miles away.

Ray Martinez sued the filmmakers. He was especially incensed by the portrayal of his wife as a stereotypical pregnant Hispanic housewife (she wasn't Hispanic) and allegations that he was a victim of racism at the APD. Many years after Ray won his lawsuit, I asked him, "How much did you win?" He said, "I signed a nondisclosure agreement, Neal." By that point we were good buddies and had been through a lot together, and I said, "Come on, Ray, how much money did you get out of that lawsuit?" He stuck to his principles: "I signed an agreement and said I wasn't going to say anything. And I won't."

He has never revealed the amount.

In contrast to *The Deadly Tower*, the 2016 documentary entitled *Tower*, produced and directed by Keith Maitland, is exceptional in its accuracy and depth. Maitland interviewed me on several occasions and used my exact words in the script he wrote for the actor Monty Muir, who portrayed the thirty-year-old Neal Spelce.

I was impressed with Maitland's technique. The use of computer animation in the film is brilliant, depicting approximately the way we all looked in 1966, with the young actors delivering dialogue we'd all said in interviews. Later in the film, the animated characters morph into the actual people themselves and how we all look more than fifty years later. Actor Monty Muir morphed into the gray-haired Neal Spelce speaking to the camera.

Viewers have asked me what I thought about Muir's portrayal of me. First of all, I wasn't sure he looked like me. Actors never do. They always look better. And he didn't quite capture my Arkansas/Texas accent. But there I was on screen—horn-rimmed glasses, suit and tie—saying what I actually said and hiding behind Red Rover. I would be a fool to complain about that handsome young actor looking more like a stylish Buddy Holly than the real Neal Spelce.

What pleased me about Maitland's approach was that the story was not about the sniper, but about the victims. In fact, the sniper's name isn't mentioned, and he wasn't shown or referred to very often. The film was about the people who were there, who lived through it, and how their lives were impacted at that moment and for decades to come.

I've seen several Tower documentaries over the years, many of them inaccurate, and *Tower* captures the true drama moment by moment. The film won several awards at festivals all over the world and should have made the cut for an Academy Award.

By virtue of circumstance—my on-the-scene reporting—I became the voice of that monumental event. I was cast into the public eye like never before. Suddenly, everybody knew my name and who I was. In the years since then, I've been recognized often as a talking-head newscaster by generations of Austinites, but the one signature moment that most people remember me for is my reporting on the radio on August 1, 1966, warning the public to stay away from the UT campus because there was a madman shooting from the Tower.

I've been asked if I feel pigeonholed by that single event. Frankly, it's not as if I'd been sentenced to twenty years in prison. Being recognized and identified with an important episode in US history and the history of broadcast journalism gives me great pride and satisfaction. To be honest, I don't mind talking about that day, because I think it has important lessons for us all—not only for the journalism profession, but for us as

In the more than fifty years since the Tower shooting I have been asked countless times to return to the campus and describe what happened on that horrible day. *Photo courtesy Neal Spelce*

a nation. True heroism, I believe, is measured in how we care for our neighbors when they are lying hurt on the hard ground.

I once said facetiously, "If the Tower tragedy is the lead in my obituary, I can live with that." It happened to a thirty-year-old man, fifty-odd years ago, and I've had a life filled with so much joy and accomplishment since then. That was only one day in a long career. I hope people will also remember the paths I've gone down as a news reporter, the places I've traveled to for a story, and the people I've touched in the many years after the guns went silent at a beautiful university campus on a scorching hot Monday in August 1966.

TOWER GARDEN AND MEMORIAL

For more than thirty years, the University of Texas tried to downplay and essentially forget the tragic events of that dark day. As UT psychology professor James Pennebaker told the *Austin American-Statesman* on the fortieth anniversary of the shootings, "UT did the same thing a lot of communities do after tragedy. They do everything they can to not think about it, to not commemorate it, to think about the future and not the past and to dismiss it as something that was an aberration."

And on the fiftieth anniversary, UT president Greg Fenves explained what had happened in the past: "In the ensuing decades, there was an instinct to shield the university by not associating it with a single crime. To not allow tragedy to define the Tower, the central symbol of this institution."

I understand the university's position from a public relations viewpoint, but ignoring the tragedy was a mistake. You shouldn't wipe out history or turn a blind eye, especially if an incident had such a far-reaching impact, not only in Austin but all over the country.

For many years there had been a deep undercurrent in the University of Texas family to recognize and memorialize the victims and bring closure. In 1999, UT president Larry Faulkner formed a committee to create a memorial in remembrance of that day. He had been a graduate student in chemistry and had just left campus when the shooting began. As he put it, "The university's stance had always seemed to be to try to erase what had happened, but with absolutely no success. It was like an injury that would never heal."

President Faulkner's committee officially designated a Tower Memorial Garden, located just north of the Tower, and included a turtle pond and grassy lawn. The garden was dedicated on August 1, 1999, and the ceremony was well attended. Many people at that event expressed their appreciation for a place where they could remember those who'd been harmed three decades earlier.

There was an elaborate design to add other features to the garden

Years later, I was joined by journalists Brenda Bell, Gary Pickle, and Phil Miller for a program at the Headliners Club to recount what each of us witnessed on the University of Texas campus on August 1, 1966. *Photo courtesy Headliners Club*

that would enhance reflection and memory, but funding constraints prevented that from happening. A small memorial plaque was added to the garden in 2007, but it didn't include the names of the victims.

It was the lack of names that didn't sit well with several of the survivors—the lack of anything specific and concrete that said, "Real people died here that day, and others still bear the physical and emotional wounds they received." In 2014, Claire Wilson, Artly Snuff (John Fox), Alfred McAlister, Forrest Preece, and other survivors and rescuers formed the Tower Memorial Enhancement Group to push for greater recognition of those who had lost their lives in the shadow of the Tower.

The group sent a formal statement to UT president Bill Powers: "We seek enhancement of the memorialization for victims of the August 1,

1966 tragedy at The University of Texas. The current plaque at the turtle pond represents a sincere effort by the university to recognize this terrible event. But we want a more substantial memorial to be made, at least displaying names of the victims who had their lives cut short that day. Our goal is to have this enhanced memorialization in place by August 1, 2016." The fiftieth anniversary.

In August 2015, members of the Tower Memorial Enhancement Group traveled to a quarry in Fredericksburg, Texas, and chose a red granite boulder, six feet tall and weighing nearly 1,200 pounds, to be the memorial stone that would bear the names of the sixteen victims who lost their lives on August 1, 1966.

At the dedication ceremony, fifty years after the bullets had rained down on campus, UT president Fenves said, "We will never eliminate the memory of the horror that consumed this campus on August 1, 1966, nor should we try. But by focusing on the good and the stories of the heroes and the lives of the survivors that are with us this afternoon, we can finally begin to remember and endure our burden of the past."

I was enormously happy that my alma mater had finally memorialized the names of the victims. The same ceremony also acknowledged and honored the students and others who'd risked their lives to rescue the wounded, as well as the brave police officers who'd put an end to the violence. Recognition and gratitude were long overdue. It was a great healing day in Austin, Texas.

I walked over and read the names on the granite monument, and I felt a rush of memories and emotions from that day when I'd sweated through my shirt and suit jacket while reporting live on the air from Red Rover. As the memorial ceremony unfolded, I was content to stand quietly in the back of the audience and savor the moment. And to remember my courageous colleagues in the news profession—many of them no longer with us—who had thrown themselves into harm's way by rushing onto campus that day to cover the story while bullets were flying all around them: Joe Lee, Phil Miller, Gary Pickle, Joe Roddy, David Swope, John Thawley, Charles Ward, Gordon Wilkison.

I will remember their names and their remarkable fearlessness for as long as I draw breath. Their actions were an inspiration to me and can serve as an inspiration to every journalist who scribbles notes in the line of fire or focuses a camera lens on the face of danger. Every day in this

INTERFECTI AUGUST 1, 1966

THOMAS AQUINAS ASHTON
DR. ROBERT H. BOYER
THOMAS FREDERICK ECKMAN
MARK JEROME GABOUR
KAREN JOAN GRIFFITH
DAVID H. GUNBY
THOMAS RAY KARR
MARGUERITE GABOUR LAMPORT
CLAUDIA RUTT
ROY DELL SCHMIDT
PAUL BOLTON SONNTAG
OFFICER BILLY PAUL SPEED
EDNA ELIZABETH ROSE TOWNSLEY
HARRY WALCHUK
KATHLEEN LEISSNER WHITMAN
MARGARET HODGES WHITMAN
BABY BOY WILSON

THE UNIVERSITY OF TEXAS AT AUSTIN REMEMBERS WITH PROFOUND SORROW THE
TRAGEDY OF AUGUST 1, 1966. THIS SPACE IS DEDICATED AS THE TOWER GARDEN
A MEMORIAL TO THOSE WHO DIED, TO THOSE WHO WERE WOUNDED, AND TO THE
COUNTLESS OTHER VICTIMS WHO WERE IMMEASURABLY AFFECTED BY THE TRAGEDY.

Every time I read the names of those killed, which are inscribed on the UT campus memorial monument beneath the Tower, I become choked up. *University of Texas at Austin/Marsha Miller* country and around the world, dedicated reporters from a new generation, cut from the same cloth as my old friends and colleagues at KTBC, hunker down in danger zones and in the halls of power to cover stories we need to hear about. They are all my heroes. They put their lives on the line to ensure that as a nation, we shall know the truth, and the truth shall make us free.

ARKANSAS TRAVELERS

People have asked me how I was able to withstand the life-and-death drama of those bullets whizzing around me while I was broadcasting the story live on the Big Wind. I always respond with a wry smile and a question for the questioner: "Do you know any nurses?" Because when it came to courage, a steady hand, and grace under duress, I had the best teacher in the world.

My mother, Fannie Lou Spelce, raised two sons mostly on her own while saving lives as a full-time nurse. She was born in 1908 on a farm near Dyer, Arkansas, a rural community of three hundred people located twenty miles northeast of Fort Smith. At age twenty, she began her nurse training at Sparks Memorial Hospital in Fort Smith, the oldest hospital in Arkansas, where she received her registered nurse certificate. That was an impressive accomplishment in the rural South in the late 1920s.

At some point, she and a fellow nurse named Marjorie read that they needed nurses in New York City, and these two good-looking young ladies decided that the big money was in the big city, so they traveled to New York in 1929 and got jobs. As my mother always told the story, they were the belles of the ball in the Big Apple, bright young southern women with natural beauty and a charming drawl. They excelled at the hospital where they were working.

New York had a major impact on my mother's formation and career. It also revealed her adventurous spirit, which set her apart. All her life, she was strong and independent and did things on her own, and that held her in good stead to raise two boys as a single mother. "Single mother" wasn't a phrase used back then, but she and many women like her had no choice, made no excuses, and went about their lives as the primary breadwinners with courage and determination, and without the support of a stable marriage.

I was born on April 17, 1936, in Fort Smith. My birth wasn't recorded until April 18, so when I registered for the draft at age eighteen during the Korean War, I was informed that my official birthdate was April 18. I thought, "Why not celebrate birthdays whenever you want?" The same thing happened to Willie Nelson, who had Arkansas roots but was born in Abbott, Texas. He celebrates both days, and probably quite a few more during the year. Willie shouldn't party alone, so I celebrate both of my days and both of his, too.

I don't know for sure how my parents met, but I suspect geography had something to do with it. Mother's family farm was about five miles from Alma, Arkansas, where my daddy was born, a slightly larger town at the intersection of the road that runs north to Fayetteville. My birth certificate says he was a Coca-Cola salesman.

Daddy was a handsome accountant/bookkeeper, articulate and smart, and although he never finished high school, he was a successful salesman in many different businesses. He had the gift of gab and would tell jokes all the time, and he was well liked. So when they met, I'm sure he swept my mother off her feet, even though she was a year older and better educated than he was.

When I was a baby, my mother found employment in Clarksville, Arkansas, working as a nurse for the two private physicians in the community—Dr. Earle Hunt and Dr. Rex Siegel—and she also worked in the town's only hospital. Sixty miles east of Fort Smith, Clarksville is a small town nestled against the Arkansas River in the foothills of the Ozark Mountains. Clarksville is where my brother, Bennett, was born in 1937 and where we grew up.

Mother and Daddy had a rocky relationship, and they separated several times when Bennett and I were children. In her later years, my mother never talked about her marriage. When someone asked her about it, she cut off the topic. She didn't want to discuss it. In fact, she didn't talk about it with my brother and me when we were growing up, even though we could see what was happening between her and Daddy. More than once, she decided to leave him in the middle of the night, threw blankets in the backseat of the car for her two boys, and drove off to another destination.

Because of their marital difficulties, we spent considerable time with my mother's family on their farm near Dyer. In my generation of children who were raised in the South and Midwest, most of us were familiar with farm life. We were from rural areas and small communities and we either grew up near farms, visited relatives living on farms, or were just one generation away from being farmers ourselves.

Going to my grandparents' farm was always a fun adventure, almost like going to summer camp. The farm was virtually self-sustaining. They raised chickens and cows, and they grew grapes and figs and corn and lots of vegetables. They also made sorghum molasses by walking a horse around in a circle, grinding the sorghum in a mill. They fed their pigs and made bacon out of them in the local slaughterhouse. Their smokehouse was used to smoke bacon and jerky, and the smell was delicious. There was a stand-alone cellar outside where my grandma stored her jars of canned fruit, peaches, pears, and whatnot down in that cool darkness. It was always a scary place to walk down into as a little boy. There were spiders and what I imagined were all manner of ghosts.

My brother and I were always running around the farm looking at mysterious things. We would climb up in a tree and eat persimmons until we got stomachaches. We ate grapes off the vine, and my grandparents raised Cain about that because they harvested those grapes for jelly. We stole watermelons with a neighbor boy, and to cool them down we'd put them in a small branch of water, not far down a dirt road, and then cut them open and eat the heart out of them. They were delicious.

My grandparents were good people, and I thought their farm was huge, but it didn't seem that big when I went back and looked at it years later. The farm and nearby community hadn't changed in a hundred years.

My mother was also an artist who captured her world on canvas. People have wondered about her paintings over the years, thinking she couldn't have been born in a time of covered wagons or when horses were used to crush sorghum for molasses. But farm life was the source of her artistic inspiration. Many of her paintings preserved the traditions of an earlier era, the commonplace things folks were still practicing in rural communities when she was growing up: quilting bees where local ladies brought covered dishes and spent all day quilting; the custom of picking up mail at the train depot on Saturdays and reading letters out loud to friends and loved ones; county fairs with clowns and booths selling canned fruit; sleepovers with cousins spending the night on pallets.

"Families were close in those days," my mother always said, "and everybody loved everybody."

Life in Clarksville

In Clarksville, Mother was in high demand as a nurse, but we didn't have much money. It was during the Depression, and we didn't own a

My mother's favorite childhood photo of me and my younger brother, Bennett (he's the one with the curly hair), occurred when she dressed us in matching sailor suits for a photography studio sitting. In her later years, as Fannie Lou Spelce began her amazing career as a folk artist, she turned the photo into one of her many acclaimed paintings. *Courtesy Spelce Family Collection*

car. We lived in a rented house next to the hospital, and later in a small two-bedroom brick house owned by Dr. Rex Siegel across the street from his own house. There was a creek that ran through town called Spadra Creek, with a concrete bridge, and you could walk across the bridge and go up the hill to the Catholic school my brother and I attended.

When Mother walked home from the doctor's downtown office every day, Bennett and I would sometimes run out to meet her, put her in

our little red wagon, and pull her home. We figured she'd been working all day and needed a lift. I'm sure it was uncomfortable for her in
that wagon, but she was always a good sport. The neighbors roared with
friendly laughter when they saw her riding in the wagon, wearing her
white nurse's uniform.

Clarksville was coal-mining country. Just up the road was a town
called Coal Hill and another town called Hartman. Whenever we took
the bus to my grandparents' farm, we would see coal miners wearing
those carbide lamps attached to their caps, the open flames fixed in front
of a reflector that gave them greater range of vision. One day, there was
an explosion in a coal mine and several miners were killed and several
others were seriously burned. Mother was called in to nurse the survivors, and seeing those miners burned like that really affected her. She
was very professional about treating patients, and this was the only time I
ever saw her shaken. She came home distraught after treating those poor
victims.

Mother worked six days a week, and on Saturdays she sometimes left
us alone in the house. Can you imagine leaving two boys alone today? She
would say, "Boys, I want you to clean the house while I'm gone." To mo-
tivate us, she bought ten-cent comic books and hid them throughout the
rooms. And so as we made the beds and swept the floor, we'd find Super-
man comics and stop and read them. We'd get lost in all those fantastic
comics about Captain America, Captain Marvel, and other superheroes.
It was a treasure hunt, but we had to clean before we read.

When she worked for the doctor downtown, his office was across the
street from the library. We'd go with her to work on Saturday mornings,
and when the library opened, we'd walk over and sit at a table and read
books for the rest of the morning. And then in the afternoons we'd go to
the double features at the Strand movie theater a few blocks away. They
played Westerns and Tarzan movies and serials and cartoons. It was an
entire afternoon of fun for a nickel or dime. I still remember the Batman
and Green Hornet serials, and of course you had to return the next Saturday to watch new episodes.

It was in that theater where I got hooked on Movietone News. I can
even remember their logo and the opening sounds of their theme song,
with a camera operator onscreen cranking a film camera and the announcer saying, "Movietone News! With the eyes and ears of the world!"
Seeing all that dramatic news had a profound effect on me. It opened my

world. I became enthralled with the medium. I didn't fully understand it at that young age, but it captured my imagination and sparked my curiosity. I saw how everyday events could be presented in moving pictures on a screen. That may have been the first step on my journey toward news reporting.

I was only five years old when America entered World War II, and I was nine by the time the war ended in 1945. I remember the era through the images of Movietone News—bombs dropping through bomb bay doors and footage of Hitler and the young Germans who were pulled in by him. In fact, one Saturday there was a movie about Hitler Youth. Actor Skip Homeier played a Hitler Youth, and that's how I became aware that they were training young people to wear the swastika on their arms and raise the Heil Hitler salute. And I certainly remember the shocking scenes of the Holocaust and seeing bodies stacked like cordwood.

The war was omnipresent, even in our small town. There was a cadre of soldiers training at the College of the Ozarks in Clarksville, and Mother volunteered to help with their USO parties. We didn't want her to leave us alone at night, so she would put us to bed and begin typing on the keys of an old typewriter, giving us the impression she was still there. When she came back home, she'd sneak in and start tapping the keys again.

There were rations with coupon books, but we didn't have a car so we didn't have to worry about buying gasoline. I remember hearing, "People around the world are in the middle of the war. They need food. Don't leave your plate until it's clean. You're lucky you've got food."

Daddy was drafted and went to the China-Burma-India Theater, where he served in the Quartermaster Corps as a bookkeeper and paymaster. He was never in combat. He sent photographs back to us a time or two, and I remember he'd grown a dapper mustache that came down from his nose and then went horizontal. I thought he was a handsome devil.

ONE-ROOM SCHOOLHOUSE

Bennett and I were educated at Holy Redeemer school in Clarksville, a one-room Catholic school, even though we weren't Catholics. Mother struck a deal with the nuns for us to attend, and they agreed to keep us at school until five o'clock, when she came and walked us home.

The school included grades one through eight, and by the time I was in the sixth grade, there were only three of us in that grade level. The nuns enforced a tough discipline. I can remember one of them walking around with a ruler and whacking knuckles. Witnessing that, Bennett and I became model students.

The class days followed a typical pattern. Second grade, here's your reading; third grade, here's your reading; fourth grade, here's your reading. Fifth grade, we'll do spelling now; sixth grade, we'll do geography. Every afternoon, while waiting for Mother, the nuns would put a book in our hands and say, "Here, read this." I remember getting a geography book and wondering, "Where the heck *is* Germany?" We didn't go outside and play or anything like that, because it would have required too much supervision.

The sisters taught us Catholic catechism, too, and I learned some Latin phrases using the highly touted *monkey see, monkey do* pedagogical method. (In fact, in high school I took Latin as a language course.) Bell-ringing was an earned privilege. Students would get selected to go out and ring the bell, and I remember being selected.

Bennett and I were unaware that our one-room learning was unusual. In our experience, it was nothing out of the ordinary. We would spend a year in one grade, half a year in another grade, and it was okay if you were nine years old and you knew what was going on up through the fifth grade. In that case, they'd advance you to the sixth grade, which was no big deal. Sitting there in a one-room school with all the students around us, including the older ones engaged in their various lessons, we could hear the exam questions in the higher grades and then the answers. This helped us progress quicker.

GORDO Y FLACO IN RAYMONDVILLE

Whenever Mother faced a serious problem she would turn to her family, because they were always very loving and supportive. After the war, she took us to Raymondville, where her brother Dude was running a grocery store. Dude offered to hire Daddy at the store as well, which was a chance for him to get back with us. But it didn't work out. To put it bluntly, Dad was a ladies' man and flirty with female patrons at the store, and that didn't sit well with Mother and her family.

When we moved to Raymondville, I was nine years old and in the sixth grade because of our flexible one-room education in Clarksville. I have no idea whether Raymondville had a better school system or not, but they took one look at me and said, "Oh no, he's too young for the sixth grade. He's only nine years old. We've got to hold him back."

There were only three months left in the school year, and Mother convinced them to let Bennett and me finish out the year in our respective grade levels and see how we'd do. I'm sure she was confident that her boys were going to excel, because I knew all the eighth-grade material by then. And it turned out that I did progress at a normal pace in the public school in Raymondville. But that first year they held Bennett back from advancing to his next grade level.

As I've thought about it over the decades, I've realized what a great education we received during those formative years with the nuns. It was rigorous, a fantastic grounding, and I believe it's the way school should be taught. In Clarksville, I was reading books voraciously during class and after school and on Saturdays in the library. Some days I would take a break and read comic books.

Raymondville had a reading program, too, and I read everything I could get my hands on. I was fascinated by Erle Stanley Gardner's Perry Mason books, and when I ran out of those, I read his mystery books published under the pen name of A. A. Fair. I was well read and well informed, and as I grew older, I decided I wanted to be Perry Mason, a trial lawyer.

It was culture shock going from segregated, mostly white Arkansas to Hispanic Raymondville. The geography was totally different as well. In Texas, if you walked barefoot on the grass, you'd get sticker burrs on your feet. All the skinny palm trees in Raymondville looked like telephone poles with potted plants on top. That was very different from the lush green forest of Wolf's Glen, a little mountain area near Clarksville where we went camping with our Boy Scout troop.

My brother and I had worn hand-me-downs in Arkansas, corduroy knickers that came down just below our knees, and we wore them instead of blue jeans to class in Raymondville. It was an open invitation for an ass-kicking, and we had our share of fights on the school grounds. I was very thin and Bennett was fairly heavyset, and I can remember them mocking *gordo y flaco*—"fatso and skinny"—and the next thing you know there was pushing and shoving and a scuffle. I don't recall ever being upset about it. I think Bennett and I just accepted it as *the way things are.*

I remember going to a softball game and hanging around under the stands, looking for dropped change on the ground—nickels and quarters—and on at least one occasion we got jumped and a fight broke out under there. Bennett and I never initiated anything, but we didn't back down. We could've run away, but we didn't. At one point I was flat on my back with a kid sitting on top of me, and the heavier Bennett came flying over and shoved him off. There were no serious injuries, and never any punishment or disciplinary consequences.

One day I got called on in class and the teacher asked, "Did you read the assignment?" I said, "No, ma'am, because I went to bed. It was dark." The class erupted in laughter. Mother would always put us to bed real early.

Sadly, my parents' attempt at reconciling in Raymondville didn't last very long. We left town in the middle of the night and were driving through Corpus Christi, 113 miles north along the Texas Gulf Coast, when suddenly there was a police car rushing up behind us, flashing its lights. Mother was really upset, so she pulled over and rolled down the window, and the first words I remember her saying to the policeman were, "I'm so glad to see you, officer! I think I'm lost and I don't know if this is a one-way street or not."

We were going down a one-way street the wrong way, but he looked into the backseat and saw two kids curled up in blankets and said, "Let me show you how to get out of here."

ON THE ROAD AGAIN

My success as a journalist has been the sum of many parts. I've always believed that the hallmark of a good journalist is curiosity, and moving to many new places and being exposed to many new things made me a curious person.

We moved to Tulsa in 1948, during the run-up to the presidential election between Harry Truman and Thomas Dewey, and Daddy was a strong supporter of the Democratic Party. (Until the day my grandma died, she would call and tell me who to vote for. It was always a Democrat.) I was twelve years old at the time, and on Halloween that year, my costume was one of Daddy's black coats and ties. I painted a mustache across my upper lip with burnt cork so I would look like Thomas Dewey. Then I taped a sign on the seat of my pants saying, "The End of Dewey."

One night in Tulsa, before Daddy came home in the middle of the night, Mother packed up the car again and we left him for Richmond, California, where Dude and several other family members had moved. By that time, Dude had become a successful entrepreneur at starting grocery businesses, and when he got established out in the San Francisco Bay Area, other members of the family had begun working for him. Two of my uncles, who were married to Aunt Marie and Aunt Inez, worked at the country grocery store that Dude had opened in Campbell, California, and the family had moved my grandparents out to a little house across the street from the store. Campbell is now a high-tech suburb in Silicon Valley, near San Jose.

Mother found a job immediately as the night emergency room supervisor at a hospital in Berkeley. She would park near the ER, and Bennett and I would sleep in the car all night long. She would come out and check on us from time to time. She put a milk bottle in the car for us to pee in. She was doing what she had to do to support herself and her sons.

While we were in Berkeley, some bank robbers showed up in the emergency room for treatment for gunshot wounds and she called the police and they came and arrested them. The front-page story was "Alert Nurse Bags Criminals."

RECONCILIATION IN CORPUS

In 1949, we returned to the comfortable and familiar small town of Clarksville, and Mother was hired again as a nurse. But right before my senior year of high school, we moved from the Ozark foothills of Clarksville to the balmy Gulf Coast city of Corpus Christi, Texas, where my father had landed a bookkeeping job. My parents had decided to make another attempt at reconciliation.

Mother worked as a nurse at the hospital, and Bennett and I attended W. B. Ray High School, in what was only the second year of the new school's existence. I was a self-taught drummer and played snare drum in the W. B. Ray Fightin' Texans band. (I had never taken lessons, but I could read drum music a little bit.) As we approached graduation, all my buddies were going to Texas A&M University and I was heading to Austin. I was ostracized by one of my friends, Durwood Thompson, who thought I was a traitor for not aspiring to be an Aggie. But A&M didn't have a law school, and if I wanted to be Perry Mason, I had to go to the University of Texas.

Daddy was an alcoholic. There was always whiskey in our house, and he abused it. One night mother said, "Let's go pick up your dad. It's late and he's in a bar and he can't drive home."

When we picked him up, he got upset and said, "Why did you have to bring the boys to see me like this?"

I remember a time or two when he was passed out on the bed at home. Daddy was outgoing and could tell a joke and slap you on the back and laugh and kid everybody. He had a great personality except when he was drunk. My teens were a nervous time because that was happening all too often.

In his later years, he joined Alcoholics Anonymous and worked hard, with pride and care, to deal with the disease. He carried an AA chip in his pocket. When I was a student at UT, he would come by and pull the chip out of his pocket to show me it had been several years since he'd had a drink.

We didn't stay in touch very well. He hadn't been a significant presence in my life. After he and Mother finally divorced, after many years of their on-again, off-again relationship, he remarried a couple of times. Occasionally he would reappear in Austin to visit me and my two children, but he didn't stay long.

In August 1980, my father was living in the Dallas area, and one day, when he was delivering a speech to fellow AA members, he stopped his remarks and said, "I need to sit down a minute" and he died of a heart attack. He was sixty-eight years old. Mother, Bennett, and I attended the small funeral in Dallas out of respect, but we sat by ourselves and didn't meet his other family in attendance.

The three of us drove back to Austin in near silence. Mother had spent so much of her young adulthood dealing with their troubled marriage and moving her two sons from place to place, supporting us on a single salary, and she'd said all she wanted to say about the man whose name I will carry for the rest of my days. His name was Neal Leslie Spelce Sr.

THE BIG LEAP

With very little self-conscious planning, and a lot of "being in the right place at the right time," my long career has been divided into three eras: I was a reporter and news director in the 1950s and 1960s, I ran an advertising and public relations firm in the 1970s and 1980s, and then I returned to television news in the 1990s.

My first major career decision came when I decided to leave KTBC toward the end of the 1960s. It was a big change, and there were a number of twists and turns involved.

To begin with, I was approached by Texas lieutenant governor Ben Barnes and Frank Erwin, chairman of the University of Texas System Board of Regents, who said, "Neal, we'd like to hire you at the university in a communications capacity." I was flattered and intrigued by that possibility. The University of Texas had always been a great love of mine and crucially important to both my personal and professional development. I said, "Sure, that would be terrific. I'll leave KTBC."

I was geared up mentally to make the big leap, and everything was ready to go. They said, "Let us get our ducks in a row and we'll come back to you and make it official."

When you get an incredible opportunity like that, you become elated and commit to leaving the past behind and embracing what lies ahead. All of a sudden it's "Things are changing dramatically for me and my family, and I've got a great future."

But I received a call from Chairman Erwin a week or two later, saying, "Neal, we won't be able to hire you. Ben and I were at the White House yesterday, and President Johnson chewed us out for trying to steal you from him. 'What are you doing taking Neal away from the TV station?'" Erwin then said to me, "I'm sorry, but we just can't do that. We can't incur the wrath of LBJ. We would love to have you at UT, and maybe that'll happen sometime down the road."

Once again, LBJ had had a major impact on my life, but this time I was disappointed. I'd been involved in broadcasting for more than a dozen years by then, ever since I was a college student, and the television news business didn't pay very well. I received a fifty-dollar-per-month raise every year, and I was told by management, "Neal, don't tell anybody about your raises. We're not giving raises to everybody." It wasn't a high-paying profession at that point, and it still isn't today, except at the superstar levels.

I wasn't unhappy at KTBC. I was very proud to be the news director at Austin's premier news station. I loved journalism and television broadcasting, but I was facing financial challenges with a growing family.

A couple of months later, a friend I knew socially, R. Miller Hicks, called me out of the blue and said, "I've got an opportunity to buy a radio station in Shreveport, Louisiana. It's called KJOE, and you're the only person I know in broadcasting. I want you to be a part of this."

Miller was eight years older than I was, an entrepreneur with real estate interests and his own business consulting company. He was a real straight arrow. He didn't cuss, he didn't smoke or drink, but he was a fun guy. He drove a convertible and took his black lab to the office with him every day, and the dog would sit beside him while Miller worked. He was a unique character, and everybody liked him.

Miller felt it was a good investment—the price was right—and he was looking for someone to manage the operation of the small daytime AM radio station. A decade earlier, when future comedy legend George Carlin had been an airman at nearby Barksdale Air Force Base, he'd worked as a disc jockey at KJOE, where he'd begun to polish his act.

I thought, "Hmm, a radio station." Although I'd been in broadcasting for years, it was the first time I'd considered a financial investment in the business. "I'm interested, Miller," I said, "but I'm a salaried employee and I don't have any money to invest."

He said, "Neal, I don't want your money, I want your expertise."

I told him that my friend Ron Rogers was managing an AM radio station in Austin. "Let me call Ron and talk it over," I said. "Would you have any objection to him joining our discussion?"

Ron and I had been contemporaries in radio-television at UT, and we'd started out at KTBC at around the same time, when we were still UT students. He'd focused on radio and I'd gone into TV. We even looked alike—both about six feet tall with short haircuts. Ron had gone off to serve as program director at WACO AM in Waco, and I'd stayed in Austin, and we'd remained good friends. Eventually, he had gravitated back to Austin and was hired as general manager of the radio station KOKE

AM, which he and his DJs were careful to always pronounce as individual letters K-O-K-E so as not to get crossways with the Coca-Cola Company.

I called Ron and said, "I don't know anything about radio, but you do. Would you want to partner with us?"

Ron Rogers had worked as a door-to-door Bible salesman in Ohio to pay for his education at the University of Texas. He loved country music, and when he was general manager at KOKE, he picked the music playlist, although that's usually the program director's job. But Ron took all the new records home every night, listened to them carefully, and brought them back the next day, deciding, "Let's put this one in the rotation."

He also did play-by-play radio for the UT Longhorn baseball team for ten years while orange-blood legend Bill Little did color, and they'd accompanied the team to Omaha for the College World Series almost every year. Ron also loved golf to a fault, and when we became business partners he'd say, "I'm playing golf this afternoon."

"Oh really?" I'd say with a raised eyebrow. "You'll be gone all afternoon out in the nice sunshine while I'm stuck in this office?"

"I'm playing with a possible client," he'd say, and that always shut down my grumblings.

For the KJOE purchase in Shreveport, Miller Hicks brought in two other partners: Sam Winters—who was with the law firm of Clark, Thomas & Winters—and Walter Caven, a lobbyist with the Texas Railroad Association who'd overheard Miller and Sam talking about the radio station at a cocktail party and asked, "How about me? Can I get in on this deal?"

Sam Winters was slim, dapper, well mannered, soft spoken, slow talking. Walter Caven was tall and thin and gregarious. He'd had varicose vein surgery that went wrong, and he ended up having to walk with a brace on his legs.

When Ron and I told Miller that we were interested, he said, "We'll provide the finances. You and Ron provide the sweat and run the station, and hopefully we'll all make some money. The five of us will be equal partners at 20 percent apiece and ride this horse together."

It was a very generous offer. We named our group the Dynamic Broadcasting Company.

Cautious by nature, and concerned with income, I didn't leave KTBC right away. Never lacking in self-confidence, I thought I could run a radio station in my spare time.

Years later, people asked me if I told LBJ and Mrs. Johnson that I was venturing into the competitive world of radio ownership. The truth is, it didn't enter my mind that they'd be concerned. Shreveport was in another state and our signals wouldn't have overlapped. In fact, I was open about it, telling friends and colleagues what we were doing.

Every Friday evening, after I signed off the air at 6:30, Ron and I would head to Shreveport, which was 320 miles away and a five-and-a-half-hour drive. Ron would pull up in front of the KTBC studio in his Mercury with a bag of burgers and a six-pack of beer, and we'd drive like crazy to get to Bossier City before last call so we could have one final drink before we went to sleep. (Shreveport was "dry" at that time.) We would work all day Saturday and Sunday with KJOE's station personnel and return to Austin on Sunday night. Every Wednesday night we'd phone the station manager to go over sales and programming.

In those days, there was a common trend in radioland known as a "trade-out"—meaning you would trade airtime advertising for some amenity other than cash. "Let me drive one of your brand-new Buicks and we'll give your dealership five sixty-second spots a day on our station." Ron and I always stayed at a Howard Johnson's motel as a trade-out for HJ commercials on KJOE.

All good things must end, of course, and eventually there were serious problems with trade-outs. Unethical employees began doing all sorts of trade-outs on the side. At a radio station we operated a few years later, I found it odd that a swimming pool company was advertising on the air. With a little probing, I discovered that the general manager had gone to the company and said, "If you'll build a swimming pool in my backyard, we'll give you airtime on the radio." The GM didn't own the station and didn't have the right to do that. It was strictly for his own personal gain.

Soon the trade-out went the way of its devious cousin "payola," which had been the practice of record companies paying DJs to play and promote selected records back in the 1950s.

When we took over KJOE, Shreveport radio station KWKH dominated the local airwaves with 50,000 watts, twenty-four hours a day, seven days a week. They broadcast the *Louisiana Hayride*, which had been an enormously popular and influential country music program for years. Elvis Presley, Hank Williams, Johnny Cash, Johnny Horton, Kitty Wells, George Jones, and many other country and rockabilly legends had performed live on the *Hayride*, which gave several of them their first public exposure.

KJOE was a little 1,000 watter, daytime only, and we changed the format from Top 40 to modern country music because it was so pervasive and well-liked, and because Ron Rogers was an expert in country music. In fact, he would later be inducted into the Country Music Hall of Fame as "The Father of Modern Country Music" in America. When we decided to go up against the big boys at KWKH, Ron explained, "Right now in radio, Top 40 is the going thing. Disc jockeys with fast-pace patter play the songs one after the other. Let's use the Top 40 format but play country music"—which is what he'd been doing at KOKE in Austin. "We'll get in and get to the music real quick—a fast pace with jingles and back-and-forth chatter like Gordon McLendon on KLIF in Dallas."

Known as "The Old Scotchman," Texan Gordon McLendon had pioneered the Top 40 rock 'n' roll format in the 1950s and 1960s. He'd built a communications empire, produced movies, and owned more than forty movie theaters.

KJOE didn't have a substantial amount of money, so we'd do what I called "guerrilla warfare." We made little stickers that said "KJOE Is Everywhere" with our call sign and the dial position printed on the sticker, and we handed them out to our staff and supporters. Every time we'd go to a public restroom, we'd slap one on the toilet—not to mention on every public bulletin board we passed by. The station received a lot of comments and praise, especially because we were playing country music without the slow-talking twang. Although we'd occasionally play the classics, like Hank Williams, Porter Wagoner, and Dolly Parton, our focus was on modern country. KJOE turned out to be very successful as a day-timer against KWKH and other competitors.

"HONEY, I'VE QUIT MY JOB"

S oon there were more investment opportunities in radioland. Our five-person Dynamic Broadcasting Company acquired stations in Beaumont and Sinton, Texas (near Corpus Christi). Ron and I also branched out on our own and created partnerships with other investors. I became involved with radio stations in Abilene, Killeen, and the Austin area.

When all was said and done, the investors and I got in, changed music formats, made the stations successful, sold them, and pocketed a little money. It was an enjoyable experience, even though there were FCC regulations that limited our acquisitions. Later on, after many of those oversight restrictions were removed, owners could purchase eight hundred stations if they so desired, and radio stations became worth millions of dollars. We were in it too damned early.

With the success of those first radio stations, Ron Rogers and I developed a taste for entrepreneurship. We were in an equity position where he and I would make money if the stations did well and we could sell them for a profit. But in those early years, we were loaded with family responsibilities, and we weren't making quite enough money in radio. So we decided to form our own advertising and public relations firm to keep us financially stable while we acquired more stations.

Knowing that the dual life was certain to be more complicated and more time-consuming, we both decided to take another big leap and leave our day jobs—he as general manager of KOKE radio and I as news director at KTBC-TV. We formed the Rogers Spelce Company, which was a plunge into the highly competitive world of advertising and PR. We were somewhat apprehensive about losing steady paychecks and taking on that level of risk, but public relations was a world that Ron and I knew well through our combined experiences in news reporting and communications.

My wife, Sheila, was pregnant with our daughter Cile at the time, and when I went home and said, "Honey, I've quit my job," it didn't go over very well. I assured her that I had a plan: "Ron and I are forming an ad agency to get clients and supplement what we're doing with the radio stations."

By then, Ron and I knew a lot of folks in the Austin business community, and we went to the banks and other commercial enterprises and said, "We'd like to handle your advertising." We were two young, energetic, and very ambitious guys.

THAT OLD CLACKETY-CLACK MACHINE

When putting radio stations on the air, we needed an information source for the news, so we had to sign up for a wire service, either AP or UPI. It was a competitive negotiation. "Okay, AP, what will you do for us?" "All right, UPI, will you match that? What will you do?"

I had always been a news junkie. Everywhere I went, I bought as many newspapers as I could get my hands on. Whenever I visited an airport or traveled to another city, I'd grab the newspapers so I could stay up to speed with local and national headlines and editorial analysis. When I voted in elections, I knew everybody on the ballot. I had often interviewed them and knew what they stood for. I was hooked on in-depth examinations of what was going on in politics.

After leaving KTBC, I was feeling frustrated because I didn't have a teletype machine and that constant stream of news within arm's reach. When our radio stations began negotiating with AP and UPI to choose a wire service, I said, "AP, you can provide a second wire-machine installation, can't you?" They said yes, and I said, "How about giving me one in Austin?" And they said, "Oh, no, only where your radio station is located."

But I had found out that the Reverend Billy Graham had an AP teletype machine in his home, so I played the evangelist card. I said, "Look, if you can put a wire machine in Billy Graham's home, where there's no radio station, surely you can give me a second machine in Austin, Texas." And they acquiesced.

I was happy to have that old clackety-clack machine with its ding, ding, ding, ding, which reminded me of being in the newsroom. By then it had become second nature to me. However, when I installed it at our ad agency, the sound drove the hell out of the people around me. They couldn't stand all that loud clacking twenty-four hours a day.

While I was gone on a trip one day, the staff built a box around the machine to muffle the noise. Their construction had a glass top so you could look in and see the copy. When you wanted to rip it off and read it, you'd lift up the top, rip off the flat-fold paper, and then close it again.

The Internet was decades away, and it eventually eliminated the need for that old teletype machine. But I still have the machine tucked away somewhere in a storage closet like a family heirloom I can't bear to lose.

Going Solo

As it turned out, the Rogers Spelce Company became financially successful, gaining clients and establishing a strong reputation. Ron and I pooled our talents. I helped him with the radio stations and kept my ownership; he helped me with the PR work. But the radio investors wanted more of his time because he was the real brains behind the day-to-day operations. Our interests and our career opportunities were beginning to diverge by the mid-1970s, so Ron and I decided it was time to split up. There were no hard feelings. We remained good friends. It was an amicable business agreement that we felt would benefit both of us.

Ron was hired by Roy Butler to manage the two powerhouse stations he owned in Austin, KVET and KASE-FM, which became enormously successful in popularity and revenues. When Butler eventually sold those stations for $90 million, I was happy to hear that Ron made out very well.

With Ron no longer involved, I changed the name from the Rogers Spelce Company to Neal Spelce Associates, and later to Neal Spelce Communications, and eventually to the Neal Spelce Company. I was on my own.

LYNDON JOHNSON IN CEMENT

On March 31, 1968, when LBJ announced that he would not run for reelection, I was at a Headliners Club party hosted at the Austin home of wealthy Texas businessman H. H. "Pete" Coffield. Former Texas governor Allan Shivers was there, and he said, "The president's getting ready to speak. Let's go turn on the TV."

The announcement came as a shock. We partygoers were stunned into silence. No one in the room had anticipated what LBJ would say: "I shall not seek, and I will not accept, the nomination of my party for another term as your president." (The teleprompter he was reading from is now in the LBJ Library.) The crowd at the party wasn't an LBJ crowd. Most of them were affluent conservatives. But Lyndon was a Texan, and Texans usually rally around their own. One person immediately started circulating a petition to urge Allan Shivers to run for president. It was a frantic move, and one that reflected the raw feelings of the moment.

That astonishing announcement meant that the Democratic field was wide open. Vice President Hubert Humphrey was LBJ's choice and the party's front-runner. But there was a spectrum of political beliefs within the Democratic Party, and the open field gave energy and momentum to candidates Bobby Kennedy and Eugene McCarthy. A significant segment of Democrats still couldn't get past their animosity toward President Johnson, and they tarred Humphrey with the same brush.

The year 1968 was one of the most tumultuous times in American history. Five days after LBJ's announcement, Martin Luther King Jr. was murdered in Memphis. Bobby Kennedy was shot to death in early June. All of that took place in a little over two months. Once again, the nation was traumatized. It had been a mere five years since President Kennedy's assassination, and that national collective pain was still fresh. When I interviewed people in my role as a reporter, it was hard for them to wrap their heads around the tragedies taking place in American politics. Every day was history in the making, and as a country, we struggled through those dark times.

Regardless of LBJ's decision not to seek reelection in 1968, he was

Unlike other presidential libraries built with private contributions, the University of Texas paid for and constructed the LBJ Library, coincidentally on the grounds where I lived for years as a student. *UT Office of Public Affairs Records, Briscoe Center for American History, the University of Texas at Austin*

keenly aware of his legacy and sensitive about his place in the long line of US presidents. As early as 1964, he'd begun to plan his presidential library, a grand repository of his life and political career, and the project broke ground on the University of Texas campus in 1967.

In early 1971, the Johnson family hired me to plan and direct the library's dedication ceremony, which was scheduled for May of that year. Organizing the event was a massive job. There were a multitude of complex elements we had to deal with. The primary question was what did the former president want?

The LBJ Presidential Library was the first presidential library built on a university campus and the largest and most expensive presidential library at that point in time. The University of Texas paid for the construction and controlled the purse strings, and that was a key factor in how the library was constructed. Presidential libraries are usually funded with private money, and a few of them are near universities. In recent years, the George H. W. Bush Presidential Library and Museum was built in College Station, on the Texas A&M University campus, and the George W. Bush Presidential Library and Museum on the Southern Methodist University campus in Dallas.

From the very beginning of my involvement, there was a race to perfect plans for the dedication ceremony at the same time that construction was still underway and rushing toward completion. That meant that my team and I had to take into account what LBJ desired, what the university expected, and what the architect had in mind. At times, the principal players got crossways with one another, as you would expect in a building process of that magnitude. After all, the dedication ceremony would be observed closely by the entire world.

The Johnson team set up my people in the Commodore Perry Hotel in downtown Austin, at Eighth Street and Brazos, which was between owners and vacant at that time. We took over one floor of the building and converted hotel rooms into offices. I built a small paid staff, and we stacked it with a huge number of volunteers who wanted to participate in the historic event. For about five months leading up to the dedication, we worked long hours, often under stress. The Johnsons were shooting for a May 22 dedication, a date that was chosen for two reasons: the historical weather records indicated that the weather was probably going to be good on that day, and university classes were out for the summer. LBJ was closely identified with the Vietnam War, and 1971 was at the height of major antiwar demonstrations on the Austin campus and around the country. That meant that additional security considerations would be brought into play.

During one private meeting with LBJ, I did something that triggered his wrath, and I found myself on the wrong end of his famous melt-you-down butt-chewings. The infamous Johnson Treatment! I can't remember what I did, but I do remember what he said: "If there's any way to fuck it up, Spelce, you will."

As usual, I sat there and took it. My situation wasn't unique. He be-

Harry Middleton, trusted White House aide for President and Mrs. Lyndon Johnson, was named the director of the LBJ Library while it was still under construction. *LBJ Library photo by Frank Wolfe*

rated people all the time, even his closest staff, as well as senators, congressmen, and his cabinet members. I was devastated, but the next day I needed a decision from him. There was something important he had to sign off on. When I tracked him down, he was at the ranch. They had a switchboard out there, and they patched me through to Mike Howard. He was LBJ's close Secret Service agent and was with him most of the time. Mike answered the car phone in the Continental. It wasn't a cellphone, of course. I also had a car phone, because LBJ insisted I get one when I was put in charge of the library dedication. It was a regular handheld phone in a box near the gearshift, with a huge, bulky transmitter in the trunk of the car. I said, "Mike, can I speak to The Man?"

He said, "Neal, you sure you want to talk to him?" He'd been there when I got my butt chewed royally. I'm sure it wasn't the first time he'd witnessed that sort of thing.

I said, "Well, I've got to, Mike."

He said, "He's out checking on his cattle right now."

I said, "But I need a decision right away."

He put me on hold, and my mind started going every which way. I sat there thinking, "What's going to happen? Is LBJ coming back to the car? Is he going to get on the phone and continue his rant?"

After a long wait, Mike came back on the line and said, "Neal, you're not going to believe this."

Was I being fired?

"The president told me to tell you that he trusts you implicitly, and whatever you want to do, he'll stand behind your decision."

A difference of night and day. I was so relieved. The day before, I'd been in the gutter, and the next day I was on a cloud.

I seldom knew how to deal with LBJ's mercurial personality. My response to his temper was to always be deferential, respectful, polite. After all, he'd served as president of the United States. My momma had raised me to respect my elders and to say, "Yes, ma'am. No, ma'am. Thank you, ma'am." Ma'am and sir. That's the way I was brought up. And to this day, I'll walk past someone sweeping the floor or busing tables at a restaurant and say, "Excuse me, sir. I need to get by."

Good manners have always been important to me, in both my personal and professional lives. I think LBJ understood that I was not a combative guy. Never was, never will be. But in my capacity as director of the Dedication Office, I wouldn't back down until I'd made my point. I'd say, "I'm not so sure we ought to do that, Mr. President." He'd say, "Why?" And I'd lay out my reasons. Then he'd say either, "Okay, I understand," or "Go ahead and do it anyway, Neal."

Liz Carpenter was a fixture in the Johnson family, and she was brought in to provide guidance and advice during the dedication planning. Liz had a notoriously strong personality with determined opinions and feelings. There was a deep, mutual attachment between her and Mrs. Johnson, and both Johnsons valued Liz's ideas and suggestions. She never came into my office and pounded the table or anything like that, but she was a force to reckon with. In dealing with Liz, my secret weapon was cherry sours. On my desk I kept a candy jar full of them, and she would come in and take the lid off and start grabbing a handful of cherry sours as she talked things over with me. I credit the cherry sours for keeping our interactions cordial and under control.

Once the library construction began to take shape, the critics weighed in. In a *New York Times* article, my friend Gary Cartwright wrote that "the LBJ library rises like the great pyramids of Egypt above all things." And in a *Texas Observer* article, the legendary Molly Ivins called it a crypt, a mausoleum, a tomb—"Lyndon Johnson in cement."

It was an unusual structure, and everybody was searching for a way to describe it. I didn't have a strong personal feeling about the architecture, pro or con. I recognized that it was different, and I accepted it as distinguished and distinctive.

The architect was the highly acclaimed Gordon Bunshaft with Skidmore, Owings & Merrill. Bunshaft had a very powerful personality and was responsible for the vision and design. Local architectural firm Brooks, Barr, Graeber and White worked with Bunshaft to carry out the details. At one point I said to Mr. Bunshaft, "You've been criticized for this being not so much a library as a memorial." He responded, "That's what it is. That's what I want it to be. I want it to memorialize the president and his presidency."

In truth, the vast archival holdings of the LBJ Presidential Library were not intended to be the dusty repository of a bygone era—mid-twentieth-century American history—but a vibrant experience for future generations that would come there and listen to the audiotapes, watch the films, study the photographs, read the correspondence and manuscripts, and view the gifts and memorabilia that President Johnson and his family had collected over a lifetime. Everything in the library was meant to educate and enlighten, to inspire, and to challenge observers and critics on both sides of the most pressing issues of one man's long and storied political career.

The library was an anomaly on a university campus with strict architectural standards. It didn't look like the rest of the university. And it soon had other problems. The travertine tiles on the outside of the building were from Italy, and a couple of years after construction, they began to come loose in the Texas heat. The lack of windows was a protective measure to preserve light-sensitive materials like photographs and papers. Initially the top floor was an open-air atrium, but it was eventually enclosed to accommodate air-controlled offices and archives, where researchers could work in comfort.

A turning point in the library's design came when LBJ decided to take a team with him to visit the Harry S. Truman Presidential Library and Museum in Independence, Missouri. The two presidents were kindred spirits. Truman was a haberdasher from Missouri, plainspoken and straightforward, who loved his whiskey with orange juice in the morning when he woke up. LBJ loved his scotch and soda. They were both well known for "telling it like it is." In Missouri, LBJ saw a replica of the Oval Office at Harry Truman's library, and I can imagine him saying something like "I want to get me one of them."

So he returned to Austin and told Bunshaft he wanted a replica of the Oval Office in *his* library, as well. However, the design plans had been completed and construction of the enormous building had been underway for a year. In a phone call on November 10, 1968, the architect's response was a polite, "We hadn't thought of [an Oval Office replica], but it's possible." LBJ implied that it was Mrs. Johnson who was insisting "it just ought to be." He said, "We just should have thought of it; we just played hell not doing it. And now we got a bunch of can't-do philosophy."

You didn't say no to Lyndon Johnson. You asked him how you could do what he wanted. Everybody who worked for him knew that. Bunshaft came back with a plan to drop in a replica of the Oval Office on the upper level of the open atrium. But space was tight, so the replica of the Oval Office at the LBJ Library is seven-eighths the size of the real Oval Office. Very few people can tell the difference.

Everything inside the replica is exactly as it was when LBJ served as president. One of the most striking features is the console built with three television sets placed side by side and tuned to ABC, CBS, and NBC. He'd watched TV voraciously to monitor current news stories and to see what was being said about him.

When visitors toured the replica of the Oval Office, they stood behind a rope that allowed them to see all the different pieces in the room, including the paintings on the wall, the rocking chair that LBJ adopted after President Kennedy put a rocking chair in that space, and the TV sets. If visitors pushed a button, they could hear LBJ's voice on a tape playback describing what they were viewing.

The windows behind the president's desk were backlit to look like real windows, but they were actually a door. The Johnson family had private quarters on that floor, with a living room, a kitchen, a dining area, and a small office for LBJ himself. (After his death, Mrs. Johnson used some of that space for her own office.) When visitors were standing behind the rope, listening to his voice, LBJ loved to open the door from his private quarters, walk out, and greet the people who were there. Of course they were shocked and beside themselves. He'd ask, "Are there any questions?" with that familiar twinkle in his eyes. He enjoyed doing that. And when people finally found the nerve to ask him questions, he answered them candidly.

THREE OUT OF FOUR

A week or so before the library opened, LBJ asked me to join him as he gave a preview tour for Horace "Buzz" Busby, a longtime aide, speechwriter, and consultant.

The library is an impressive experience for a first-time visitor. As the three of us walked past exhibits on the first floor and entered the Great Hall, we turned and looked up—a true "wow" moment—at the glass wall covering the full width of the building. It rises four stories, showcasing red buckram boxes, each with a gold presidential seal, that contain forty-five million pages of LBJ's papers from his long public life.

We walked up the grand staircase to a massive twelve-foot-tall polished gray granite pylon that dwarfed us, even the very tall LBJ. Each of the pylon's four sides was almost four feet wide. Buzz was a short man, and it had a powerful pull for him, especially when he started reading the quotes on each side. The words were etched into the stone and highlighted with a bronze tone. LBJ had selected four quotes that he wanted to be remembered for:

A President's hardest task is not to do what is right, but to know what is right.

The Great Society asks not how much, but how good; not only how to create wealth, but how to use it; not only how fast we are going, but where we are headed. It proposes as the first test for a nation: the quality of its people.

Until justice is blind to color, until education is unaware of race, until opportunity is unconcerned with the color of men's skins, emancipation will be a proclamation, but not a fact.

Horace Busby, left, with Governor John Connally and LBJ aide Warren Woodward at the LBJ Ranch, wrote three of the four LBJ quotes memorialized in the LBJ Library. *Photo by Neal Spelce*

I have followed the personal philosophy that I am a free man, an American, a public servant and a member of my party, in that order always and only.

As Buzz walked around the pylon, he was smiling. And then LBJ said, "Buzz, three of those quotes are yours." Not bad for a speechwriter.

I have one little regret to this day: I never did find out which three Buzz had written for LBJ.

Buzz was also credited with writing the "I will not seek, and I will not accept" speech, when LBJ announced that he would not run for the presidency in 1968.

When Horace Busby died in 2000 at the age of seventy-six, the *Washington Post* wrote that he "was regarded by many in press and political circles as Johnson's finest speech writer."

He first showed his writing talent while serving as editor of UT's student newspaper, the *Daily Texan*. He left the University of Texas two credits short of graduation to work for the former International News

Service at the Texas State Capitol. In the late 1940s, LBJ came calling on Buzz to write for him during the US Senate race.

Buzz left politics for a while and started a newsletter, *The Texas Businessman*. But LBJ soon convinced him to join his White House staff as a confidante, consultant, and writer. During the tumultuous 1960s, he was occasionally referred to as "LBJ's other self." After leaving the White House, Buzz moved to California and published *The Busby Papers* for a host of clients.

THE FINAL TOUCHES

LBJ had a phrase—"Let's put the big pot into the little pot"—meaning let's take this big job and make it manageable. When it came to planning the library dedication, that was our guiding light. Our PR agency had never arranged a ceremony of that importance before, and sometimes we had to improvise. For example, the president wanted to invite everybody—VIPs, foreign dignitaries, ambassadors, former leaders in Congress—but at that time in Austin, we had only two upscale hotels. The Driskill was built in 1886, and the Stephen F. Austin was built in 1924, so there wasn't much in the way of modern deluxe accommodations. But in looking at the list of invitees, we realized that everyone on it was a VIP who would want a private suite.

Someone on my staff mentioned that there was a private women's dormitory called Hardin House, west of the campus, that was designed with a living room–bedroom area on one side of a suite, and a matching area on the other side, with a common bathroom between them. In effect, they were two-bedroom suites. As soon as the university ended its spring semester in 1971, UT began a massive cleanup and revamping of Hardin House, readying it as a hotel with fresh linens and towels, new bedspreads, and the finest toiletries. The university dipped into its art collections and hung original art on the walls. So when VIPs walked in, they were walking into amazingly beautiful suites. All of this was done from scratch, under the guidance of volunteers Carolyn and Tom Curtis, in a welcoming Texas spirit, to take good care of the folks who were coming to Austin at the request of President and Mrs. Johnson.

The hotel needed a staff, so we went out into the community and recruited a large number of volunteers to play hotel staff. In the lobby of Hardin House, we set up popcorn machines and music to create a festive atmosphere. Henry Ford II was prevailed upon by LBJ and local Lincoln-

Mercury dealer Roy Butler to provide a fleet of Ford Motor Company cars, mostly Lincoln Continentals, and we assigned volunteer drivers to pick up dignitaries at the airport. (In those days, Austin's taxi service was limited.) Land Commissioner Bob Armstrong, who later ran unsuccessfully for governor and then served as the deputy secretary of the interior, volunteered to be a bellhop and opened the doors of the cars and greeted their passengers, welcoming them to town.

The planning committee decided to hold the dedication ceremony on the lawn outside the LBJ Library because there wasn't enough room inside the building to handle the large number of guests. At the last minute, the UT groundskeepers put down sod around the new outdoor fountain and on the overlook where I had once lived in a fraternity house. (The house had been demolished to make way for the Sid Richardson Hall complex adjacent to the library.) A couple of days before the dedication, the slope below the library was covered with grass.

We arranged the chairs in the seating area alongside the fountain, and we built a platform for the speakers and special dignitaries, who were a selection of national and statewide leaders. President Richard Nixon and three of the top four officials in succession for the presidency were seated on that platform, out in the open, including Vice President Spiro Agnew, House Speaker Carl Albert, and Secretary of State William Rogers. US Treasury Secretary John Connally, Lieutenant Governor Ben Barnes, and officials from the university were also part of the platform party.

Because of UT campus unrest and LBJ's unpopularity with students, we felt it was very important to secure a large perimeter around the football stadium, the law school, the performing arts center, and the new library, extending the boundary to nearby Interstate 35. The security teams made the entire area a no-pass zone and cordoned off several acres. Even so, the planners remained concerned that security points might be breached by aggressive demonstrators.

Security was a massive group effort that involved local, university, state, and federal law enforcement agencies, the fire department and EMS, and the Secret Service. We had meetings on a regular basis to coordinate their roles. Fortunately, they were all very professional and experienced, and they knew what to do in any given scenario. I asked a lot of questions: "What's the UT Police response if this happens?" "Where is EMS going to be parked?" "General, how many National Guard troops can we expect?" All my questions were answered satisfactorily and with great patience.

On the day of the dedication ceremony, National Guard troops were stationed out of sight under the stadium, at the ready, in case things got out of hand. Secret Service and agents from the Bureau of Alcohol, Tobacco, and Firearms (ATF) were sequestered in the law building. The public didn't see these backup forces. Austin police officers, Department of Public Safety troopers, and Texas Rangers were assigned to the barricades, prepared to stop protesters from breaching the perimeter.

The security measures worked. Demonstrators did show up and carried signs and painted obscene words on their foreheads and chanted the usual, "Hey, hey, LBJ, how many kids did you kill today?" But with the students gone for the summer, it was a crowd of only a thousand protesters. The shouting and chanting were far enough away from the celebration that they didn't disrupt it or cause any problems. Law enforcement was able to contain the demonstration. Afterward, however, protesters followed some of the dignitaries back to Hardin House and clashed with the Tact Squad in the street. Thirty were arrested there, the only arrests of the day.

A Special Gift

Prior to the dedication ceremony, the White House staff contacted me and said, "President Nixon would like to do something special for President Johnson. It's going to be in private, before the dedication begins. And it's a secret, a real surprise. We don't want LBJ to know about it."

They had reproduced a replica of a portrait of President Andrew Jackson that was one of LBJ's favorites and had hung prominently in the Oval Office during his presidency.

Nixon's staff added, "We don't want a crowd, Mr. Spelce. President Nixon just wants to make a nice personal gesture to thank President Johnson for his service to the country."

I said, "Let's set it up for the two presidents to meet in the replica of the Oval Office, where President Nixon can make the presentation."

Everybody agreed. "Please keep it secret, Mr. Spelce."

"Yes, certainly."

"It's gotta be a surprise."

When President Richard Nixon gave a thoughtful gift to LBJ in a private meeting just before the library dedication ceremony, it became apparent to Nixon I had lied about it. *LBJ Library photo by Frank Wolfe*

"Yes, I understand."

Anybody who ever worked with Lyndon Johnson—or for him, around him, near him, or within a fifty-mile radius—knew you didn't want to surprise The Man. At all. Ever.

So I lied to President Nixon's staff and phoned LBJ as soon as I could. I said, "Mr. President, he wants it to be a surprise." And he said, "Neal, don't worry, I'll handle it. Thank you for letting me know. I really appreciate Dick Nixon for doing this."

Shortly before the ceremony, we ushered a small party of Nixon aides and his Secret Service detail up to the "seven-eighths" Oval Office, with an aide carrying the portrait and President Nixon grinning from ear to ear because he was going to surprise LBJ with this great gift. Nixon made brief remarks and then presented the portrait, saying, "Mr. President, we have a gift for you."

LBJ reached into his suit pocket, pulled out a 3x5 index card, and started reading. "I certainly do appreciate this gift, Mr. President, and I can't tell you how much it means to me."

When he finished reading the remarks, he looked over and winked at me, and put the card back in his pocket. Everybody in the room laughed. I was very fortunate that I was not added to President Nixon's infamous enemies list.

The Big Day

May 22 was an unexpectedly windy day, and we were afraid it was going to rain, but the weather turned out to be beautiful. The male guests were dressed formally in suits and ties and the women in their finest, because it was a one-of-a-kind moment in the history of our nation.

As the ceremony began, it was my job to walk with LBJ and Richard Nixon and guide them through their paces, silently gesturing for them to turn here, descend these stairs, stop there and wave. It shook me a little when I realized that walking right beside me was the Marine officer

The dedication of the LBJ Library on May 22, 1971, was a one-of-a-kind moment in the history of our nation. I'm on the right, walking with two presidents. *LBJ Library photo by Frank Wolfe*

who was carrying the *football*, as it's called, the black briefcase carrying the launch codes for our country's nuclear weapons. That briefcase goes wherever the president goes, and it contains the instructions on what the president should do and where he should go in case of an emergency situation or attack.

The Marine's lips weren't moving, but I heard him saying, "Turn left, Mr. President. Go straight. There are steps ahead, so be prepared to take those steps. When you get to the top, here's what's going to happen." The Marine and I hadn't discussed or coordinated where I was leading them, but to the public, it looked as if the presidents were well rehearsed and striding with confidence and grand purpose. There were no blunders. The Marine and I had done our jobs.

The Reverend Billy Graham delivered the opening invocation. He was LBJ's spiritual adviser and a key part of his life. The president listened to him. When LBJ was buried two years later at the Johnson ranch, Billy Graham presided over the rites at the president's request. I don't know that observers would've called Lyndon Johnson a religious man. He attended church, but he wasn't someone who wore religion on his shirtsleeve. He respected ministers and the clergy, and he would include their voices in the rollout of his various social programs, especially ministers in the African American churches.

In his remarks, President Nixon was very gracious in his praise of the former president, even though they were political enemies. That day, the two men reached across partisan lines as if to say, "You were the president, I am the president, we understand each other and what we've both gone through in this job."

LBJ's own address perfectly summed up the new presidential library: "It is all here: the story of our time—with the bark off. This library does not say, 'This is how I saw it,' but this is how the documents show it was. There is no record of a mistake, nothing critical, ugly, or unpleasant that is not included in the files here. We have papers from my forty years of public service in one place, for friend and foe to judge, to approve or disapprove. I do not know how this period will be regarded in years to come. But that is not the point. This library will show the facts—not just the joy and triumphs, but the sorrow and failures, too."

I had heard President Johnson rehearse his remarks the day before the dedication ceremony, when he said to me, "Let me read this to you, Neal, and see what you think." He was walking into the restroom as he spoke,

LBJ at the podium during the library dedication, where he said "It is all here: the story of our time—with the bark off." And there is quite a lineup behind him—US Speaker of the House Carl Albert (partially obscured by Pat Nixon), President Nixon, Secretary of State William Rogers, UT Board of Regents Chairman Frank Erwin, US Treasury Secretary John Connally, Texas lieutenant governor Ben Barnes, Texas Speaker of the House Gus Mutscher, Mrs. Johnson, Postmaster General (later LBJ School dean) John Gronouski, Vice President Spiro Agnew (partially obscured by LBJ), UT Chancellor Mickey LeMaistre, and the Longhorn Band. *LBJ Library photo by Michael Rusnak*

and in true LBJ fashion, he unzipped and began guiding his stream while he read those words aloud from an index card. By that point, nothing surprised me about our informal meetings.

After all the remarks were concluded on the platform, I accompanied Presidents Johnson and Nixon as they walked in front of the fountain and then went up the long slope of stairs to the plaza above. It was my idea that when they reached the plaza, they would wave to the audience below while the Longhorn Band was playing "The Eyes of Texas" and people were clapping, and we'd turn on the silent fountain for the first time in public. When we cued the fountain, a beautiful plume rose into the air and the strong winds blew the cascading water over the audience, drenching all of them dressed in their finery, women and men alike. It wasn't exactly a gully washer, more like a soft rain.

At that historical juncture, it was hard for me to disagree with what Lyndon Johnson had said a few months earlier: "If there's any way to fuck it up, Spelce, you will."

It was a faux pas, but it quickly became a laughable moment because everyone was in an upbeat mood, enjoying the celebration, and they had great respect for LBJ and his family. Fortunately for me, The Man didn't put me in a headlock after the dedication was over. We turned off the fountain once we saw that it was spraying the audience, and when the guests eventually made their way into the library and began attending other functions, we turned the fountain back on so that everyone could see the cascade in all its glory from a distance. It really is a great fountain, with travertine marble containing the pool of water. It would have been a majestic surprise if the wind hadn't flared up.

Frank Erwin, chairman of the University of Texas System Board of Regents, was a force of nature. Highly controversial and unpopular with UT students because of his hardline opposition to student demonstrations, he was a *git 'er done* guy. When somebody in power needed something, he made it happen. He was instrumental in persuading the university to approve of, and pay for, the LBJ Library. And he'd found the money to make the Hardin House renovation possible. His imprint was on everything at the dedication.

Our team met with "Chairman Frank" on a regular basis to go over what we were planning for the ceremony, what we needed a decision on, and a number of issues that required discussion. At one point, as the date was quickly approaching, Frank said, "You know, Neal, everybody will want a drink when the program is over."

Frank Erwin was no amateur when it came to drinking.

I said, "Mr. Chairman, I'm sorry. This is university property and it's forbidden by law to serve alcoholic beverages in a university facility."

He looked down his Ben Franklin reading glasses at me, paused, and said, "All right, Neal. I understand."

I went on to say, "Think of the publicity. If we go through all this planning and have a great ceremony, Mr. Chairman, and someone comes back and says we've broken the law, or if someone gets arrested, we'll never live it down."

"Okay, fine, Neal."

UT Regent Chair Frank Erwin got the last laugh on me after I told him it was illegal to serve liquor on campus. He quietly hired bartenders who suddenly wheeled out many portable well-stocked bars for the guests following the official LBJ Library dedication ceremony. *Photo courtesy Headliners Club*

I thought I'd won the battle. But on the day of the ceremony, shortly after the fountain sprayed everybody and the show was over, portable bars were wheeled out with full whiskey bottles stacked on top, and formal bartenders started pouring drinks. Everywhere I looked there was another bar, and another. I didn't know if Chairman Frank had used his own nickel or the university's nickel. It wouldn't have surprised me either way.

I couldn't do anything about it, of course. When Frank saw me staring at him, shaking my head, he grinned at me with a scotch in hand. I thought, "Erwin, you son of a bitch."

In keeping with LBJ's tradition at the ranch, Texas barbecue was served to guests sitting at long tables arranged underneath striped awnings that were rippling in the wind: Henry Kissinger, Dean Rusk, Barry Goldwater, William Westmoreland, future Watergate figures Bob Haldeman and John Ehrlichman, Julie Nixon Eisenhower and David Eisenhower, and three thousand other VIP attendees. It was quite a feast, with a large and cheerful family atmosphere, the kind of celebration the Johnsons had always enjoyed, and the perfect conclusion to nearly four years of construction and six months of intense planning for that day.

One of my most enjoyable moments at the dedication was meeting actor Gregory Peck. He and his wife, a former Italian journalist named Veronique Passani Peck, were close friends with the Johnsons. The Pecks returned to Austin a time or two after that, and on one occasion I complimented him on his role as Atticus Finch in *To Kill a Mockingbird*.

He was gracious, saying, "Thank you very much," and he confided a story about Harper Lee, the author of the novel. "She was on the set from time to time," he said. "I remember walking along a sidewalk for a quick shoot, and after we finished the take, she came over and said, 'Mr. Peck, watching you do that scene, I thought I was seeing my daddy.'"

The character of Atticus Finch was based on her father, an attorney in the Deep South.

Gregory Peck told me, "I was overwhelmed. I really thought, 'That's the highest praise an actor can get.'" And then she went on to say, "Your stomach pooches out just like his did."

He looked at me with that handsome smile and said, "That'll bring you down a notch or two."

For me personally, the library dedication had been a once-in-a-lifetime experience. I had rubbed shoulders with university leaders, nationally acclaimed architects and builders, law enforcement professionals, the staffs of two American presidents, and hundreds of generous volunteers. When the dedication was finally over, I felt incredibly proud of the major role that my team and I had played in one of the significant historical events of the twentieth century. But after months of nonstop adrenaline rush—day after day, around the clock, especially in those final weeks leading up to the ceremony—I was completely spent. A skinny guy to begin with, I had lost ten or fifteen pounds because of the constant energy the work required. My mind never slowed down. I was always thinking, "What about security? What about the food? Have we checked the sound system? What about the weather?"

As the barbecue was winding down and those three thousand guests began to leave the grounds, President and Mrs. Johnson went upstairs in the library and took their shoes off to relax and decompress. I can't remember what time Sheila and I left, but it was dark when we got home. Suddenly the adrenaline was gone, after five months of stress, and I just collapsed. I was wiped out, but I felt satisfied and tremendously relieved.

The euphoria didn't last long. There was work still to be done. My team and I returned to the library the next morning, a Sunday, to help clean up and make sure everything was in its proper place. There was also the Hardin House and a tremendous amount of tidying needed there. One of the volunteers, former KTBC cameraman Gary Pickle, a good friend of mine to this day, recently reminded me that he helped to round up the cars used to ferry the VIPs. They were loaners, fleet vehicles, fancy cars. As he said, "Dignitaries just left them where they were. We had to wander around Austin picking up cars."

In the days following the dedication ceremony, I received thank-you notes from LBJ, Mrs. Johnson, Richard Nixon, and Spiro Agnew. I was so grateful for those personal notes that I've preserved them behind glass for fifty years. They're hanging on a wall in my home office.

LBJ wrote, "Dear Neal: You gave us a successful beginning to what we hope will prove to be a worthy project. The good memories of May twenty-second are going to stay with us always, and whenever we turn our thoughts to that day, we are going to be thinking of you, too, with gratitude and admiration. You did an outstanding job arranging every-thing for the dedication ceremonies, tying a thousand and one details to-gether during days we know were never long enough." He added, "Mrs. Johnson and I thank you on behalf of all the guests who were here, and most of all, we thank you on our behalf for a perfectly planned day."

Ever the warm and gracious lady, Mrs. Johnson wrote, "Dear Neal: I know you must be exhausted, but I hope you are happy, because the Dedication couldn't have been better and you deserve a lion's share of the credit. Everyone has been singing your praises and if you're not careful you're going to be putting on every dedication that's held in Texas or any other place for that matter! To say we couldn't have done it without you is an understatement, but I'm sure you have heard every superlative by now. Please know that Lyndon and I will never forget all you did and will be forever grateful."

She signed her note, "Lady Bird."

TOM JOHNSON: THE PEN IS MIGHTIER

When Tom Johnson came on board at KTBC in 1971, following a stint in the Lyndon Johnson administration (Tom is not related to LBJ), I was already transitioning out of TV news. But in the short time we worked together, he was very supportive of my role as the news director and we took a liking to each other.

Tom had been a White House Fellow and then served as an aide to LBJ. When the president left the White House and returned to Texas, he invited Tom to work for KTBC at an executive level—a measure of LBJ's high regard for him. Tom was given an office next door to Jesse Kellam, the longtime general manager of KTBC, and Tom served in effect as the assistant general manager. A year later, because of his impressive leadership and charisma, he was named an executive vice president at KTBC.

I admired Tom for being a strong proponent of good solid news coverage, reporting straight down the middle and not leaning one way or another. I'll always be grateful to him for hewing to that hard journalistic discipline, old-school style.

Tom Johnson's career in the news media had begun in high school, when he was a sports stringer for the *Macon Telegraph* in Georgia. He was from a family of modest means, so the newspaper publisher funded his college education at the University of Georgia and then at the Harvard Business School. The publisher also recommended Tom for that White House Fellowship. Because of his newspaper background, Tom was assigned to work in Press Secretary Bill Moyers's office, and Tom and Bill became very close friends.

Tom was an inveterate note-taker, which gave him a special window into LBJ's presidency. He was the guy in the room who was always capturing the details on paper. With his sharp mind absorbing everything—nothing escaped him—Tom's recollections of those crucial years in American history are highly prized.

Soon after President Johnson's death in 1973, his family began asking themselves, "What are we going to do with all our assets?" It was that time in a family's life when the patriarch dies and they have to decide, "Now what?"

They decided to sell the television station and keep the Austin Cable System and the radio stations, switching the call letters to KLBJ AM and FM. Within months of LBJ's death, they sold KTBC-TV to the Los Angeles–based Times Mirror Company. Tom Johnson coordinated many of the negotiations for the sale, and he did his usual masterful job. The Times Mirror folks were so impressed with him that when the sale was wrapping up, they said, "Tom, we want you to work for us." They also owned the now defunct *Dallas Times Herald,* and they hired Tom as editor in 1973 and then promoted him to publisher of that newspaper in 1975.

When Otis Chandler relinquished his publisher's position at the *Los Angeles Times* in 1980, he chose Tom Johnson as the first non-family member in one hundred years to fill that prestigious and powerful post. Tom's work in LA caught the attention of Ted Turner, who had started a twenty-four-hour cable news network called CNN, which was headquartered in Atlanta. In 1990, Turner recruited Tom to head up that network, and Tom began the day before Saddam Hussein invaded Kuwait. CNN's historic, exclusive coverage of the Gulf War propelled the network into televisions throughout the world and won CNN virtually every award in TV news.

A year later, when Mikhail Gorbachev resigned as the Soviet Union's president and that "union of republics" ceased to exist, the fierce competitors ABC and CNN jockeyed to negotiate the exclusive rights to broadcast Gorbachev's formal signing of the documents that would end the USSR and issue in a new era in global history.

ABC's Ted Koppel secured permission to film Gorbachev's last days in office, but Tom Johnson visited the resigning leader in person in Moscow and talked him into an interview and exclusive rights to cover the signing itself. Gorbachev was well aware of CNN's growing worldwide influence and joked with Tom: "You built your empire better than I built mine, but be sure to give enough power to your republics."

At the signing ceremony, as the CNN cameras were showing the world that epic shift in power taking place after nearly seventy-five years of one-party Communist rule, Gorbachev tried to sign the document but his Russian-made pen didn't work. Tom quickly reached into his pocket, pulled out his personal black Montblanc fountain pen, and handed it to him, saying, "Here, Mr. Gorbachev, use mine." The president glanced at the pen and asked with a wry smile, "American?"

Tom Johnson's personal pen was used in that once-in-a-century historical event. How important was that one little pen in Gorbachev's hand? It dissolved a global power that had dominated a scattering of small Eastern European nations since World War II, promulgating an ideology that had fueled a dangerous Cold War that had divided the world for decades.

Years later, when Tom was chairman of the LBJ Foundation—the nonprofit organization that supports the LBJ Presidential Library and the LBJ School of Public Affairs at UT Austin—he invited Gorbachev to speak at the library and introduced him. Gorbachev was interviewed by library director Mark Updegrove through an interpreter, and the former Soviet president addressed the world issues of the day. When the interview concluded, Tom appeared again and said, "Mr. Gorbachev, you may remember that I took my pen back on that historic day in Moscow. So I want you to have a new pen exactly like that one."

He presented Gorbachev with a new black Montblanc fountain pen.

Tom had donated the original pen to the Newseum in Washington, DC, which for many years collected and displayed historical materials and memorabilia from the news media and spotlighted the role of the free press in American history.

Ever since he was a young man, Tom had impressed a great many influential people with his intelligence and high energy as a take-charge guy who could always be counted on to grab hold of the situation and get things done, no matter what it was. But in spite of his soaring success, there was another facet to him that few people knew. In fact, I didn't know about it, either. He suffered from severe bouts of depression.

When he was publisher of the *Los Angeles Times* and the pressures became too intense, he would sometimes retreat to a small room and lie on the floor to escape the stress. He had hired trusted assistants who kept things running smoothly, and they protected and covered for him: "No, Mr. Johnson is not available right now. How can I help you? I'm sorry, you'll have to check back later."

The same thing happened when he went to CNN. He took his assistant, Joan Klunder, with him from Los Angeles. She and Tom's other executive assistant, Ashley Van Buren, managed the Chief Executive Office when his depression consumed him.

Tom Johnson, right, with LBJ Foundation leaders—former LBJ White House counsel Larry Temple and former Texas lieutenant governor Ben Barnes. *Photo courtesy Headliners Club*

He was a man who'd been at the pinnacle of power everywhere he went, and yet there were times when he'd been incapacitated by that dark illness. The good news was that Tom found psychiatric help with Dr. Charles Nemeroff of Emory University and was treated with an antidepressant that finally worked. He still experiences bouts of depression, but they're not as severe as they were in earlier years. He's written many articles and appeared on several televised shows about his experiences and how to handle depression, and he became an articulate spokesman on that subject, advising readers and viewers to seek professional medical attention and find the proper medication. He's also a strong advocate of talk therapy.

Because of his loyalty and his long association with the Johnson family, Tom has become one of the major keepers of the LBJ flame. He sends news of interest to a private mailing list made up of those who have been close to the Johnsons. For instance, he notified us in July 2015 that "General Jim Cross died today." Cross was the pilot of Air Force One during LBJ's presidency and a good friend to the president and Mrs. Johnson. General Cross had even written a book about his time in the Johnson circle. Tom keeps those personal contacts—and those memories—knitted together. The mailing list, sadly, is getting smaller as the years pass.

Tom has been urged to write his life story in a memoir, and he presented his meticulously researched and insightful recollections to an audience a few years ago at the Headliners Club in Austin. His life story was well-illustrated, insightful, and powerful. If this is an indication of what the completed Tom Johnson memoir will be, the world will be treated to an important historical record that will make news and likely become a best seller.

Tom has long been retired from CNN and lives in Atlanta with his delightful wife, Edwina. They visit their children and grandchildren in other parts of the country and return to Austin frequently. Someone asked him how he's spending his time in retirement. The answer was quintessential Tom Johnson: "Helping my friends and family."

1972 CIVIL RIGHTS SYMPOSIUM: "IF OUR HEARTS ARE RIGHT"

L BJ wanted to host a symposium on civil rights in his new presidential library, and so library director Harry Middleton arranged for a symposium to take place in December 1972. Civil rights were the cornerstone of Lyndon Johnson's Great Society and an issue dear to his heart. He asked Middleton to invite every major civil rights leader in the country. Racial equality and inclusion were burning issues in 1972, as they still are today.

The auditorium below the library could seat a thousand people, and it was filled to capacity with an audience eager to hear the influential speakers and panelists. There was a large media presence. The opening address was delivered by retired Supreme Court chief justice Earl Warren, and the symposium participants included Julian Bond, Henry B. Gonzalez, Barbara Jordan, Burke Marshall (head of the Civil Rights Division at the Justice Department during the civil rights era), and Clarence Mitchell of the NAACP, among others.

I volunteered to assist backstage in the green room, which was set up with easy chairs for the speakers to relax in. They gathered there for refreshments and last-minute grooming, waiting to be called onstage. At one point I was visiting with Vernon Jordan—at that time the executive director of the United Negro College Fund and president of the National Urban League—and civil rights activist James Farmer, who was from East Texas, had lived in Austin as a child, and became the founding director of the Congress of Racial Equality (CORE). Mike Howard, the ever-present Secret Service agent, pulled me aside and said, "Neal, The Man wants to see you." I thought, "Here we go again. What have I done wrong now?"

Mike led me to the men's room and said, "He's in there." I said, "Oh no." He said, "Yeah, and I'm not going in. You go on in."

LBJ was sitting on the commode and had some concerns about a few minor details. Vintage LBJ. The word *crude* comes to mind. Forget the

Congresswoman Barbara Jordan and civil rights leader Vernon Jordan with LBJ at the December 1972 Civil Rights Symposium moments prior to LBJ's last public speech. LBJ died in January 1973. *LBJ Library photo by Frank Wolfe*

niceties and the things you do or don't do in a professional situation. As far as he was concerned, there was something important he needed to discuss or have done, and it didn't matter to him where and how he was delivering the instructions. Some leaders take a meeting while on a treadmill. LBJ preferred the throne.

Sound was being piped into the green room so we could all hear what was going on in the auditorium. Feelings were raw out there. The atmosphere was very tense. Dissenters were standing up and shouting at the speakers, occasionally disrupting what was being said. Emotions were also bubbling up from those who felt that the symposium wasn't the time or place for that. I don't know what the audience expected. It was a symposium on an issue that was critical to everyone. But those were unpredictable times filled with a fiery intensity.

While LBJ was milling around in the green room, visiting with symposium participants, I noticed a military doctor hovering near him, watching him carefully. After all, the former president had suffered two heart attacks in the four years since leaving the White House. The doctor was concerned that LBJ was getting caught up emotionally in what was happening between the speakers and those vocal elements in the audience.

When it was his turn to speak, LBJ shuffled awkwardly up the stairs to the stage, and I noticed him slipping a nitroglycerin tablet under his tongue to settle the pains in his chest. A scattering of audience members continued to be riled up, and at one point, someone yelled and charged the stage. Security moved in to restrain him, but LBJ said, "No, wait. This is important to him. We need to hear what he has to say. Sir, what are your concerns?"

It defused the situation for a moment. But the man was still angry, and the president said, "I hear you. I understand what you're saying." He was putting into practice his favorite axiom, "Come, let us reason together."

I don't know what the angry young man would have done. Maybe he just wanted to get in LBJ's face. When I looked into the wings, I saw the military doctor standing there in his long military coat, observing the former president's every move.

It probably wasn't wise for LBJ to have participated in that volatile event. He'd been sick the night before, and he began his remarks in a soft-spoken voice, with low energy and appearing somewhat frail. He admitted to the audience, "My doctor admonished me not to speak at all this morning, but I'm going to do that because I have some things I want to say to you."

Over the course of his thirty-minute speech, his passion for civil rights was ignited and he showed signs of LBJ the decisive leader in his prime, caring and perceptive and devoted to the cause of equality for all citizens. He ended his address with stirring eloquence: "And if our efforts continue, and if our will is strong, and if our hearts are right, and if courage remains our constant companion, then, my fellow Americans, I am confident *we shall overcome.*"

It was the last speech Lyndon Johnson would ever deliver. A month after the symposium, he died from a massive heart attack at his ranch.

LAYING THE MAN TO REST

Lyndon Johnson died on January 22, 1973. He was only sixty-four years old. Even after his doctors' warnings over the past two years, he'd begun to smoke again and his weight was fluctuating. When I was around him, he wasn't eating like a heart patient. Bypass surgery was ruled out by pioneer heart surgeon Dr. Michael DeBakey after an examination in Houston, when he determined that the former president wouldn't survive the procedure.

On the day he died, LBJ asked Secret Service agent Mike Howard to bring him a glass of milk. Mike was very close to President and Mrs. Johnson, and he was the one who discovered the president's body in bed with a telephone in his hand. LBJ was airlifted in his private airplane to Brooke Army Medical Center in San Antonio, where he was pronounced dead on arrival.

I found out about his death late in the afternoon, when Tom Johnson phoned me. It was like when the fire bell rings and a Dalmatian jumps up on a fire engine and you rush out. I rushed from my PR office in downtown Austin straight to KTBC. Tom was, in effect, running the television station at that time.

When I arrived at Tom's office, he told me he'd already contacted Walter Cronkite at CBS. He knew Walter very well, and when news came that Lyndon Johnson had died, Walter was on the air. Tom met some resistance when he tried to get through the CBS switchboard. He said, "This is Tom Johnson. I'm a spokesman for President Lyndon Johnson. I need to speak to Walter Cronkite right away." They said, "I'm sorry, he's on the air. He can't talk now." Tom insisted, "Yes, he can. Tell him it is very urgent. President Johnson died moments ago."

Walter had had a cordial, professional relationship with LBJ during his presidency and had aired five exclusive interviews with the former president at his ranch in the years after he'd left office. The final interview had taken place only ten days before Tom's phone call. When the CBS staff finally gave the message to Walter, he said, "Tom Johnson. Sure, put him through. I'll talk to him on the next break."

Soon after LBJ died, a military honor guard escorted his flag-draped coffin into the LBJ Library's Great Hall, where he would lie in state. *LBJ Library photo by Frank Wolfe*

I helped organize and direct more than thirty thousand mourners, who stood in long lines outside the LBJ Library around the clock to pay their last respects. *LBJ Library photo by Frank Wolfe*

Tom said, "Walter, President Johnson died this afternoon. You're the first newsman we're calling." With the telephone receiver still in his hand, Walter Cronkite announced on the air that President Lyndon Baines Johnson had died a short while ago at his ranch in Texas.

I was very moved when Tom told me I was the first person he'd called after speaking with Walter.

LBJ's death triggered an enormous amount of activity. When a US president dies, protocol dictates that the military is in charge of everything. They begin immediately to implement the extensive plans that have been put in place and are well rehearsed. But we knew it would take a while for military officials from San Antonio to arrive in Austin with the body. In the meantime, Tom Johnson said, "Let's call a news conference. We've got to get the word out."

We held the conference in the large staff room on the fourth floor of KTBC. We crammed in all the press we could possibly manage. News reporters from all over the world began flying into Austin to cover the story.

As far as the Johnson family was concerned, everything was planned by the book. Actually, in three-ring binders. Here's what happens at the LBJ Library, here's what happens in Washington, here's what happens at the ranch. Even though his death was somewhat sudden, LBJ and Mrs. Johnson had made secret plans with a special Department of Defense office that handles all presidential funerals. They had reserved plots side by side at the family cemetery on the Johnson ranch.

His body was taken to a funeral home for preparation. That evening they brought the casket to lie in state at the LBJ Library. The line started forming outside the library almost immediately and it never let up. Mourners were there all night. They stood in line and moved slowly into that grand building, walking up the steps in the Great Hall to where the casket was stationed beneath the massive granite pylon that bore LBJ's four favorite quotes. There was a military guard positioned on each side of the flag-draped casket, and family members, staff, and close friends stood there silently for quite some time. By the time the casket was removed from the library and sent to lie in state in the Capitol rotunda in Washington, DC, more than thirty thousand people had filed past President Johnson's casket in Austin to pay their respects with prayers and tears and fond farewells.

LBJ Library Director Harry Middleton with LBJ at the library in March 1971. When LBJ died, Middleton ordered a count of the mourners and laughingly said later, "I know that someday LBJ will ask me how many people came by and viewed the casket, and by God I'm going to know." *LBJ Library photo by Frank Wolfe*

I helped work the line that night like a church usher, quietly instructing those who had come: "Please step inside here. When you walk by the casket, be respectful but please keep moving. The line is very long."

There was an irreverent yarn that made its way around press circles a few days later. Someone saw his Republican friend walking past the casket and asked, "What are you doing here? You were always opposed to LBJ." And the friend replied, "Yeah, I just wanted to come by and make sure the son of a bitch is dead."

Harry Middleton famously prearranged for a count of the people who viewed the casket. When asked why, he said, "I know that someday LBJ will ask me how many people came by and viewed the casket, and by God I'm going to know."

At the time of his death, I'd worked for Lyndon Baines Johnson for nearly twenty years. I'd interacted with him dozens of times during my career at KTBC. I'd traveled with him to Asia, to the Kennedy compound in Hyannis Port, and to Missouri to visit former president Harry Truman, and I'd spent numerous hours with him at his ranch. I'd served as director of the planning committee for his presidential library. After so many years in his orbit, I'd realized that LBJ was very fond of me. He was a complicated man, but I liked the guy. And I certainly liked Mrs. Johnson. She was such a loving, caring person, and they had very graciously included me in the extended Johnson family.

At the beginning of my career, I was in awe of The Man, but the more I was around him, the more comfortable I felt, even though I'd get my butt chewed out by him from time to time. I can't remember being singled out for anything I thought was unfair or off-base. And sometimes in the next moment after a reprimand, he would compliment me and say, "Come on over here, Neal," and throw one of those long arms around my shoulders. He was a paternal figure in my life, for sure, and it wasn't the proverbial love-hate relationship. I had nothing but admiration for him.

In our professional relations, he never treated me as "just a reporter" or "just an employee at the TV station." I always had the sense that I belonged there, even though I wasn't out campaigning for him and I didn't serve on the White House staff. I wasn't part of his inner circle like Tom Johnson, who was like the son he never had, or George Christian, who worked closely with him as his White House press secretary. But there were numerous occasions when I participated in the laughter and camaraderie surrounding LBJ and felt his warm and welcoming embrace.

Yes, I knew how controversial he was, and I experienced firsthand the many facets of his personality. He was all of that, but it didn't change my personal feelings toward him. I was genuinely distraught when I learned of his death. You can't interact with someone who is so brilliant—and believe me, LBJ was brilliant—and who has such deep concern for our nation and its progress as a Great Society, without feeling the pain of his loss when he's gone.

On the evening when mourners were filing past the casket in the presidential library, Tom Johnson said to me, "Neal, I'm going to leave and fly to Washington and help arrange what will happen there. We'll take the body to the Capitol, where he'll lie in state, and then we'll have the eulogies and funeral service at the National City Christian Church. But afterward, he's coming back home to be buried at the ranch. Will you be responsible and in charge of the burial at the ranch?"

I said, "Certainly, Tom. I'm glad to help."

For the next few days, none of us got any sleep. First we were hit with the news of President Johnson's death, and then we had to act and react and just keep going, because there was so much to do.

The Johnson family cemetery is a short walk from the ranch house down a little country lane that follows the Pedernales River. The cemetery had been there since 1905, when LBJ's great-grandmother was the first to be buried in that grove of live oak trees. Generations had been laid to rest there. A little three-foot-high rock wall surrounded the cemetery, blocking the occasional floodwaters from reaching the grave markers. That cemetery had found a special place in LBJ's heart. "I come down here almost every evening when I'm at home," he once said. "It's always quiet and peaceful here under the shade of these beautiful oak trees."

When I drove out to the ranch to oversee the burial preparations, it was a bitterly cold January day, gloomy and drizzling rain, the sort of day you'd expect for a funeral. Exhausted and sleepless, I'd thrown on a suit and tie, which is what I wore every day, and a friend of mine had given me one of those plastic see-through raincoats to ward off the chill. It didn't help very much.

The grass had turned brown, but those huge live oaks all over the LBJ property still had their foliage and wouldn't drop their leaves until later that year. When I arrived, the grounds were muddy, and I was concerned about setting up chairs for the service at the gravesite. I was relieved to find that the military had already taken charge. There was a frenzy of activity. Telephone company folks and military men were stringing lines for their communications, and news networks were beginning to appear in their large mobile trucks. In 1973, the networks used fat round cables that ran from a truck about the size of an eighteen-wheeler. A studio inside the truck contained backup generators, access to telephone lines, and screens to monitor the cameras that had been placed around the cemetery.

When I hurried over to the cemetery on foot in the pouring rain, a huge network truck was pulled up right beside the rock wall. A general wearing a raincoat strode over to me and asked, "Can I help you?"

I introduced myself and said, "I'm here representing the Johnson family. I'm in charge of coordinating the burial for them."

He said, "Fine, we appreciate that."

I looked at the truck and said, "General, this is not going to work. This truck is overpowering and distracting. It will take away from the dignity of the ceremony. We can't let it stay here."

He said, "Well, sir, you know that the television networks are here per a prior agreement."

I said, "Yes, sir, but we just can't have that truck looming over everything."

He responded with military precision. "Don't you worry, Mr. Spelce. We'll take care of it."

I almost saluted.

I came back early the next day, and bless their hearts, the military had moved that big eighteen-wheeler out of the way, at a greater distance from the cemetery, and had covered it with military-style camouflage netting draped over a tree. Now the truck more or less blended in. If you looked closely, you could tell something was there, but it was far enough away and no longer a problem. The general had handled it in fine fashion. I wouldn't have thought about camouflage or cover, but he'd said they would solve the problem, and in the snap of a finger, it was done.

I don't know what the general told the television folks to make that happen, but I was very pleased that he'd respected my request. I had the cachet of representing the Johnson family, and he didn't question my credentials or my authority. And all I had going for me was Tom Johnson saying, "You need to take care of this, Neal. We trust you with the responsibility."

At one point during the preparations, I noticed a big black Lincoln Continental limousine driving down the country road toward the cemetery. Two men wearing heavy topcoats with fur collars stepped out into the cold wet weather. They were dressed to the nines, and I thought, "Oh, this says wealth."

They were the advance team for the Reverend Billy Graham, who would be speaking at the service. They didn't stay long. They got the lay of the land and then crawled back into their heated limo. I'm sure they reported to the Reverend Graham, "This is what the setup looks like. This is how it'll take place."

LBJ had rubbed shoulders with the wealthy and the powerful, but he'd grown up with dirt-poor farmers and understood poverty and the common man. That was part of his appeal. He had once said to Lady Bird, "When I die, I don't want just our friends who can come in their private planes. I want the men in their pickup trucks and the women whose slips hang down below their dresses to be welcome, too."

There were security concerns about the dignitaries who would attend. It was designed to be a private ceremony, not open to the public. And yet in keeping with President Johnson's wishes, the family invited guests who had touched their lives—neighbors and old friends who worked the farms nearby and owned businesses in the little towns close to the ranch.

In January 1973, the Hill Country was experiencing very wet and bitterly cold weather, and on the morning of the burial ceremony, there was another chilling rain. Fortunately, it had stopped by early afternoon and the service went off without a hitch.

The military checked credentials at the gate and directed the cars and shuttle buses as they entered the premises. It was like a church setting but outdoors, with volunteer ushers showing guests to their seats. Family members were seated on the front row, near the tall granite headstone that memorialized the president. The Fifth Army Band from Fort Sam Houston in San Antonio began the service by playing "Ruffles and Flourishes" and "The Star-Spangled Banner." Anita Bryant sang "The Battle Hymn of the Republic." Eight military pallbearers stretched the American flag over President Johnson's coffin. Flags flew at half-staff at the ranch house in the distance, including LBJ's own personal flag, a blue field with his initials in the center and surrounded by five white stars.

Hundreds of mourners stood outside the rock wall, paying their respects. Support personnel from the ranch, former White House staffers, and Secret Service agents were among them. It was a bucolic setting and very somber. I remember seeing Jewell Malechek, the wife of ranch foreman Dale Malechek, dressed in black and crying her eyes out when the hearse rolled by, bringing the casket for interment.

John Connally delivered brief but eloquent remarks. He'd been a very close friend and supporter of Lyndon Johnson since 1938. In addition to serving as governor of Texas, Connally had also served as secretary of the navy under President Kennedy and as secretary of the treasury under President Nixon. Five months after LBJ's death, John Connally would switch parties, becoming a Republican.

I was charged with overseeing LBJ's burial underneath sprawling live oak trees at the family cemetery alongside the Pedernales River on the LBJ Ranch. *LBJ Library photo by Frank Wolfe*

The former governor described Lyndon Johnson as a "complex man" and his presidency as "a triumph for the poor, a triumph for the oppressed, a triumph for social justice and a triumph for mankind's never-ending quest for freedom." And he added, "Along this stream and under these trees he loved, he will now rest. He first saw light here. He last felt life here. May he now find peace here."

The Reverend Billy Graham, probably the most prominent Protestant clergyman in America at that time, had the last word. He said that President Johnson's "thirty-eight years of public service kept him at the center of events that have shaped our destiny. To him, the Great Society was not a wild dream. It was a realistic hope. And it seemed to me that those that knew him would agree that the thing nearest his heart was to harness the wealth and the knowledge and the greatness of this nation and help every poor and every oppressed person in the country and in the world."

Both speakers touched on the toll that the Vietnam War had taken on President Johnson. The Reverend Graham said that it was Lyndon's destiny to be involved in "a war that he never wanted, and to search for a peace that he did not quite live to see achieved. As President Nixon said on Tuesday night, 'No one would have welcomed peace more than Lyndon.'"

From time to time, Mrs. Johnson smiled in appreciation at the tributes to her husband. Her daughters and other family members remained dignified as well, some showing their emotions, some not, each one handling grief in their own way.

The service ended with a twenty-one-gun salute from the Texas National Guard, who fired howitzers from a cattle pasture nearby. A wreath sent from President Nixon was placed at the foot of the coffin by General William Westmoreland, who had led US forces in Vietnam.

After the ceremony, there was a reception for VIPs and personal friends at the ranch house, where coffee and sandwiches were served. I couldn't join them. I had to supervise the disassembling of that very complicated construction—the chairs, the trucks and their television cables, the cameras. I was on the scene to answer any questions that arose. It had been a grueling amount of work in such a short timeframe, but somehow we all survived it.

LADY BIRD'S SENSE OF BEAUTY

Mrs. Johnson loved the outdoors. When she was growing up in a plantation home on the outskirts of Karnack, a community in deep East Texas near the Louisiana state line, she was always outside and enthralled by the beauty of nature. That's the way she grew up, and it influenced her national beautification project on behalf of the National Park Service when she was the First Lady. When the Johnsons returned to Austin in 1969, she continued those efforts, spearheading the Town Lake Beautification Project. She was an active, nurturing presence for the rest of her life.

Mrs. Johnson was enamored of wildflowers and worked out a deal with the Texas Highway Department to beautify the landscape alongside Texas highways. She had a very gracious way of coaxing, and I can almost hear her saying, "Don't you think it might be a good idea when your highway maintenance crews are out there keeping up the roadways that they scatter some wildflower seeds? We'll have beautiful wildflowers blooming all through the spring. Won't they give color and improve the scenery over what's now just tall grass and weeds?"

The highway department embraced her initiative. In fact, Mrs. Johnson gave awards every year at a ceremony held in the little auditorium at the Johnson ranch for highway department personnel, supervisors, and maintenance people who were singled out for their efforts to plant wildflowers throughout the state. She inspired a worldwide movement to appreciate "the smallest sprout and the tallest tree," in her own words, and to enhance every environment with smartly planted wonders of nature that are native to their soil.

In 1982, Mrs. Johnson founded what is now called the Lady Bird Johnson Wildflower Center, nearly three hundred acres of gardens, woodlands, and an arboretum on the outskirts of Austin. It's a unit of the University of Texas at Austin, and its staff members conduct research, teach children and adults about sustainable landscapes, grow native plants and trees, collect all manner of seeds, and consult with personnel at similar centers and research facilities around the world. They freeze certain seeds

Upon first seeing it, Mrs. Johnson fell in love with Fannie Lou Spelce's *Arkansas Peach Season* painting. Soon thereafter, she and LBJ bought eight of Mother's paintings and gave them as Christmas gifts to family members and close friends. *Courtesy of Spelce Family Collection*

to preserve them for reproduction, so that we never lose those particular flowers and plants. The Wildflower Center hosts nearly two hundred thousand visitors a year. It's a wonderful tribute to her legacy and the perfect complement to the LBJ Library and the LBJ School of Public Affairs on the UT campus.

"Oh My, I Love It"

Mrs. Johnson had first seen my mother's paintings reproduced on Christmas cards that our PR agency had sent out during the holiday season, and shortly before LBJ's death, she asked to see some of the actual paintings. We set up a time for her to visit our home, and when she walked in the front door, one of the paintings was only ten feet ahead. She clasped her hands and said, "Oh my, I love it." It was *Arkansas Peach*

Season, a painting of that fine season in Clarksville, Arkansas, but it also looked like the Texas Hill Country, where peaches are a major crop.

Mrs. Johnson fell in love with the painting and raved about it to her husband when she returned to the ranch. He expressed an interest in acquiring some of Mother's paintings, and in November and early December 1972, my brother, Bennett, shuttled paintings to and from LBJ's personal assistant at the LBJ Library, Martha Tiller. She had them transported to the ranch for LBJ's consideration.

The former president acquired eight paintings, which became his personal Christmas gifts that year for Mrs. Johnson, their two daughters, and close friends such as John and Nellie Connally and ranch foreman Dale Malechek. Two of the paintings are still hanging in the Johnson ranch house, now operated by the National Park Service.

In gratitude for the purchases, Mother painted a picture of a young Lyndon Johnson sitting in his overalls on the front porch of his boyhood home, which she rendered based on a photo in a book in the LBJ Library. We have a photograph of Mother presenting that painting to LBJ himself, saying, "I thought you would like to have this, Mr. President."

Mrs. Johnson had the painting reproduced in small, framed prints that she personally inscribed and gave as Christmas gifts in 1973, the Christmas following President Johnson's death.

LADY BIRD, FLY AWAY HOME

Mrs. Johnson outlived her husband by thirty-four years, dying on July 11, 2007, at the age of ninety-four. She had suffered a stroke, and she lingered in ill health. Although she wasn't able to speak, she was very alert and conscious of what was going on. I visited her in the hospital on a couple of occasions, and we could communicate. She would react to my words with facial expressions.

Cactus Pryor was always a favorite of the Johnson family, especially Mrs. Johnson. As I mentioned earlier, they admired and trusted him so much they asked him to greet and provide entertainment for John and Jackie Kennedy at the Johnson ranch on November 22, 1963, where the First Couple was planning to spend the night. Cactus was making final preparations at the ranch when the world received the news that President Kennedy had been shot in Dallas.

Cactus would always end his programs on the air by saying, "This is Cactus Pryor. Thermostrockimortimer!" For decades, listeners wondered what that word meant. He confided in me the origin of the word and I swore to not tell anyone. I haven't.

I ran into Cactus one day shortly after he visited Mrs. Johnson in the hospital, and I asked him how she was doing. He told me that her daughter Luci was sitting at her bedside and had said to him, "Cactus, Momma has always wanted to know—and would like for you to tell her now—what you mean by thermostrockimortimer."

"Well, what did you tell her?" I asked.

He smiled that roguish smile at me and said, "I told her it means 'I love you, Lady Bird.'" And he and I both damned near lost it.

It sounds somber, but after her stroke, we knew that Mrs. Johnson wasn't long for this world. Her friends and loved ones would visit her at her home in West Lake Hills overlooking the city of Austin. It was a home she'd picked out herself and where she lived in her later years.

Lynda and Luci, other family members, and close friends began planning for the memorial service, and once again, we relied on the three-ring binder and the military's expertise. I was part of the group that made those plans, and the family asked me to be the spokesman whenever Mrs. Johnson died. I was soon joined by Elizabeth Christian, the daughter of George Christian, LBJ's White House press secretary from 1966 to 1969. Elizabeth had her own PR firm in Austin and was a key partner in providing the arms and legs of the planning.

When we were fairly certain that it had come down to the last two or three days of her life, I took a hotel room in downtown Austin to be available on a moment's notice. Elizabeth and her husband, Bruce Todd, a former mayor of Austin, spent the night in Elizabeth's office, and one evening I joined them and their staff in a long vigil. The media continued to call us: "Any word yet? Any late word?"

Liz Carpenter, Mrs. Johnson's friend and trusted assistant for many years, visited her in her home, and when she left, a media friend with the *Houston Chronicle* called Liz for an update. For some reason, Liz said, "I just left Mrs. Johnson. She has died."

I don't know what Liz was thinking. Fortunately, that reporter called us to confirm. "Liz tells me that Mrs. Johnson has just died," she said.

I said, "No, we don't know that. *Hold!*"

I phoned Tom Johnson, who was there at the bedside. I said, "Tom, Liz just told a news reporter that Mrs. Johnson has died."

He said, "No, that's not right, Neal. I'm right here beside her. She's resting peacefully and she's still with us."

I got off one phone and switched to another, telling the reporter, "Thank you for contacting us. I'm glad you double-checked. I can confirm that I spoke to someone at her bedside just now, and Mrs. Johnson is resting comfortably."

A Catholic priest was with her, administering last rites, when she finally passed away. Tom called me to say, "Neal, Mrs. Johnson died at 4:18 this afternoon."

That was all our team needed. Everything was ready, and our meticulous planning kicked in. We sent out a statement immediately, and it went viral. We held a news conference, and there were many respectful questions from the press. As it turned out, because of my association with the Johnson family over many years, I was able to supply a few details that I pulled up from my memory and experience.

A reporter asked, "Broad question. What is Lady Bird's legacy?"

I said, "You know her legacy nationally, with the National Parks and her efforts to combat the roadside clutter of billboards. But here in Austin, it's Town Lake."

I explained that when she came back to Texas after her husband's presidency was over, Mrs. Johnson had been appalled at the appearance of Town Lake, the body of water cutting through downtown Austin. It was a mud pen, and she took it on as a personal project. She urged friends and family members to join her cause, and she found an ally in her old friend Mary Lasker of the Lasker Foundation, who'd previously donated thousands of flower bulbs and other plantings when Mrs. Johnson was beautifying the Potomac River and Pennsylvania Avenue.

Always genteel but persuasive, Mrs. Johnson asked Austin mayor Roy Butler to create the Citizens' Committee for a More Beautiful Town Lake. To head the committee, the mayor called on Les Gage of the Gage Furniture family, and Carolyn Curtis, a Johnson family friend whose father was the longtime general manager of KTBC. Their task was to landscape the area, control erosion, and construct hike-and-bike trails along the banks.

After the beautification was completed, and for the rest of her life, Mrs. Johnson would walk the trails with Carolyn and other friends and point out things that needed attention. She was always looking for ways to make Town Lake more user-friendly and easy to maintain. It was something in which she took a great deal of pride.

A few years before Mrs. Johnson's death, George Christian and Larry Temple persuaded the Austin City Council to rename Town Lake as Lady Bird Lake. George and Larry told her about it before it was to be announced, and Larry Temple disclosed to me that "she vehemently said she did not want her name on the lake because she thought she would be blamed every time it got dirty." He said, "George and I agreed to her request to withdraw the name change and we privately said it could wait until after her death."

After her death, the Austin City Council did indeed change the name to Lady Bird Lake in her honor, saying, "We know she didn't want to do that, but we feel it's appropriate."

Once I'd explained her legacy and the press conference was over, Tom Johnson said to me, "Neal, I didn't know all that. It was great that the reporters could walk outside and see what Mrs. Johnson had accomplished."

As the Johnson family spokesman, I broke my own rule to allow photographs of Mrs. Johnson's casket arriving for a very small, private ceremony at the University of Texas Lady Bird Johnson Wildflower Center. *Photo by Kelly West/Reuters*

She was carried to the LBJ Library in a natural wood casket covered with wildflowers, and like her husband, she lay in state at the top of the marble staircase while thousands of mourners walked past to pay their respects.

One of her wishes had been to say one final goodbye to the Wildflower Center. The Johnson family wanted to keep the ceremony small, avoiding a huge crowd showing up at the center, even though a lot of folks wanted to be there. About fifty guests were invited, special friends and acquaintances through the Wildflower Center, people who had worked very closely with her and others who had supported the center.

The *Austin American-Statesman* has always employed great award-winning photographers. At the time of the memorial services, Zach Ryall was the paper's chief photographer, and he'd also guided the newspaper's direction in recent years, advancing from overseeing the photography to overseeing all the digital aspects of the newspaper. As I was coordinating the ceremony at the Wildflower Center, I told Zach that his access was limited: "You can photograph the hearse pulling up, the casket being unloaded and going into the center, but we don't want to disrupt the private moments inside."

The media was very gracious in abiding by those wishes. But Zach came up to me and said, "Neal, I know you said no photographers inside, but let me show you this great shot."

It was an image framed through the center's archway, with beautiful plants draping the entrance and the handsome architecture of native stone. He said, "Imagine this. Look here and look there."

He envisioned a photo of the casket being escorted through the archway, and he convinced me it was a moment that needed to be captured on film. I said, "We've told the media that they can't come in here. But you're right. We've got to have that image for history."

So I broke my own rule. Once again. But as always, it was for a good cause.

Zach stationed his photographer at that spot, crouching down behind a little rock wall with the perfect view. Zach said, "It won't be disruptive. He'll never move, and he'll wait until everything is over before he gets up and leaves."

The photograph was magnificent.

The official memorial service was held at Riverbend Church in Austin's West Lake Hills, overlooking the wooded landscape that Mrs. Johnson loved so much. In Bill Moyers's eulogy, he said, "She seemed to grow calmer as the world around her grew more furious." And he praised her for being a thoughtful and soothing influence in her husband's life, helping to negotiate "the civil war within his nature."

The service was planned and run by others, but I was backstage with Elizabeth Christian and members of four former First Families, who were all very gracious people: Laura Bush and Barbara Bush, Rosalynn and Jimmy Carter, Hillary and Bill Clinton, and Nancy Reagan. I made sure they were lined up and knew where they were going when we ushered them out to their seats on the front row.

Shortly before the service began, I took a quick break and ran to the restroom, and then returned to guide the dignitaries to their seats. In my public role as the sole usher, I stood facing the First Families and the entire audience. Everything was going as planned, the music was playing, and the view of the hills outside the windows was spectacular. When I walked to my seat three or four rows back and sat beside Elizabeth, I

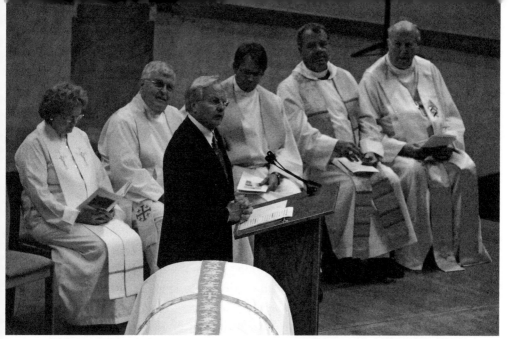

Bill Moyers, whom I replaced at Austin's KTBC-TV while both of us were still UT students, has had a lifelong association with the Johnson family. He delivered a moving eulogy for Mrs. Johnson, a fellow East Texan, at her funeral. *University of Texas at Austin/Marsha Miller*

I personally escorted Nancy Reagan, Rosalynn Carter, Jimmy Carter, Laura Bush, Bill Clinton, and Hillary Clinton to their front row seats at the Riverbend Church funeral service for Mrs. Johnson. *University of Texas at Austin/Christina S. Murrey*

straightened my suit, looked down, and realized that my fly had been unzipped the entire time. I was incredibly embarrassed and wondered if anyone had noticed. Suddenly I remembered that old Bob Hope joke about the three ways you can tell when you're getting old. The first thing you do, you forget names. The second thing is you forget to zip up. The third thing is you forget to zip down.

The original plan was that after the service, the hearse would bear her casket from Riverbend Church out to the family cemetery at the Johnson ranch, where she would be buried next to her husband. But because so many people had expressed their love and admiration for her, and they couldn't attend the service, we announced that the funeral cortege would begin at the State Capitol, roll slowly down Congress Avenue, and pass along the Town Lake beautification trail.

The outpouring of love for Lady Bird Johnson was an unforgettable sight. Thousands of people lined the city streets and Highway 71 to bow their heads, doff their hats, wave, salute, and raise signs with thoughtful sentiments, however they felt like expressing their fondness and respect for that remarkable lady. Parents and grandparents, children, all sorts of mourners were waiting for her to pass by. Out on the highway, pickup trucks were parked with passengers sitting in the beds, waving and praying. It was a very touching tribute for miles and miles out into that rocky countryside that was such a part of her, the hearse traveling along a road she knew and loved so well.

The family followed the hearse in their own vehicle, with Luci and Lynda waving back to the people and thanking them for being there. It was a very quiet procession, no sirens blaring, just a serene and dignified homage in keeping with Mrs. Johnson's own personal style.

It started raining that day, and I was asked by the press, "Is this going to curtail any of the services?"

I said, "No, Mrs. Johnson would love the rain."

People in the Texas Hill Country know that rain is a blessing. With her affection for natural wonders and that special part of Texas, she would've welcomed the rain coming down and nourishing the earth as she made her final journey to rest beside her husband. It was a private ceremony at the ranch, smaller and less complicated than President Johnson's burial, and the family didn't invite television coverage. I attended the ceremony, but I wasn't there as a news reporter. I was burying a friend.

MAD MEN, AUSTIN-STYLE

After Ron Rogers and I dissolved the Rogers Spelce Company in the mid-1970s, I opened Neal Spelce Associates. The company's first office was located in a small building across from the State Capitol. I had been on television for many years in Austin and had a broad-reaching identity—what the kids nowadays call a *brand*—so our agency decided to use my name recognition. *Neal Spelce* was attached to everything we did at Neal Spelce Associates, for better or worse. The downside was there was too much *me*. Clients began to say, "We want *you* to handle the account, Neal." I was getting locked in and overwhelmed. An acquaintance from a competitor agency once told me he'd made a pitch to a potential client and thought he'd done really well. After the client had packed up and was walking out, he turned and said, "Now you're with Neal Spelce, right?"

The name recognition hadn't always been accurate or comfortable. One evening when I was having a beer with my KTBC colleagues at Scholz Garten—the famous beer garden once frequented by LBJ and his political crowd and many of Austin's premier writers and artists—there was a table of folks watching us as if to say, "Hey, they're the local TV guys." That happened now and again.

An attractive woman left that table and came walking up to me and said, "They tell me you're Neal Spelce."

"Yeah, guilty as charged," I said. "Afraid I got caught."

She said, "No, you're not Neal Spelce."

I said, "I am Neal Spelce. What makes you think I'm not?"

She said, "Because I've slept with Neal Spelce and you're not him."

I couldn't resist asking the next question: "Well, was I any good?"

She said, "Not particularly."

Whoever was using my name out there did not perform as well as he probably thought he did.

CHASED BY THE BEAR

During my journey in radioland, I discovered that I didn't mind taking risks in business ventures, but it wasn't as if I'd been trained as an MBA and had the formal schooling to run a company. In fact, I'd never been adept at handling commercial finances, so I brought in my brother, Bennett, a certified public accountant, and said, "Bennett, you handle the money and I'll handle the people."

Bringing a family member into the business is often a recipe for disaster. I understood how stubborn and adamant Bennett was—our mother often called him "bull-headed." When we were growing up, we'd fight like brothers do sometimes, but we quit fighting when he threw me into a wall and broke the sheetrock. I remember saying, "Okay, I don't think we're going to fight anymore."

The upside was that Bennett is very witty—he loves wordplay and jokes—and although he's more reserved than I am, he can be tougher in negotiations. I valued his judgment because he was usually right. He would say, "You can't spend the money on that." "We need to get more revenue from this group." "We've got to watch this." "Let me negotiate the lease for more office space when we get ready to expand."

Instead of falling into an old familial bashing of heads, I called upon my diplomatic skills and we were able to work together really well. Bennett used to say, "Neal is the outside guy and I'm the inside guy. I run the agency and Neal goes out and works with clients and brings business in."

He often used a humorous analogy: "Neal is like the pioneer who says he's going to bring back a bear if we'll skin it. And then the next thing I know, I hear Neal outside the door shouting, 'Open the door! Open the door!' So I open the door real quick and Neal comes running through with a bear chasing right behind him. 'I got your bear!' he's yelling. 'You skin him. I'll go get another one.'"

A GOOD WORD

Beginning with our friendship at KTBC, Tom Johnson and I have maintained an excellent working relationship for decades. For instance, after LBJ's death, portions of the Johnson ranch were sold, and the cattle were part of the dispersal sale. The remainder of the ranch was given to the National Park Service. Tom asked me and my agency to publicize details of the sale of assets.

It was deeply satisfying to me personally when Tom began recommending me everywhere. Phone calls started coming out of the blue: "Tom Johnson says we need to hire you." I was grateful for his confidence in me, and when those calls came, I responded with no questions asked.

The ad agency grew to more than thirty employees, which was impressive for Austin in the 1970s. We were fairly successful at making pitches. We won some accounts, we lost some. But that's the nature of the business. A seasoned graphics designer named Al Boyd came to me and said, "Neal, I'll show you how to make money in advertising if you'll bring me on board." He advised us to stop outsourcing our design work and bring it all in-house. So we added advertising design to the company.

As we continued to grow, we moved to larger offices, eventually downtown to the black monolith of the Austin National Bank Tower at Sixth and Congress. I wanted to lease the office number 1560 because that was the dial position for my last radio station and I thought it would be easy to remember. But 1560 wasn't available.

In time, we began to transition the accounts from me to my staff, who were excellent co-account executives very capable of taking over the projects. We hired Howard Falkenberg away from a local radio station, where he was serving as the news director, and he turned out to be a fantastic communications strategist. He was the only person to whom I ever entrusted the title of president at my company. I was the titular head, and my name was on the door, but Howard was there in the conference room when I couldn't be there, running the show and taking care of everything.

I had a commonsense approach to surrounding myself with talented thinkers. It was a collaborative process, like making a movie rather than writing a novel. I wasn't trying to be a visionary like Elon Musk, building an entirely new kind of car or flying to Mars. My strength was connecting with people, which I'd always done as a news reporter, and I gave our clients what they wanted—with a dash of imagination. The key was not to push a wild idea, but to offer a variety of specific possibilities that zeroed in on what they really needed. Let's rent the Goodyear Blimp? Sure, that's a great idea. But how does it translate into raising money for your project and making it a grand success? I learned very early on that it was never about me and my "brilliant" strategies. I always counseled my staff to assure the clients of the great commercial results they'd achieve if we all put our heads together, brainstormed, and reached mutual agreement.

In the early days of advertising, representatives would go into a client meeting and say this is who we are, this is the experience and expertise we'll bring to your account, so hire us. Deals were struck over general impressions. But that eventually evolved into clients saying, "Show us what you can do for us." And that's when it became necessary to pitch the account with a very creative presentation.

One example of that is what my agency did for the Estates at Barton Creek, when the area was being developed by John Connally and Ben Barnes. The Barnes-Connally Partnership owned land that abutted the Barton Creek greenbelt and wilderness area west of Austin. (One wag said, "I don't know how Barnes did it, but he managed to get his name listed first in the partnership!") The two men envisioned large upscale homes and a golf course and conference center. Our challenge was to attract builders, investors, and home buyers to a planned community that didn't exist yet. We wanted to run some ads, but there was nothing to advertise. It was a stunning, untouched area of woods and creeks, but how could we convey the fact that there would be homes built there and a wonderful place to live and raise a family?

The creative team at our shop came up with an idea to put an ad in *Texas Monthly* to show that the Estates at Barton Creek would have great appeal for families. We dressed two kids in yellow rain slickers with book satchels and photographed them walking through a lush green paradise to illustrate how safe and family-friendly the area would be. The photograph was gorgeous because we shot it in green woods after a rain. The kids' slickers were luminous and the trees had an almost magical sheen.

The Barnes-Connally Partnership had borrowed a lot of money to develop the Estates at Barton Creek, and the company dissolved when the partners were caught up in the real estate bust of the late 1980s. Both John Connally and Ben Barnes declared bankruptcy. The court seized all of Connally's assets from his home and his ranch, and then took those valuables to Houston in 1988 and auctioned them off. As their prized possessions and personal keepsakes were being claimed by the highest bidders, John and Nellie Connally sat in the front row with the dignity and resolve they'd shown as the state's First Couple, when Big John served as governor. When asked why they were attending the auction, John Connally replied, "We want to play out the whole hand. I guess there's some degree of self-flagellation involved."

Connally had worked with the auctioneers to prepare a catalog of everything that was being sold and even stood up at the auction to describe

Throughout my life, I was fortunate to be involved with many famous folks such as Oveta Culp Hobby (left), President Eisenhower's secretary of health and human services, and former Texas governor John Connally and with his wife, Nellie Connally. *Photo by Neal Spelce*

the importance of certain possessions to jack up the bid price. Several of his friends had raised money and arranged to purchase items that meant something special to the couple, and those items were later returned to the Connallys.

One of the items they auctioned off was a painting by my mother. LBJ had purchased it and had given it to the Connallys as a Christmas gift a month before his death.

I had interacted with John Connally a few times when I was a newsman, but I didn't fully understand how intelligent and charismatic he was until we were fellow board members for Cable Advertising Systems, a company that sold advertising time on cable networks. At board meetings, I always made it a point to sit beside him and ask him questions whenever I could, channeling my former reporter persona, and he was remarkably open and informative. "Governor, what can you tell me about what's going on at Ford Motor Company from your board member's perspective?" "What's happening with the stock market?" He was a fount of knowledge, and he also had a great sense of humor.

One day he and I walked out of the Barton Creek Country Club and stopped to talk, and I got up the courage to ask him about the JFK assassination. "Governor, you've heard all these theories about how many shooters were involved." He said, "There was just one."

He talked about the wounds he received that day in Dallas. "I've hunted all my life and I know the sound of rifle fire," he said. "I heard those shots, and there was only one rifle firing. And it was fired by one man."

He was convinced that Lee Harvey Oswald, and only Lee Harvey Oswald, had committed the horrible deed.

The Only Paid Ad

When we expanded the graphics department at Neal Spelce Associates, one of the artists we hired was Becky Levy. Her husband, Michael Levy, was a UT law student at the time, and as a young couple they shared one car, so he would pick up Becky when she got off work. One afternoon Mike said to me, "Neal, let me show you something." He had a sheaf of pages. "I've got this idea. I want to start a magazine."

I said, "Mike, you haven't finished law school yet."

Mike Levy is not a Type A personality, he's a Type A Plus Plus, a go-get-'em bundle of energy and imagination. "I'm going to finish law school," he assured me, "but take a look at what I'm planning. When I was an undergraduate at Penn, I read a magazine in Philadelphia called *Philadelphia Monthly*."

He described his vision for a magazine he wanted to call *Texas Monthly*.

"Mike, Philadelphia is small compared to the state of Texas. Covering Texas is a huge undertaking."

He said, "Texas has all the best stories," and he went on and on in detail. I famously responded, "Mike, you're going to lose your ass."

The rest is history. (Recall that I was also the guy who said, "Nothing important ever happens in a motorcade.")

Mike Levy received his law degree, but I don't think he ever practiced a day of law. He started *Texas Monthly* with a small group of friends and extraordinary writers, and over the next five decades it became a hugely successful enterprise and a major venue for world-class journalism. Our two companies had offices in the Austin National Bank Tower and I remained good friends with the Levys.

In the very first issue of *Texas Monthly*, our advertising agency bought a full-color ad on the back cover, generally the most expensive page in a magazine, and that probably paid for the magazine's next month's rent. As I thumbed through the pages of that first issue, it seemed to me they were printing ads for free to make the magazine look professional and gain advertising momentum. I suspected that a jewelry store, for example, wouldn't advertise in a startup magazine. I said, "Mike, is mine the only paid ad in your magazine?" He started laughing. He was printing free ads for businesses with clientele he *hoped* would read his new magazine.

NEWS JUNKIE

ecoming a news junkie began with my watching Movietone News
at the picture show in Clarksville when I was a boy, and that strange
moment witnessing LBJ descend from a helicopter in Raymondville. It was a fascination that grew stronger during my years as a reporter for the Johnsons at KTBC, tagging alongside LBJ in Asia, helping
him plan the dedication of his presidential library, and overseeing him
laid to rest at the family ranch. Standing in his long shadow, observing
him behind the scenes on many occasions, was the best course in political science I could ever take. Those experiences fed my addiction to news
and politics. It's why I gravitated toward national party conventions and
presidential inaugurations, as well as state and local politics, throughout
my career.

Mario Cuomo: Hamlet on the Hudson

A good friend of mine, attorney Gordon Wynne from Wills Point,
east of Dallas, was also a producer of Broadway musical extravaganzas,
inaugural galas, and the Hallmark Hall of Fame television series. He had
a great love for music and pageantry, and he was hired to handle the
production of the 1984 Democratic National Convention in San Francisco. The convention's keynote speaker was New York governor Mario
Cuomo, who was sometimes called "Hamlet on the Hudson" because
of his *to be or not to be* indecision to run for the presidency. Neverthe-
less, Mario Cuomo was an outstanding speaker and a rising star in the
Democratic Party.

Gordon called me and said, "Neal, we work with each of the speakers
to get them ready to walk onstage, and we want them to do as good a job
as possible when they speak. If we pay your expenses, would you come
out here and work with our speakers?"

It was volunteer work. My PR firm wasn't hired, so I didn't receive a
salary. I asked if I could bring my son, Allen, who was in college at the
time, to experience a national political convention, and Gordon agreed
to give us food, lodging, and travel.

At the Moscone Convention Center in San Francisco, there was a room set up with a podium and teleprompters, and the speakers would come in and go through their speeches. I was asked to work with Governor Cuomo and a few others.

Making a speech at a political convention is unlike any other speech you've ever delivered. It's usually before a packed, roaring crowd in a huge arena, with a multitude of delegates on the convention floor and surrounding the stage. They're all partisan, of course, and many of them show up wearing crazy outfits—funny glasses and hats with the names of their favorite candidates and every imaginable sign and placard. Their craziness is an enthusiasm-building device that becomes the measure of a convention's success.

A political convention is a magnificent event. The candidates walk to the podium with music booming and the crowd cheering and applauding. The television cameras are zeroing in, the lights are swirling around, and the spectacle can take your breath away. For even a seasoned speaker, the plunge into that environment can be overwhelming. You can get knocked off your game when you hear your voice echoing over the audience and bouncing back and forth while thousands of ecstatic delegates are milling around on the floor. Unless you're the keynote speaker, the scene is chaotic, with handshaking and hugging and celebrations throughout the arena and every conceivable distraction.

As producer, Gordon Wynne always stood near the podium, wearing a headset and directing the stagecraft. He decided that when the primary speakers came out—for nominations, keynote speeches, acceptance speeches—the crew would take the houselights down to quiet the din on what would become a nearly dark floor. There was also an ulterior motive. Gordon didn't want the cameras showing all those crazies cutting up. Yes, they were there to represent the large cities and small towns and out-of-the-way places in America, and they were all convinced that *their* candidate would be the next president of the United States. But Gordon felt that the average television viewer had only a limited tolerance for the silliness.

The TV people said no, we can't take the lights down because we want to show crowd reaction. Ultimately, Gordon and the networks reached a compromise: when there was applause or an outburst of emotion, they'd bring the lights up a bit to capture the audience responding.

Governor Cuomo came to San Francisco not with a delegation, but with his son, Andrew Cuomo, who would follow in his father's footsteps and also become the governor of New York. Cuomo arrived with his speech already written. I had no idea what he was going to say. He went through the speech with me, and part of it criticized President Ronald Reagan's "Shining City on a Hill" speech.

We worked side by side. Cuomo would rehearse and then turn to me for my input. I reminded him, "Governor, the teleprompter will be following your pace. It's not gonna scroll ahead of you or drag behind."

I added, "And don't worry about the cameras. They're gonna take you from several angles. There's gonna be a camera shooting over here, over there, and one straight ahead. Don't worry about them because that'll distract you. Just be aware that when you finish a sentence and the applause starts, the cameras are gonna show you, too, so don't look down or scratch your nose or grab a drink of water."

When the time came, he handled the speech to perfection from the outset, opening with, "Please allow me to skip the stories and the poetry and the temptation to deal in nice but vague rhetoric. Let me instead use this valuable opportunity to deal immediately with the questions that should determine this election and that we all know are vital to the American people."

He enjoyed his moment in the spotlight, and his confidence and charisma came across very well. He won enormous praise for that speech, and it ignited the popular sentiment, "Why didn't we nominate Mario Cuomo this year instead of Walter Mondale?"

When he walked off the stage, I was busy working with another political figure, who was preparing for the podium. As the applause died down, Governor Cuomo came looking for me, saying, "Where's Neal? Where's Neal?" He wanted to thank me. I had done my job, and he had done his. Eighty million people had listened to his speech, and it is considered one of the best speeches ever delivered at a US political convention.

Ann Richards: Backwards and in High Heels

Four years later, at the Democratic National Convention in Atlanta, a minor political figure named Ann Richards with a big silver pompadour hairstyle and a charming drawl was selected to make the keynote speech. Many people began asking, "Who the hell is Ann Richards?" The state treasurer of Texas, not a governor or senator?

The hierarchy of the Democratic Party was aware of her humor and appealing verbal skills because she'd seconded the nomination for Geraldine Ferraro as vice president at the convention in 1984, but she was unknown on the national stage.

As soon as Ann was chosen as the keynote speaker, she and Mario Cuomo had a phone conversation. "You did a great job last time, Mario," she said. "I need your advice." He said, "Do you know this guy there in Austin by the name of Neal Spelce?" She said, "Of course I know Neal."

I had known Ann for many years prior to the 1988 convention. For one thing, Ann and I ran with many of the same Austin crowd, mutual friends who were famous in their own right as writers, artists, and musicians.

Besides that, Ann had served as a Travis County commissioner before being elected as the state treasurer, and I'd covered her race against Johnny Voudouris, a wealthy businessman who owned a successful custodial company that serviced the US military. The good old boys had lined up against Ann. Singer and Austin radio personality Sammy Allred maintained that "Johnny Voudouris looks like Steve McQueen" and wrote a little song for him, a campaign ditty. Because county commissioners are in charge of roads in Travis County, Johnny Voudouris's campaign spread photos of him leaning against a road Caterpillar or some sort of front-loading heavy equipment. It implied, "Macho men, we build roads. This job ain't for little ladies."

But Ann ran as Ann. She never tried to be someone she wasn't. She didn't have to climb onto a big dirt-mover or a Sherman tank. She remained true to herself, her values and principles, and she won.

In Ann's phone conversation with Mario Cuomo, he said, "You need to hire Neal." So she called me and said, "Neal, do you want to help me on this?" I was happy to make myself available, knowing that I would be a paid consultant this time.

According to Ann's friend Jan Reid in his book *Let the People In: The Life and Times of Ann Richards*, Ann's writing team of Suzanne Coleman, Mary Beth Rogers, and Jane Hickie began working with veteran Washington speechwriter John Sherman to polish and strengthen Suzanne's first draft. It underwent several rewrites over the next few months, and yet Ann still wasn't comfortable that she had it exactly to her liking.

Gordon Wynne wasn't producing the 1988 convention, but Ann trusted Gordon and hired him to come to Atlanta and help with her speech. Taking his usual approach, Gordon acted like a conductor in the orchestra pit: "When she comes out, take the lights up . . . take the lights down . . . play this music . . . follow my cue when the music is up." He had the typical disagreements with the convention managers over lighting and other details. "No, we've got our way of doing it," they said. "No, you do it this way," he insisted. And Gordon prevailed.

Ann was a great speaker and a great performer. She knew how to play to an audience with perfect charm and wit. In Texas, we knew how popular and charismatic she was. The crowds would walk away enthralled with her. There was nothing I could teach her about timing and delivery, so I worked with her on the same mechanical things I'd focused on with Mario Cuomo: Here's where the cameras are. This is the shot they're going to get. Here's where the teleprompter is. When I asked her what she was going to wear, she said, "Damn it, Neal, I don't know what to wear."

I suggested that it be something to complement her color and striking hair, and not to distract the viewers with jewelry. I've always advised, "Don't wear a lot of fancy jewelry around your neck or earrings. They will detract from what you say. People will be wondering, 'What in the world is she wearing?' They're not going to hear the important words you're delivering."

I advised her that the dress should be plain. "No ornamentation and no print or anything like that," I said. "You want the cameras to frame an image that focuses on your face, so you can convey your message through your eyes and your words."

When that historical moment arrived and the orchestra kicked off "Deep in the Heart of Texas," she walked out onto the convention platform waving and wearing a light blue dress that complemented her silver hair. It left an eye-catching and memorable impression. She ignored my advice in part and wore a tasteful string of pearls and small clusters-of-pearl earrings. She always did things her way, and that's why we admired her so much.

During rehearsals, I was impressed with several great lines in her speech that we all knew would be critical to its success. Perhaps the most unforgettable was, "Poor George, he can't help it—he was born with a silver . . . foot in his mouth." She was talking about the presidential candidate George H. W. Bush, of course, who came from a very wealthy family.

Ann was good friends with the comedian and actor Lily Tomlin, and that line was written by Lily's partner and writing collaborator, Jane Wagner.

I worked with Ann Richards for days in Atlanta on her 1988 Democratic National Convention keynote address. She wowed the crowd. *Photo by Wally McNamee, Wally McNamee Photographic Archive, Briscoe Center for American History, the University of Texas at Austin*

Another great line was aimed at women voters and everyone who supported women's rights: "Twelve years ago, Barbara Jordan, another Texas woman, made the keynote address to this convention, and two women in 160 years is about par for the course. But if you give us a chance, we can perform. After all, Ginger Rogers did everything that Fred Astaire did. She just did it backwards and in high heels."

Ann was a master at self-deprecation, and that showed up in her anecdote about junior high basketball: "Tonight I feel a little like I did when I played basketball in the eighth grade. I thought I looked real cute in my uniform, and then I heard a boy yell from the bleachers, 'Make that basket, bird legs.' And my greatest fear is that same guy is somewhere out there in the audience tonight, and he's going to cut me down to size."

Ann and Suzanne Coleman sent the final draft of the speech to the party headquarters there at the Omni Center, and the official response was, "No, no, no, we've got to cut out these jokes. Keynotes are a serious business. You're doing great on content, but don't use the jokes."

Ann was devastated.

Stepping out of line as usual, I said, "You've got to use that humor, Ann. It's *you*. It's sincere. It's not somebody standing up there reading a boilerplate speech that editors jammed together and insisted, 'You ought to say this.' The country needs to see your personality in action."

She said, "I know, I know, but they're saying . . ." I said, "Well, let's tell them you're not going to leave out the humor." So she tried again and they said no again. It went back and forth. Finally, I said, "The teleprompter is located down below the podium. There's an operator sitting down there who can make changes instantaneously. He's a functionary, not a party hack, and he'll follow orders from a man like me wearing a nice suit. If push comes to shove, I'll go down there at the last minute and insert those lines in the teleprompter. I'll put them back in. Nobody will know except the teleprompter operator."

She laughed and said, "I hope it doesn't come to that."

But that was the decision we made, and we were serious. Nobody was aware that we were prepared to go rogue.

Ann didn't back down and finally won the argument, thank goodness, and I didn't have to convince a teleprompter operator that I was a party bigwig making last-minute changes.

There were other behind-the-scenes machinations taking place at the same time. In past conventions, reporters and network commentators had asked in advance, "What's the keynote speaker going to say? Will you give us a copy of the speech?"

Of course, it's imperative to keep the remarks a secret for the element of surprise, so we concocted a plan. I suggested, "Let's leak it to a few key people."

Ann's team asked how we were going to do this, and I said, "First of all, you've got to let Mario Cuomo see it, because reporters are going to ask him. All he needs to say is, 'I've read her speech and you're going to love it. It's fantastic. You're going to forget about me when you hear Ann Richards.'"

Governor Cuomo agreed to that with a huge smile.

I also suggested that they give the speech to my old friend and CBS colleague Walter Cronkite, "the most trusted man in America," and ask him not to reveal the content. Ann knew him as well, and she contacted him to say, "Walter, here ya go. This is what I'm going to deliver."

With that familiar twinkle in his eye, Walter looked into the camera and said, "We can't reveal what's being said in the speech by Ann Richards tomorrow, but I'm convinced that this state treasurer from Texas will wow the crowd."

His insider's knowledge built up the anticipation for her speech, and when she finally delivered the address, she dazzled the delegates and millions of television viewers alike. "Poor George." "Ginger Rogers." "Bird legs." Here was this unglamorous lady, by Hollywood standards, a Texas gal with her old-school hairstyle and country plain-talk, but Ann's sharp observations and downhome humor brought the audience to its feet several times, applauding and cheering wildly.

Texas attorney general Jim Mattox was the only Democrat on the convention floor not cheering after Ann's speech. Patricia Kilday Hart captured that image in a *Texas Monthly* article: "As Richards enjoyed her big moment, her chief rival for governor, Attorney General Jim Mattox, was sulking in the thunderous ovation rocking the Omni Center. . . . He sat petulantly in the front row, glaring at delegates waving 'Ann Richards' signs, applauding weakly, and sitting glumly through her best lines. He spent the next day telling interviewers that the speech had been okay but no big deal."

It was a portent of things to come. Mattox campaigned against Ann two years later, in the 1990 Democratic Party primary for governor of Texas, and lost. When she moved into the Governor's Mansion in 1991,

Ann Richards became only the second female governor in the history of the Lone Star State.

Azie Taylor Morton: With Liberty and Justice

My UT friend and classmate George Dillman developed a close friendship with Azie Taylor Morton (1938–2003), who would become the first and only African American to serve as treasurer of the United States. George and Azie both labored intensely, behind the scenes and without fanfare, to execute the complex credentialing operations at several national Democratic Party conventions. It was a thankless but vitally important job—especially with warring factions within the party demanding all manner of credentials and seeking access to the convention floor—and they put in back-to-back sixteen-hour days to keep on top of it.

On September 12, 1977, when Azie learned that President Jimmy Carter had named her US treasurer, it was her close friend, George Dillman, who escorted her to a congratulatory dinner that evening in Washington. She served as treasurer from 1977 to 1981. Azie's signature was on all paper currency during that time.

Azie Taylor Morton had been raised by her maternal grandparents in the tiny Central Texas community of Dale, twenty-eight miles east of San Marcos. She never knew her father. Her mother was deaf, and because Dale had no high school for African Americans, Azie attended the Texas Blind, Deaf, and Orphans School in Austin. An exceedingly bright person, she graduated from high school at age sixteen and then graduated cum laude from the historically black Huston-Tillotson College in 1956. Afterward, she excelled in a number of governmental positions.

At the 1980 Democratic convention—when Azie had been US treasurer for about three years—George Dillman learned that she hadn't been assigned any official role in the convention and wasn't going to be recognized, even though she was the first African American treasurer of the United States. That set George in motion. He called his close Texas friend Gordon Wynne, who was the convention production coordinator, and suggested that Azie should lead the opening Pledge of Allegiance. Not necessarily a big deal, but Dillman and Wynne turned it into a momentous occasion.

When the networks began their live broadcasts, the house lights dimmed and a spotlight was focused on Azie as she was introduced. The live orchestra began softly playing "Battle Hymn of the Republic," and the crowd hushed. All eyes were on Azie as the conventioneers stood with her to recite the pledge.

The current news was all about US hostages being held in Iran. Azie began by reading from the teleprompter what Dillman had written: "All Americans, whatever your political party or persuasion, or wherever you may be, join hearts and hands" in prayer for the Americans held hostage in Iran. Her preacher-like delivery soared as the orchestra continued playing the "Battle Hymn" in the background, and she seamlessly transitioned into "I pledge allegiance . . ." The stirring music kept building, keeping time with her delivery cadence, and her voice reached a crescendo with the ending: ". . . with liberty and justice for all!"

It was mesmerizing. There were cheers. There were tears. What a historical moment.

Azie moved to Austin after her Washington service. She spent a lot of time with former congresswoman Barbara Jordan (who had her own national spotlight moments). I was blessed to help Azie in a few small ways, in one instance recommending her to be a paid board member for Austin's homegrown Schlotzsky's sandwich franchise. And I found it fitting that in 2018, a street running alongside Austin's beloved Zilker Park was renamed Azie Taylor Morton Drive. It replaced what was formerly known as Robert E. Lee Drive.

A TRUE MAVERICK

In 2008, I was keeping an eye on the presidential primaries, and after Arizona senator John McCain won the most delegates in Louisiana's convoluted Republican caucus/primary, he appeared at a televised news conference. To my surprise, his presentation was horrible. He didn't do a good job at all. At the same time, Barack Obama was thrilling large audiences nationwide with his fantastic oratorical skills—the antithesis of John McCain.

McCain had never considered himself a great speaker; he was always just himself. But it was near the end of the long primary season, and I could see that he was showing signs of exhaustion. It's a common problem. With those grueling schedules, I'm amazed at how candidates keep their heads on straight. They're pushed and rushed here and there, and they have to catch some rest whenever they can and then be on their toes again.

Right after that speech, I was at the Headliners Club in Austin and I ran into Mark McKinnon, who was McCain's media adviser at the time. Mark had attended UT and had served as editor of the *Daily Texan*, the university's nationally acclaimed student newspaper. A former Democrat, he'd become personal friends with George W. Bush in the 1990s and had directed the media strategies for the younger Bush's gubernatorial and presidential campaigns. I knew Mark well enough to tell him I thought McCain did a poor job in his remarks in New Orleans. Mark said, "Oh we know, Neal, we know."

At some point during that summer of 2008, Mark left the McCain campaign when it became clear that Obama would be the Democratic nominee. Mark had great respect for the future president, and he didn't want to work against the election of the first African American candidate and a unique historic moment for the nation.

When the McCain team began preparing the senator for the Republican National Convention that summer, Mark contacted me and said he'd recommended that McCain hire me to help him with his speech presentation. Mark knew I'd worked with Mario Cuomo and Ann Richards on their speeches at Democratic conventions in 1984 and 1988, but the party didn't matter to Mark or McCain.

Not long after our conversation, McCain's campaign manager, Rick Davis, called me and said, "McKinnon gives you high marks. Let's talk and see if there's a way you can help the senator with his keynote address."

I had met John McCain once before. I was in New Orleans working with James Earl Jones on a television series, and we were having dinner at Commander's Palace when McCain walked in and sat at a table with a friend. James Earl looked over and said, "That's John McCain. I really admire him." I asked if he'd ever met him, and he said no. "Come on," I said to that great actor with the deep, distinctive voice, "let's go say hello."

We walked over to McCain's table, and I said, "Senator, Neal Spelce." The senator looked at me in the way all politicians look at strangers and said, "Neal, how are you?" as if we were best friends. I said, "I want to introduce you to James Earl Jones."

That was my first interaction with John McCain.

A few weeks before the Republican convention in St. Paul, Minnesota, I flew to the McCain campaign headquarters in Washington, DC, for a meeting with the senator, his campaign manager, Rick Davis (Steve Schmidt would join the campaign later), and his longtime trusted speechwriter, Mark Salter. I knew McCain wouldn't remember that exchange in New Orleans because I was just a guy who facilitated his introduction to James Earl Jones. As we got started, I gave them my analysis of Barack Obama's charismatic speechmaking ability in comparison to McCain's, and I didn't hold back. I said, "Obama is an outstanding orator, but he's tied to the teleprompter, and the teleprompter has its limitations. For some reason he wants the teleprompter script to be up high, so it's almost like he's an elitist looking down his nose at the audience. If you watch his speeches, he never looks directly at the audience. That's because he's reading the teleprompter."

We knew that Obama would be coming out in a Greek temple setting at the Democratic convention in Denver. I said, "He's gonna look like a Greek god emerging on high. A 'Hey, look at me, speaking from Olympus' sort of deal, rather than communicating directly with the people."

I reminded the McCain team that conventions were primarily television events, and the most important audience was not the one in the arena. A speaker could belch and the crowd would cheer, because they're committed party people. The audience McCain needed to reach was sitting at home, drinking beer, watching TV, and saying, "Let's see what McCain has to say," and "Let's see how Obama is handling himself."

I said, "Senator, we know what Obama's gonna do, and you can't compete with that." He said, "I know that, Neal. I can't do it his way." I said, "You don't have to. In fact, you shouldn't try. His eloquent voice will ring to the rafters, but it's gonna be 'Look at what a great speaker I am.' A little too elitist. Your audience is the common folks sitting at home."

He smiled and said, "Neal, you realize that this is the most important speech of my life." And I said, "No pressure, huh, Senator?"

So we talked it through, and I recommended that they position the teleprompter directly in front of him but down low on the same sight line as the television cameras, so that while he read the words on the teleprompter, it appeared that he was looking straight into the eyes of the people in their living rooms, addressing them in an intimate way. I told him he would be tempted to respond to the raucous delegates in the big hall—screaming supporters dressed in funny hats holding clever signs. But I urged him to get past that and talk to the television cameras as if he were speaking to a person sitting on a couch. Lower your voice, I said. You don't shout at someone sitting across from you in a living room.

Rick Davis said that convention directors had been planning the logistics and the visual design of the arena stage for a year or more, and they weren't set up for my recommendations. But he gave me the authority to fly to Minnesota and do whatever I needed to do to make my idea work.

At the Xcel Energy Center in St. Paul, I ran into some resistance but managed to get my points across. Avoiding a standard podium or pretentious Greek columns, McCain's TV consultant Fred Davis constructed a ramp that ran out from the regular stage into the midst of the delegates. I recommended that we station a huge sixty-inch television monitor at the end of the ramp, which we'd use as a teleprompter. The monitor was positioned right in front of the bank of television cameras that were stacked for coverage, and that meant John would be looking into the cameras as he was delivering his remarks.

I can't count how many times the senator rehearsed his speech in the final weeks before the convention. At every hotel we stayed in while campaigning, we booked ballrooms of various sizes and re-created the format onstage in St. Paul—the same setup, the same distance from the

I traveled on the campaign trail with Senator John McCain for weeks, preparing him for "the most important speech of my life, Neal"—his presidential nomination acceptance address at the Republican National Convention in 2008. *AP Photo/Stephan Savoia*

teleprompter and cameras. Some nights we had to cancel the rehearsal because John was too tired to practice.

His speechwriter was Mark Salter, who'd been writing for the senator for twenty years by then. The *Wall Street Journal* called Salter "the chief creator, shaper, and enforcer" of the McCain public image, and he eventually collaborated with John on seven books. Salter was a thoughtful person who knew McCain so well he was once called "McCain's alter ego." Salter was a great writer, but his early drafts of the convention speech were a little too oratorical for my taste. I wanted it to be more of a one-on-one conversation than a grand, soaring speech to the masses.

It had always been my philosophy that all television communication is one on one, because viewers are not sitting in a coliseum; they're right there in their armchairs, lying in bed, grabbing a bite in the kitchen, or somewhere in the comfort of their own home.

I didn't get all the changes I suggested for the speech, because Mark loved an elegant turn of phrase. And to his credit, it was a very good speech.

The night before the convention address, John was feeling the pressure. He'd say, "Let's go through it again," and I would walk around the hotel conference room and listen to him, not meeting his eye but studying the monitor to see how he was coming across. After one of his deliveries, the staff members applauded, full of compliments. I said, "Okay, that's it, Senator." He said, "Let's do it again," and I said "No, sir." He said, "*What?*"

True to his reputation, John McCain was sometimes prickly, a navy guy and top gun pilot. He was also down to earth, no nonsense, straightforward, without pretense. It was the way he grew up, and the defiant character he'd forged after five and a half years in a prisoner-of-war camp.

I said, "You nailed it, Senator. I want the speech that you just made— the way you delivered it—to be imprinted in your brain." He pushed back, saying, "You mean we can't rehearse it again?" I said, "No, sir. What you just did is perfect for you and your style. You can't get any better."

I had enormous respect for John McCain. I got to know him as we traveled together on those final days of the campaign. One night on the road, we were meeting in his hotel suite and he said, "Let's order Chinese. Somebody call P. F. Chang's." It was in those relaxed moments, when we were sitting around and chatting, eating late-night fast food with his team, that I really got a feel for his personality.

It was the same when we went to his Hidden Valley ranch retreat outside Sedona, Arizona. The approach was in high desert mountain terrain, but the ranch was down in a verdant valley with lush grass from the stream flowing through it. He had spent quiet hours in that ranch house for a long time. He loved to grill dinner there, and one evening we were all sitting around laughing and cutting up, really relaxed, drinking beer—his wife, Cindy, was the beer distributor for Anheuser-Busch in Phoenix—and here comes John with a Mason jar, shaking it, talking about this and that, shaking the jar, and I finally said, "What the hell is in that jar, Senator?"

"Not a secret sauce," he said, grinning, "just salt and pepper." He was blending it to sprinkle on the meat he was grilling. "And by the way, you can get good meat at Costco."

Always down to earth.

The ranch house walls were covered with the original cartoons that political cartoonists had drawn about him and then given to him as gifts. I enjoyed walking around and reading those cartoons, the favorable and unfavorable, the flattering and unflattering. LBJ had done the same thing at his ranch house, displaying visual images pro and con. It took a confident personality, with a tough hide, to smile at the constant criticism they received in public office.

One evening in a city I can't recall—because they all blended together after a while—John called my hotel room and said, "Neal, do you want to join us for dinner? The Secret Service has found this little restaurant down the street."

There were half a dozen of us at dinner, and John started asking me about President Johnson. I didn't know if he had had an association or friendship with LBJ, or if he held any animosity toward the man who was serving as president when John's plane was shot down over Hanoi.

John was fascinated by my stories about my old boss. After a few choice anecdotes, I turned that around, as reporters do, slipping into my inclination to ask questions rather than respond to them. It must've been the warm spirit of fellowship in the small gathering around the table, because I felt bold enough to say, "Senator, tell us about the Hanoi Hilton." And to my surprise, John McCain opened up.

He talked about both of his arms and one leg breaking when he ejected from the airplane, and how his captors had crushed his shoulder with a rifle butt and bayoneted him when they dragged him out of the lake. They refused to treat his injuries at first and let him heal on his own, then later performed poor surgeries on him. Angered by his defiance, they broke one arm a second time and dislocated his shoulders by bending him over a rod. In typical McCain fashion, he said, "But I wasn't going to show them I was in pain."

His injuries explained why whenever you saw John McCain waving on the campaign trail, he couldn't raise his arms above his shoulders.

"I remember when they brought me back to my cell after that torture session," he told us at dinner. "The other American prisoners were outside, and they saw them dragging me along, because I could hardly walk. My buddies started clapping. I grinned at them and pilot-signaled a 'thumbs up' that I was okay."

He also told us that the North Vietnamese had asked him for names of key naval officers. John's father and grandfather were both four-star admirals in the US Navy, and John had attended the United States Naval Academy, following in their footsteps. He admitted to us that he didn't do well academically. He wasn't a top graduate, but he got through. As a pilot, he earned his captain bars, but he was never going to make admiral.

While John was a prisoner of war, his father was appointed commander in chief of the Pacific Command, putting him in charge of all US forces in the Vietnam theater. The North Vietnamese tried to take advantage of that situation, thinking, "His daddy is very important, so the son must be a high-level operative. This guy knows information we can use."

They tried to draw names and information out of John. He said, "When they wanted names, I ticked off the names of the offensive linemen for the Green Bay Packers."

Eventually, in a gesture of appeasement to John's father, his captors offered to let John go home. But he refused to go unless they freed the rest of the prisoners as well.

"Later on, when my time came and they finally decided to release me," he said, "they took me to a hospital and cleaned me up and treated whatever they could see, and then they brought in a television camera for propaganda purposes, put a microphone in front of my face, and said, 'Were you treated well here at the hospital?'" John responded, "Yes, but why the hell didn't you sorry sons of bitches do this when I was in prison and being tortured? To hell with you!"

Defiant to the very end.

Patriot and Hero

John McCain was a true patriot and a great American. He flew into imminent danger on an air mission into enemy territory, knowing he might die, and he suffered for that action. It takes a heroic nature to go into combat, survive being shot down, and endure the brutality of being a prisoner of war.

As a senator, he was often described as a maverick. He made tough decisions that weren't politically correct, expedient, or in lockstep with the party line. He adamantly opposed the use of torture by the United States, for example, because he had experienced torture himself. "As I have argued many times," he said about that controversial subject, "the methods we employ to keep our nation safe must be as right and just as the values we aspire to live up to and promote in the world." In another speech, he said, "It was wrong to use these methods. . . . it undermined our security interests, and . . . it contradicted the ideals that define us and which we have sacrificed much to defend."

He was his own man. He didn't walk around with an American flag draped around his shoulders, but he loved this country dearly and wanted us to be the moral compass of the world.

Toward the end of John's life, someone said to me, "Don't you think that John McCain ought to give up his Senate seat, now that he's been diagnosed with terminal brain cancer, and let someone else fill the seat?"

I said, "The John McCain I knew in that brief period of time was a real fighter. He doesn't give up."

He came out of his war experiences with an unbending determination to be the kind of public leader who did what was right at all times. He wasn't going to step aside for anything, especially not cancer.

SHE'S ALASKAN, RIGHT?

I was traveling with the McCain campaign when he and his advisers were trying to decide who should be selected as his vice presidential running mate. I overheard several conversations about potential candidates, but I wasn't a policy guy with the campaign—I was only there to help communicate ideas and strategies—so I didn't participate in those discussions.

When Sarah Palin was selected, I wondered, like everyone else, "Who is Sarah Palin? Who is this governor of Alaska?" The media and the rest of the nation received the information at the same time I did.

Bless her heart, Sarah was only four months out from having baby Trig, who was born with Down syndrome. When it came to their children, the Palins were a loving and accepting family; still, having a child with significant physical and mental challenges could not have been easy for Sarah and her husband, Todd. And then there she was, suddenly thrust into the most visible political spotlight in the world. I knew that even though Sarah had a strong family network—and had worked out the career-and-home balance as governor of Alaska—the hard-hitting, nonstop McCain campaign was going to be a monumental challenge for the mother of a four-month-old baby with special needs.

Imagine her situation: being separated from her baby, saddled with a very rigorous schedule, lacking rest, a thick briefing book in her lap constantly, trying to learn Senator McCain's positions on health care, the environment, gun control, the Middle East, and dozens of other issues. When her very long days ended, she was on the phone back home to her husband and kids, missing them and the new baby and hoping everything was as normal as possible.

When she stumbled big-time in a series of disastrous interviews with Katie Couric, many Republicans began calling for Palin to be dropped from the ticket. I was sitting with John McCain in his Washington-area campaign headquarters, viewing film and prepping for the debates, when campaign manager Rick Davis walked in and said, "Neal, can I see you for a minute?"

He pulled me aside and said, "The senator has suggested that Sarah Palin take time off from the campaign for right now. He's offered her his ranch to prepare for her debate with Joe Biden"—the Democrats' vice presidential candidate. Rick gave me a serious look and said, "She really needs some help."

So I left the McCain campaign, in effect, and went to work with Governor Palin.

I'd watched her on the campaign trail, standing in the audience to hear her speak, but I hadn't met her in person until our get-together at John's Hidden Valley ranch. I sensed that she was bright and articulate, but she was at a very low point when we began a quick rehearsal for the debate.

When you prep for a debate, it's best to have someone portraying a moderator and someone portraying the opponent, with the moderator asking questions and the stand-in candidate responding back and forth to replicate the debate structure. It became obvious that Sarah was exhausted and unable to concentrate. Her mind was overwhelmed by all the briefings, and she couldn't hold her thoughts. She wondered aloud, "What am I trying to say?" So we cut the rehearsal short to give her time to catch up on her rest. "We'll get back at this tomorrow after a good night's sleep," I said.

When we walked away from that first rehearsal, I thought, "Sarah is not up to speed at all, and not just on information. She doesn't seem *steady*."

The campaign team did a wonderful and very smart thing. They brought in her husband, her children, and the baby to spend the next few days with her. It was very relaxed. Sarah was getting rest. She had her family around her. She was holding and hugging her baby. The daughters were taking care of the baby, and her husband was there comforting her. Their family dynamic was positive, strong, and nurturing. It was good medicine.

With Sarah on the mend, gaining emotional strength and confidence from her family, we decided to leave the confines of the house and take the debate rehearsal down to the creek and set up there. My thinking was, "Sarah's an Alaskan, right? She'll enjoy hearing the water rushing and the leaves blowing around in the cool breeze, with everybody sitting around on the lush green grass and breathing the clean air."

Once we got started, Sarah was more alert, but she still didn't have a firm grasp of the information. At one point, she said, "I'll tell you what. Let's stop now. Let me study this briefing book and we'll come back this afternoon."

Dressed in jeans and a sweatshirt, she took the briefing book, sat cross-legged under a tree, and relaxed. The children were all running around outdoors, having a fun time, and their joy seemed to energize her. You could see an amazing change taking hold. She started absorbing those briefing pages, picking up facts and figures, and gaining knowledge about the issues. So much so that after another rehearsal or two, she gave an answer to which Steve Schmidt responded, "No, no, Governor, that's not the senator's position. The senator believes *this*, not what you just said. You need to reinforce his position."

She said, "Steve, that's not what I believe." He said, "John McCain is the candidate for president. You're the candidate for vice president." She said, "Well, okay, but after we're elected, I'm going to change his mind."

Feisty. I admired her spirit.

One problem we encountered during rehearsals was that Sarah kept referring to Joe Biden—actually the guy playing Joe Biden—as Senator "O'Biden." I said, "Governor, it's Senator *Biden*. You're mixing up Biden with Obama. It's Biden." She said, "Okay, I've got it," and a few minutes later called him O'Biden again. "I just can't get it out of my head," she said.

Someone suggested, "Why don't you just call him Joe?"

She said, "I don't know him well enough. I've never met him. I can't just call him Joe."

Someone else suggested that when she was shaking his hand just before the debate started, to say, "Good to meet you, Senator. May I call you Joe?"

Sarah agreed that she needed to get his permission.

After the debate, we found out that Senator Biden was caught off guard by the request to call him *Joe*. He was distracted trying to figure out if referring to him in such a familiar way was a devious political strategy.

Joe Biden had been in the Senate for thirty-five years. He was very active on committees and especially knowledgeable about foreign policy. Everyone predicted that he would destroy Sarah Palin in the debate. But I think if anybody looked at that debate with an objective eye and analyzed it carefully, point by point, they would've said that Sarah Palin won. He was a much more experienced politician, but he was overconfident and impatient and she took it to him.

All the Candidate's Men

Fred Davis—"Hollywood Fred"—had a reputation for shooting fantastic television commercials. He'd shot a commercial for Texan John Cornyn when he was running for the Senate the first time. Fred showed it to me when I stopped by his house in California. He said, "Neal, what do you think about this?"

It was a long shot of the Big Bend region of Texas along the Rio Grande, an unbelievably beautiful vista. Suddenly I was thinking, "What's that way down there? Who is that white-haired guy?" It was John Cornyn walking through the rocky terrain.

I don't know what it took to get that shot. But when he was working with the McCain campaign, Hollywood Fred set up a shoot high in the mountains of Arizona. It was rough territory in high elevation, and it wasn't easy getting up to that mountaintop. Fred scouted out the location, set up the cameras and equipment, and filmed John McCain sitting on a rock, talking. It was an elaborate Hollywood production that had necessitated ferrying truckloads of equipment up into the mountains. Fred even hired a helicopter to fly around over the scene, filming panoramic views of rugged Senator McCain way out in the middle of nowhere, sitting on that rock.

We did one shoot inside a supporter's home in North Carolina. It was a normal house. There were two eighteen-wheelers sitting out front with equipment and lighting, and the crew was wandering around the yard. The scene was John McCain sitting in a chair, talking. A simple concept, but the production was phenomenal and the commercials were effective.

Rob Portman played a key role in the campaign. He'd served as director of the Office of Management and Budget under George W. Bush, and Rob knew the ins and outs of budget and financing. He was also physically fit, thin, a runner, and passionate about his workouts. He was selected to portray Barack Obama in the debate rehearsals.

Rob had read Obama's books, and he and the campaign staff had done the research and pulled together a lot of information. He'd learned everything he possibly could about the Democratic candidate so he could respond in the way Obama would respond. Because Rob did such a remarkable job, John was well rehearsed. He was never surprised in the debates by anything Barack Obama said. I'm sure the Obama campaign did the same thing on their side.

Rob was more than a debate stand-in. He was a veteran politician, and at one point he said, "Neal, I don't think the senator's right on this issue." It was a financial issue. I said, "Have you talked to him about it?" He said, "I'm working on him, but I'm not sure he's going to see it my way."

Rob Portman has gone on to serve as an influential US senator from Ohio.

All campaigns have people who are "volunteers" on a very high level. Some of them are lobbyists. Veteran lobbyist Charlie Black had worked for a number of Republican candidates and campaigns dating back to 1972. His law firm, in effect, loaned him to those campaigns, and he functioned as a senior adviser.

When I began traveling with Senator McCain, I rode with the senior advisers in a panel van, which carried eight or ten of us. Charlie Black realized that I hadn't traveled in motorcades with presidential candidates before, and he said, "Neal, let me give you some advice. There are three things you need to be aware of. First of all, if you see any food, eat it. Second, if you see a restroom, use it. You never know when you're going to find another one."

"The third one is serious," he said. "When John or any candidate is making an appearance, and a motorcade is waiting for him to leave, you position yourself between the candidate and the motorcade and you get to the motorcade before the candidate does, or you're going to be left behind." He said, "The minute that candidate gets in his vehicle, boom, the Secret Service is saying go, go, go. They take off, they don't linger. Make sure you jump in the van before he gets to his vehicle."

I followed that advice, and I never got left behind.

The Three Amigos

In his final days, John McCain said, "In retrospect, I wish I had selected Joe Lieberman as my vice presidential running mate." He added, "That's nothing against Sarah Palin."

US senator Joe Lieberman was a Democrat and Al Gore's vice presidential running mate in 2000. Six years later, Lieberman lost the Democratic primary in his home state of Connecticut, so he ran as an independent and was reelected to the US Senate.

During McCain's presidential campaign, I saw him and Joe Lieberman working together, side by side, and laughing a lot. Before one of the debates, we were all sitting in the green room, reviewing last-minute details with John and listening to the clock go tick, tick, tick. The time was quickly approaching for a historical debate with millions of people watching, and it was a little tense in the room. Joe Lieberman stood up and started dancing and singing whoo-oop, a-boop-a-doop, oop, oop. He looked at everybody and said, "Come on, let's have some fun." It broke the ice and we all started laughing.

Senator Lindsey Graham from South Carolina was the third member of their trio. I got to know him fairly well during those months. He and Joe Lieberman were John's two best friends, and they accompanied him on the campaign trail. They had a respectful, close relationship.

I was impressed with Lindsey Graham because he was a smart lawyer and had served as a judge advocate general in the US Air Force and later as a defense attorney. He and John served together on the Senate Foreign Relations Committee and had traveled together worldwide, sometimes on junkets to the Middle East and into war zones. They were very close friends. From time to time, Senator Graham would help John with a suggestion or two, saying, "John, just a minute. Maybe you ought to rephrase that in this way." John listened to him and valued his advice.

John McCain will be remembered for who he was, how he served, and what he stood for. He was an independent thinker who didn't worry about what people thought of him. He wasn't interested in racking up accolades, awards, and more medals. Sure, he ran for president a couple of times and didn't make it. I can hear him saying, "No guts, no glory." He was a good man.

CELEBRITIES, POLITICIANS, AND A FEW RASCALS

When Darrell Royal was hired as the head football coach of the Texas Longhorns at the end of the 1956 season, he hadn't yet built a national reputation. He'd played quarterback, defensive back, and punter under Bud Wilkinson at Oklahoma. I certainly agreed with Jan Reid in his *Texas Monthly* article in 1982: "Royal was the kind of player he later loved to recruit: a fast, undersized halfback converted to a quarterback because of his feel for the fake, read, and pitch of the option, a sprint-out passer equally at home in the defensive secondary."

After college, Darrell went on to coach at four universities and even the Edmonton Eskimos in the Canadian Football League, but he wasn't among the coaching elite. When he was selected as the new head coach at UT, I was a young reporter at KTBC-TV. Our news director, Paul Bolton, turned to me and asked, "Who is Darrell Royal? You ever heard of him?"

I actually knew who Darrell was because he'd been in the same Delta Upsilon fraternity at the University of Oklahoma that I was in at UT. Whenever our chapter drove up to Norman for regional meetings, we Austin DUs would bring a case of whiskey because Oklahoma was dry. That's how we paid for our trips. We delivered whiskey to the frat parties, and they paid a good price for it. I guess you could call us bootleggers.

I read the DU fraternity alumni magazine faithfully, and I was aware that Darrell had become a successful coach in smaller but respectable places.

Darrell was an immediate hit in Austin. When he took over the team, they'd gone 1–9 that season, the worst in Longhorn history. He turned the team around, going 6–4–1 in his first season (1957) and taking the team to the Sugar Bowl. Darrell never had a losing season. With him at the helm, the Horns won three national championships and eleven Southwest Conference championships. He built big powerhouse teams on defense and perfected the wishbone option on offense, a successful innovation during the 1960s and 1970s. He did such a magnificent job coaching the Longhorns that the university eventually renamed the stadium in his honor—the Darrell K Royal–Texas Memorial Stadium.

One of Darrell's many strengths was his knack for cultivating alumni support. Every week during football season, he'd have lunch with the Austin Longhorn Club and bring in the 16mm film from the previous game. He would show the film and talk it through: "Here's what we did and why we did it, and here's what we didn't do." Those of us who attended the luncheons really enjoyed this great insider look at UT's football games.

In the 1966 season, the Horns lost back-to-back games to Oklahoma and Arkansas, two of Texas's most bitter rivals. When I attended the lunch the next week, there was grumbling at the tables and one of the alums said, "Coach, you've lost two games in a row. Now what?"

Darrell responded, "We don't ever want to lose. But before coming here I was thinking about what that famed jurist Oliver Wendell Holmes said to young lawyers: 'You're never going to win them all. You're going to lose a trial sometimes. A case is going to go the other way. But take that as a learning experience. It builds character, and you'll learn from your losses in the courtroom, just as much as you'll learn from your victories. And so bear that in mind. Losses are not always bad.'"

The crowd got quiet, and Darrell looked around the room and said, "After those two losses, I've thought a lot about what Oliver Wendell Holmes said. And I say—'Piss on Oliver Wendell Holmes.'"

His team went on to win five out of the next six games that season, including a Bluebonnet Bowl victory against Ole Miss.

Another very smart thing that Darrell did was to invite professors to be guest coaches at home games, a tradition that won the support of many UT faculty members. He'd welcome a selected professor to attend the pre-game meetings with the coaches, take part in the player rituals, and roam the sideline with the team. Later on, Darrell did the same with country musicians. Long before actor and Longhorn mega-fan Matthew McConaughey became "minister of culture" at the University of Texas, Darrell invited Willie Nelson and other country music favorites to be guest coaches on the sideline.

Darrell had always been a huge country music fan, and sometime in the early 1970s he started hosting picking-and-grinning sessions at his home in the Onion Creek neighborhood in far South Austin. It wasn't

Edith Royal told me that UT Coach Darrell Royal became so enamored of life in Austin that when asked if he would consider taking his national championship football coaching skills to the professional level, Darrell refused, saying "Last time I checked they didn't have a pro football team in Austin." *Photo by Neal Spelce*

what you'd call a mansion, but it had a spacious living room area that was perfect for large gatherings. He and Edith invited friends and celebrities to join them there all the time. Darrell would say to musicians, "When you finish playing at the Saxon Pub, come on out. We'll do a little picking at the house. I'll have some folks come over."

Darrell and I established a connection early on because of our shared college fraternity, and I was at their home for several of those jam sessions. As far as I know, Darrell didn't sing or play the guitar, but during those evenings he was always in his element and beaming with happiness, laughing and enjoying himself and encouraging the entertainers. "Can you play that song called _____?" "Didn't you sing _____ that time at Castle Creek?" The performances were spontaneous and magnificent, and the magic lasted into the wee hours.

Around that same time in the early 1970s, Darrell called me at my PR firm and said, "We've got a real problem when we go into homes to recruit players, Neal. We need to talk to the mommas and the papas to convince them that the University of Texas is the right place for their boy, and how much we'd love for him to join the team, and how well we'll take care of him while he's in Austin. But the problem is that damn television sitting in their living rooms. Every time we go into a living room to talk to these folks and try to have a serious conversation, they keep glancing at what's playing on their TV. They look at me and say, 'Oh yeah, coach, we hear ya,' but they're distracted by watching the TV program out of the corner of their eyes. It's just awful."

Darrell was an ingenious guy. To solve that problem, he'd bought what is now an antiquated type of slide projector, a big box that you'd feed slides into one at a time. He wanted to use that in their presentations. The idea was that the images would be projected onto the TV screen, and it would also play audio to accompany the slides. So the TV program would have to be turned off.

Darrell said, "Neal, let's put together a program that our coaches will carry with them whenever we visit parents and their sons. This way we can say, 'I brought along this presentation about Longhorn football and the University of Texas. Do you mind if we turn the TV off so we can project this on the TV screen?'"

Under his direction, my firm produced the slides and the narration. The presentation touted the UT traditions and championship football teams and the integrity of a world-class university. It explained how the athletics program helped its athletes with their studies, directing them toward graduation and a college degree. The plan worked! When Darrell and his coaches finished the presentations, they never turned the TV set back on. They left the projector showing its last UT image while they continued the conversation with the parents about why their son should commit to being a Longhorn.

One of Darrell's most appealing qualities was he was so down to earth. Anyone could approach him. I had a friend who said, "Neal, I'd like to talk to Coach Royal about investing in an Oklahoma company that's making parts for Pulsar Watches." They were the world's first electronic digital watches.

I introduced the two men, and my friend said, "Darrell, you're a leg-

Darrell Royal (center) with Gregory Peck and Veronique Peck when the actor received a ceremonial key to Austin from Mayor Lester Palmer. *Photo courtesy Headliners Club*

end in Oklahoma, even though you're down here in Texas. This little company in Chickasha sure would like to have you as an investor."

Darrell pulled out his checkbook, wrote a check for $10,000, and handed it to him. That was a lot of money in the mid-1970s.

First of all, I was surprised that Darrell had that much money in a checking account. But that's the way he was. Frankly, I think he wrote the check because of our friendship. He didn't know this guy, and I didn't know the company.

A few months later, my friend invited Darrell and me to a ceremony for the expansion of the plant in Chickasha. "Darrell would be a big draw," my friend said, "and it would be terrific publicity for the company he's invested in." I talked to Darrell and he said, "Sure, let's try to work it out."

They flew us up there for the ceremony, and although Chickasha was not a big town, the event was packed. It looked like the entire population turned out because Darrell Royal was there. He was introduced and said a few short words to congratulate those involved in bringing jobs to the area.

On the evening after the ceremony, the company held a banquet at the local country club, but sitting through another banquet didn't appeal to Darrell. He called an old lawyer friend (I never knew his full name) and said, "I'm in town. How about us having a beer together?"

Darrell's friend picked us up and we went to a little roadhouse bar out in the country where lots of eighteen-wheelers were parked. We ordered beers and I went to the jukebox to pick a few country songs I thought Darrell would like. I noticed men going through a door into the back of the place, and I got to thinking, "This may be a whorehouse."

Darrell was sitting at the bar, talking to some of the truck drivers, and I walked over and said, "Darrell, we about ready?" He said, "Yeah, but we're waiting for my friend." That's when I realized that the attorney had slipped into the back, too.

One of the truckers looked up at me and nodded toward Darrell, asking, "Is this guy a friend of yours?" I said yes, and the trucker said, "He says he's Darrell Royal." I said, "Yeah, that's right." Skepticism crossed the truck driver's face. He said, "He can't be Darrell Royal. He's a trucker."

Darrell had been talking truck-driver talk to those guys and hadn't said a word about football. The coach was at the top of his profession, but he never talked about himself or what he did for a living. He'd once said, "The way you measure a man is how he treats somebody who can't do anything for him." And that night in Chickasha was a perfect example. Those truck drivers couldn't do anything for Darrell, but he'd always related to the common man and was interested in their stories.

Darrell Royal was also a tough negotiator and a master at public relations. Every season, when Texas played the Oklahoma Sooners at the Red River Shootout in the Cotton Bowl stadium, the Longhorns stayed at a Marriott Hotel in Dallas. It was an established tradition. But at the end of the 1970 season, when the Horns were selected to play Notre Dame in the Cotton Bowl, the manager of the Marriott was a Notre Dame graduate and cut a deal with the Fighting Irish to stay there instead of the Longhorns. When Darrell heard about that, he said, "What do you mean they booked the Marriott? We book them every year. We're a solid customer. Notre Dame may never stay there again!"

Texas had to book another hotel, and Darrell Royal was quietly furious.

The Marriott was building a hotel in Austin at the same time, and its sales staff had started to book rooms and meetings in advance, preparing for a full house when the hotel opened its doors. But the Austin trade associations and business organizations responded with, "We're not gonna book our meetings and conferences with the Marriott because of what you did to the Longhorns in Dallas. We'll patronize someone else. And we're gonna cancel what we've already booked."

All of a sudden, Marriott was getting hurt big-time in the wallet.

My PR firm had been hired by the Marriott organization to handle the opening of the new Austin facility, and a hotel executive gave me a call, saying, "We've got a problem." I said, "Yes, sir, I know all about that. You've got a real big problem." He asked, "What can we do?" I said, "You've got to work it out with Darrell Royal." A short time later, he called back to say, "Coach Royal won't talk to us. He says to hell with us."

After that, a fellow whose last name was Marriott called me and said, "Can you get me a meeting with Coach Royal? I really need to sit down with him." I contacted Darrell, and he said he didn't want to meet with anyone named Marriott.

I knew where Darrell sat at Longhorn basketball games, always on the aisle in a certain spot. So I took a chance and went to a basketball game with Mr. Marriott, and he sat down on the steps next to Darrell and said, "Coach, we're sorry. That Dallas manager stepped out of line and we apologize for his decision. We'll do anything to get you back."

Mr. Marriott made Darrell an offer he couldn't refuse: "We'll give you free hotel rooms at the Marriott here in Austin for all your home games."

Marriott knew that the night before every home game, Darrell removed his team from the distractions of campus by booking them into an Austin hotel. That way he and the assistant coaches could control the atmosphere, have team meetings, serve the right kind of food to prepare for the game the next day, and get their game faces on.

A few months later—to show respect for the Texas Longhorns—my firm recommended a football theme for the grand opening of the Austin Marriott hotel. We even brought in the Dallas Cowboy cheerleaders to perform. Darrell Royal didn't show up for the opening ceremony. He'd made his point and struck a deal with the Marriott folks that greatly benefited the football program, but it wasn't his kind of party.

Darrell's leadership skills were evident to those outside the world of sports. On one occasion I was with LBJ and Jesse Kellam, the general manager of KTBC-TV, just the three of us talking in the downtown federal building where LBJ had a suite of offices. We started discussing football, and LBJ said, "You know, Darrell Royal would make a great president of the United States."

LBJ was an admiring fan of the coach and how he conducted the Longhorn football program. I thought, "Wait a minute. Politics and football? Do they mix?" But LBJ went on to praise Darrell Royal up one side and down the other, and I realized that in the unlikely event that Darrell ever ran for office, I'd vote for him.

WILLIE NELSON: RIDING WITH SHOTGUN WILLIE

The Redheaded Stranger is a legend in the world of music, and not just country music. Willie Nelson is one of the best songwriters and vocalists of his time. He and I became acquainted because, back in the day, we moved in many of the same circles.

Wally Pryor—Cactus Pryor's brother—called me one morning and said, "Guich Koock and Willie Nelson are looking at a piece of property out west of Austin. They're thinking about setting up some sort of an amusement place—a tourist attraction—and they're trying to figure out a good piece of land to develop. I've got a pickup truck, and I'm going out there to drive them around the ranch. You want to come along?"

Wally had been a swim-team champion as a UT student and later became the very popular "Voice of the Longhorns," known for his colorful commentary from the press box during football games. He'd also been a director of local programs at KTBC-TV.

Guich (pronounced "Geech") Koock was a sometime entertainer with a quick wit from a venerable South Austin family. He'd won second place in a singing-cowboy contest on TV and was the co-owner of Luckenbach, Texas, a community about eighty-five miles west of Austin and the subject of a popular song by Waylon Jennings. When asked about his first name, Guich's stock retort was "Daddy raised dogs and they got all the good names."

I contributed a case of Mexican beer to that misadventure, which also included Darrell Royal. Wally was driving the pickup, and I was standing up in the truck bed with Willie and Darrell, the three of us holding onto the cab with one hand and drinking beer with the other. It was a beautiful piece of Texas Hill Country land near the LBJ Ranch. We were studying all those acres of ranchland passing by, and at some point Wally

One of the rare times Willie Nelson wore a tuxedo was when we honored Willie and his wife Connie at the Headliners Club. *Photo courtesy Headliners Club*

yelled out the window, "Hang on, boys! We're gonna bounce out of here and get on the road and ride around to the other side of the ranch."

Wally started driving fast, and the three of us in the truck bed were hollering, "Woohoo, woohoo, don't make us spill our beer, Wally!" He made a quick turn, and Willie said, "You're going to kill us all. Slow down, Wally!" And then Darrell turned to me and said, "You know, Neal, if we're killed here today, nobody's going to know you died."

He was right. It was a sobering thought. Willie Nelson and Darrell Royal killed in a pickup accident, along with an unidentified minor figure. The story of my life. I said, "True, Darrell, but the ride was worth it."

The only death that occurred as a result of our beer-drinking-driving-and-dreaming was the deal itself. Nothing ever came of it.

THE SILVER SPURS HALL OF FAME

When I was a UT student in the 1950s, I was a member of the Silver Spurs organization. Founded in 1937, the Silver Spurs take care of Bevo, the real live longhorn steer that's the UT mascot, including on road trips across Texas and to other states. We were sometimes mistaken for the Texas Cowboys, who manage Smokey the Cannon, which they fire at football games. The Cowboys are the ones who wear black Stetsons and chaps.

In 2004, I got a call from the president of the Silver Spurs Alumni Association, and I thought the usual, "Oh lord, they're gonna ask for more money." But the president said, "Neal, you're one of the first to be selected for what we're calling the Silver Spurs Hall of Fame."

The Silver Spurs Alumni Association was funding construction of the Silver Spurs Bevo Center, located in Darrell K Royal–Texas Memorial Stadium. It's a museum that commemorates the history and tradition of Bevo and the organization's role in his handling.

It's quite an honor to be in the company of my good friends Lowell Lebermann, Sam Perry, Dan Burck, and sports legend Diron Talbert. We're all pictured on plaques in the Bevo Center in the stadium. I don't think they have the time and money to take mine down and put somebody else's up, so it'll be there for a while.

WALTER CRONKITE: THE MOST TRUSTED MAN

In the mid-1990s, I became deeply involved in producing a syndicated TV series of short segments titled *An American Moment*, featuring

Charles Kuralt as the narrator. Charles was best known for his very popular *On the Road* series, which had run for twenty years on CBS, and our series was similar in format and in its Americana charm. The segments started airing in 1997, but Charles died suddenly in July of that year, and we transitioned the production to feature the barrel-voiced James Earl Jones.

Walter Cronkite had talked to Charles Kuralt and saw what we were doing with *An American Moment*. After Charles's death, Walter contacted me and said, "Neal, I wonder if I could do something like that?"

Walter and I had been longtime colleagues and friends, dating back to my days at KTBC-TV, and later as fellow members of the Headliners Club. He'd generously supported my career, at one point cutting an audiotape that signed off his *CBS Evening News* broadcast with, "This is Walter Cronkite. Stay tuned now for my friend Neal Spelce." It was an incredible boost to my ratings, and I was very grateful to him for that endorsement leading into my local newscast.

Walter had retired in 1981—way before he should have. In those days, CBS had a mandatory retirement age of sixty-five, but Walter didn't want to go gentle into that good night. There were raw feelings. However, CBS provided an office for him in the building and gave him a staff and a secretary, so he was able to continue his projects. They took care of him; they just didn't want him as the news anchor anymore. That job went to fellow Texan Dan Rather.

After our discussions about *An American Moment*, Walter and I developed a contract with his attorney to produce a syndicated program we were calling *Walter Cronkite Answers*, which was Walter's suggestion. The spots would be a minute and a half long, with a ninety-day shooting schedule. The concept was different from what we were doing with the Charles Kuralt series. We would go out and seek questions for Walter, and we'd tape his responses. "Walter, what were you thinking when you removed your glasses and announced that President Kennedy had died?" "Walter, how did you feel at the moment when Neil Armstrong stepped on the moon and said, 'That's one small step . . .'?" Questions like that. We intended to avoid political issues, although Walter had strong personal opinions about history and politics.

We taped a few samples and printed fancy brochures that we could put in front of potential sponsors to inform them about the show: "Here's the gist of the program. It'll be an audience-builder because, at the end

FOR NEAL, my guide, guardian and friend. With warm wishes!
Charles Kuralt

One of the most gratifying media experiences of my life was when we pioneered a very successful nationwide TV series about our country, *An American Moment with Charles Kuralt.*
Photo courtesy Neal Spelce

I helped noted actor James Earl Jones, a lifelong stutterer, work through his vocal issues when he succeeded the late Charles Kuralt on *An American Moment with James Earl Jones. Photo courtesy Neal Spelce*

of the episodes, Walter will say, 'If you have a question, contact this local station.'" We were confident that our series would generate audience interest at each individual station throughout the country.

In television and other fields of entertainment, a "Q-Rating" is a measurement of how popular and familiar your "brand" is. Although Walter had been retired from the *CBS Evening News* for almost twenty years, he still had the highest Q-Rating of any news personality on television in the late 1990s. Over the decades, he'd created an intimate connection with his viewers. People had always *listened* to him. They believed him and hung on his every word.

Once we had our concept ready to go and the contract signed, I thought, "This is going to be a slam dunk. Everyone still loves and trusts this man. We're not going to have any problem finding a sponsor." But we did.

The most common objection was, "He's too old. He's past his prime. We want to appeal to a younger demographic." I pointed out that the Q-Ratings indicated he was well recognized and highly respected by young folks, but that didn't change the potential sponsors' minds.

We approached one maker of a vitamin supplement whose target audience was older people, and the company paid us to visit them and make a pitch. When we arrived, their advertising agency was invited to sit in, and the ad reps shot a hole in our project. They were promoting Alex Trebek, the *Jeopardy* host, and choosing Walter would take money away from their agency. We were puzzled and insulted that the company would choose a game-show host over a superstar journalist, so when we got home, we returned the vitamin company's money to them.

Walter asked, "What happened, Neal?" I said, "Walter, we're still trying, but we just don't have the acceptance in the advertising community that we thought we would."

To this day, I regret that we couldn't launch that project for the great Walter Cronkite. Our timing was off. Cable channels were in their infancy and not very active or "niche" at that point, but I'm convinced that if it had been a few years later we could have approached a cable channel and said, "We'll sell our program to you, and you go to your pharmaceutical sponsors and sell it to them."

Today, there are dozens of cable channels that focus on an older demographic that still watches cable news and other "lifestyle" programs aimed at seniors. We were ahead of our time.

"The most trusted man in America" CBS-TV's Walter Cronkite, along with his wife, Betsy, were honored by two longtime friends, George Christian and me, at a Headliners Club event. *Photo courtesy Headliners Club*

Walter and I shared many moments over the years, and on a couple of occasions I was fortunate to see him in rare form. One of those moments happened at a fancy private party hosted by Lowell Lebermann in Austin on Walter and Betsy's anniversary. It was quite stiff and formal: tuxedoed waiters passing drinks and hors d'oeuvres on silver trays, a classical pianist providing background music, people on their best behavior and talking in hushed tones.

Then the music stopped. It got quiet. The silence was broken by the upbeat sounds of ragtime pounding on the grand piano. In the open space near the piano, Walter was dancing a jig—by himself, oblivious to his surroundings, with his Scotch-filled glass spilling onto the expensive carpet. His eyes were closed as he danced around muttering, "I just love Scott Joplin!" It was a welcomed and endearing sight during what was no longer a stilted party.

BILL MOYERS: TAKE TIME TO FLOAT

Bill Moyers had served as LBJ's press secretary from 1965 to 1967, and even though things became strained between him and the president, Bill stayed close to the Johnson family for many years, primarily through his friendship with Mrs. Johnson. She was born and raised in Karnack, Texas, which is only fifteen miles from Bill's hometown of Marshall. They were kindred spirits, two children of rural East Texas, more Deep South than any other region of the state.

Bill had come a long way from that summer I'd spent in Marshall, when he and I had shared the same gazebo stage on those sultry musical evenings deep in East Texas. He was always up-front as the young emcee, introducing the program, and I was stationed at the back of the band, banging on my snare drum. I was impressed by his confidence and poise, although I probably didn't make much of an impression on him. Little did we know that our paths would cross many times from that point forward—with the Lyndon Johnson connection as the linchpin.

After leaving the Johnson administration, Bill became the publisher of the daily newspaper *Newsday* for three years, then turned toward a career in television. He'd hosted the news program *Bill Moyers Journal* at PBS, and a few years later he went to work for CBS (1976–1986), first as a senior correspondent and eventually as the senior news analyst when Dan Rather was hosting the *CBS Evening News.*

But what really solidified Bill's reputation and screen visibility were the documentary series he launched in the 1980s, beginning with *Joseph Campbell and the Power of Myth* in 1988. He became a very popular figure with viewers and won numerous awards and distinctions, including a Lifetime Emmy Award, a Lifetime Achievement Award from the National Academy of Television Arts and Sciences, and induction into the Television Hall of Fame.

Bill and I have maintained a long-distance friendship over the decades. We talk, we laugh. He did something very special for me when I had five bypasses in open heart surgery. Bill had had heart surgery himself, and he sent me the sweetest personal note. The sentence that has remained with me is, "Don't forget to take time to float every day." In other words, settle down, take it easy, relax. That was excellent advice from an ordained minister who'd written books about philosophy and faith.

DAN RATHER: COURAGE

Dan Rather is known for his bulldog tenacity as a news reporter. He became a household name by wading into the teeth of hurricanes to get the story and report it. (*"It's blowing in right here where I'm standing on this seawall."*) He was punched in the gut and knocked to the floor in the 1968 Democratic National Convention in Chicago for trying to interview delegates. He grew facial stubble, dressed in traditional Afghan attire, and was smuggled into Afghanistan to cover stories about the Afghans fighting against the Russian invaders. And there was no network correspondent more dogged than Dan Rather in his pursuit of the facts in the Watergate investigation. When Dan began to ask President Nixon a tough question at a televised public appearance at Jones Hall in Houston, an irritated Nixon asked Dan, "Are you running for something?" To which Dan responded, "No sir, Mr. President, are you?"

His aggressive television persona helped to create the tough *60 Minutes* style of relentless, in-your-face investigative journalism. When Dan's reporter instincts are stirred in his blood and he goes on high alert, he pursues the story until the facts are established and the details are ready for the public to hear.

But the truth is that Dan is totally different when you meet him in person and get to know him. He's polite, kind, and solicitous of other people's opinions. Texas boy that he is, raised in the small Texas town of Wharton, fifty miles from the Gulf Coast, it's always *yes ma'am, no ma'am, thank you ma'am,* and *please sir.* He's a family man who married a young woman named Jean Goebel from the even smaller town of Winchester, Texas, and they've raised two children in a marriage that's lasted for more than sixty years.

What is missing in the usual profiles of Dan Rather is how generous and thoughtful he is. He was famous at CBS for his "Rathergrams"—handwritten notes to colleagues that said, "Thank you so much. You did a great job on that story yesterday. I really appreciate your hard work."

If you meet Dan in a social situation, his usual response is, "Let's not talk about me. Tell me about you. What do you do?" If he's met you before, it's the old standard Texas phrase, "How's Momma and them?" Basically, "How are your wife and kids? Are they grown yet? Catch me up." Reporters have a knack for remembering names—it's part of the training—and Dan is remarkably good at it.

Contrary to his attack-dog reputation, Dan is an old-school gentleman with an admirable talent for diffusing confrontations. The two of us were having lunch one day in Lakeway, a suburb on the hilly outskirts of Austin with a fine view of Lake Travis, and a redneck-looking guy dressed in a gimme cap and jeans was hovering around outside, waiting for us to leave the restaurant. When we walked out, he approached Dan and said, "I really wish you'd do a better job of reporting on the oil business." He looked like he might be a roughneck from the oil fields.

Dan said, "I'm sorry you feel that way, sir. My daddy grew up in the oil patch and worked in the oil patch, and I have a great affinity for people who work in that business."

"Well, you ought to talk about it on TV."

"I appreciate what you're saying," Dan said with a smile.

Dan didn't take issue with the man; he accepted his criticism. I tried to hustle us out of there, worried that the guy might try to whack Dan upside the head. It wouldn't have been the first time he'd been attacked physically by a stranger.

The most rewarding side of celebrity is when people are polite and excited to recognize you. They say, "We appreciate your reporting! Thank you!" And they often tell you a personal anecdote about something you covered that affected their lives. My response is always, "Thank you very much. I sure appreciate you watching—and your kind thoughts." Those encounters are very gratifying.

Another time with Dan: In 2012, he'd published a book titled *Rather Outspoken: My Life in the News*, and that year the Texas Book Festival asked me to interview him in the House of Representatives chamber in the State Capitol.

Dan drew a large crowd that filled all the seats on the House floor and most of the visitors' balcony. I was the moderator and introduced Dan. Because he and I were close friends, we didn't talk it over beforehand. We just knew each other. When it came time for questions, there was a line of people at the standup microphone in the main aisle of the chamber, and someone asked, "Mr. Rather, who are you supporting for president of the United States?"

By that time, Dan had left CBS but was hosting the news program *Dan Rather Reports* on Mark Cuban's cable network, and airing his political opinions was probably unwise. I interrupted and said, "Sir, that's

Texas state representative Elliott Naishtat greeted Dan Rather and me at the 2012 Texas Book Festival, where I moderated a presentation by Dan about his latest book to a packed Texas House Chamber. *Alberto Martinez*/ American-Statesman

a good question, but that's not why Dan is here today. He's here to talk about his book."

I cut it off, but then the crowd started mumbling and grumbling, so I tossed out one of my old standard jokes: "Look, I know the problems when people who are on television get into politics. I was wrong so many times about politics, they made me an honorary weatherman."

The audience laughed, and Dan said, "I'm going to use that line from now on."

One of the things that most people don't know about Dan is that he loves music and musicians. Country music was an important part of his life growing up. I remember one occasion when we were cutting a promo together on the banks of what is now Lady Bird Lake and Dan said, "Neal, what have you been listening to lately?" I said classic country music—booze and women and heartache—and he said, "Really, like what?" I started singing a few tunes, and we ended up laughing and singing "Smoke! Smoke! Smoke! That Cigarette" together.

An interviewer once asked him what he liked to do for relaxation, and he said bass fishing on Lake Travis while listening to Willie Nelson music. Which explains why Dan called me one day to ask if I could help him contact Willie. "I want to interview him for *60 Minutes*," he said, "but I can't get past his gatekeepers. Do you have any suggestions?"

I told him that the one person who knew Willie as well as anybody was former Longhorn football coach Darrell Royal, so I called Darrell and he contacted Willie. A few hours later, Darrell phoned me to say, "Willie doesn't want to do it." I said, "Really? Why?" And Darrell said, "He's uncomfortable about the marijuana thing."

This was at a time when Willie was being harassed for dope-smoking just about everywhere he went. His tour bus was constantly being searched. Willie's position was, "I don't want to get into that. I know Dan wants to talk about music, but I just don't want to expose myself."

I called Dan, and he said, "I can understand that. I want to focus on his music, but I understand where he's coming from."

On another occasion, I was talking with Dan and his wife, Jean, and I asked about his interview with Dolly Parton: "She's funny, she's witty," he said, and then Jean piped in: "Dolly said, 'Dan, you haven't asked me about my breasts. I see you've been looking at them.'" It was a very rare moment when Dan Rather was flustered by a remark.

Dan's retirement from CBS in 2006 ended his brilliant career in broadcast journalism on a sour note. The problem had begun two years earlier, when Mary Mapes, a producer for *60 Minutes Wednesday*, received documents asserting that George W. Bush had benefited from favorable treatment in being accepted for the Texas Air National Guard, a deferment that kept him out of the Vietnam War.

Ben Barnes, the lieutenant governor of Texas during that era, confirmed that he'd made phone calls on Bush's behalf. But when Dan aired the story, the program was met with a firestorm of criticism because the documents could not be authenticated. They appeared to be typed on a computer with superscript capability rather than on a manual typewriter common in the 1970s.

CBS conducted an investigation using an independent panel, and although they couldn't determine that the documents were fraudulent or that a political agenda was in play, the network fired Mary Mapes and three others involved in the story's production.

That cut Dan to the quick. He had devoted forty-four years of his life to CBS. There was no more loyal company man than Dan Rather. He thought that William Paley and the people who started CBS hung the moon. Edward R. Murrow was an icon for Dan, a role model he emulated. He was such a CBS man that he once sent me a letter in which he substituted "e-y-e" for the letter *I* all the way through, because the CBS logo was an eye. "Eye thought eye would write you a note," it began.

After the documents incident in 2004, Dan stayed on at the network for a couple of unhappy years and then retired. He issued a statement that said, "I leave CBS News with tremendous memories. But I leave now most of all with the desire to once again do regular, meaningful reporting. . . . As for [CBS's] offers of a future with only an office but no assignments, it just isn't in me to sit around doing nothing. So I will do the work I love elsewhere." One door closes, another one opens. For the amazingly energetic Dan Rather and his curious mind, leaving CBS has allowed him to pursue several fascinating opportunities in cable television, satellite radio, social media, and book publishing.

Mary Mapes wrote a book about the Bush-documents affair that was adapted into a 2015 movie entitled *Truth*. I kidded Dan about it because the handsome Robert Redford played Dan Rather. It was a small movie, no explosions or car chases. Dan thought the filmmakers did a good job, although they portrayed the dapper Ben Barnes as a Texas cigar-chomping country bumpkin, which couldn't be further from the truth.

In his early days as the anchor of the *CBS Evening News*, Dan signed off with a single word: *Courage*. It's a word that captures the essence of Dan Rather. A virtue imbedded deep in his soul. His entire career has been defined by him bravely forging into news stories like a soldier charging into battle. He has always been fearless, and we're a better-informed nation because of his stellar work over a long and distinguished career.

Soon after leaving CBS, Dan told Sam Skolnik, a reporter from the *Seattle Post-Intelligencer*, "In many ways, on many days, [reporters] have sort of adopted the attitude of 'go along, get along.'. . . What many of us need is a spine transplant. . . . Whether it's city hall, the state house, or the White House, part of our job is to speak truth to power."

Amen, Brother Dan. Courage.

Here's Johnny!

One of my strangest experiences at the advertising firm happened one day as I was sitting in my office and the receptionist buzzed me to say the usual: "There are a couple of gentlemen here to see you."

Attorney Ernie Kuehne was a button-down lawyer, coat and tie, but his client was a burly guy wearing a Hawaiian shirt, kind of scruffy-looking, in stark contrast to his lawyer. Attorney Kuehne began, "A week ago, my client here broke some Americans out of a Mexican jail."

Studying that burly guy on the other side of my desk, I wouldn't have predicted he was a mastermind who could pull that off. But he was the type of guy who would fit into a crowd that would do something like that.

The lawyer said, "We'd like to get him on Johnny Carson to tell his story about what he did."

I said, "Okay, tell *me* the story."

The burly guy's name was Don Fielden and he was a long-haul trucker who'd won a Purple Heart as a Marine in Vietnam. When he began to talk, I noticed he had missing teeth. He pulled out a piece of paper on which he'd drawn the plan to free an American prisoner at the jail in Piedras Negras, a Mexican border town across the Rio Grande from Eagle Pass, Texas. He'd visited the prisoner more than once, scouted the situation, and developed his scheme.

As he told me the story, I thought, "That's a story Johnny Carson probably would like."

In fact, Fielden was very funny. Not so much in a tell-a-joke way, but his description of the jailbreak was both dramatic and humorous. He said, "We wanted to make sure we handled the guards, so I asked someone to teach me the Spanish translation for 'Put your hands up.' But I got it wrong. I'm not sure what I said, but they didn't put their hands up. They got the picture when I started motioning with my shotgun."

The American prisoner was a young man who'd been busted for possession of a large quantity of marijuana in Mexico, and he was rotting in jail with a long sentence. Don Fielden had been hired by the prisoner's father in Dallas to break the kid out.

The lawyer said, "My client here is on the run. The authorities on both sides of the border are looking for him, but he hasn't been arrested yet. We've got to be careful. Do you think you can get him on Johnny Carson?"

I said, "Let me work on it and figure out the best way to approach this. I do think it's a fascinating story and Johnny Carson would love it."

After they left my office, I called Frank Maloney, a friend of mine who was a retired assistant district attorney and prosecutor, and told him the story. Frank said, "Neal, you aren't a lawyer and you don't have attorney-client privilege. You could be brought in as an accessory for aiding a fugitive who's being sought by the law. We prosecute people for abetting criminals. I advise you not to touch this thing in any way, shape, or form."

I thanked Frank and said, "I don't want to go to jail at this stage of my life, Frank. Maybe later."

I called the lawyer back and declined to be involved. He was disappointed, but I told him, "It's not something we're able to do."

Later that year, in the fall of 1976, the journalist Jan Reid wrote an excellent story in *Texas Monthly* about the Piedras Negras jailbreak, and he mentioned my meeting with Fielden and Kuehne. More than forty years later, Jan's story has been optioned for film. It will make a terrific movie. I decided that if I ever met Johnny Carson, I'd tell him the story and say, "I wish I could've called you, Johnny." But I never got the chance before he died.

CARL THE CONSPIRACIST

Sometime around 2012, a conspiracy theorist that I'll call "Carl" was convinced that on the night before President Kennedy was assassinated, I was in Dallas having dinner at the home of Clint Murchison Sr., a wealthy Texas oil man, along with several other conspirators, and that we were fine-tuning details about how the president would be killed the next day.

This lunacy began when I received a call from Carl saying, "Neal, you don't know me, but I'm compiling stories about old Austin. I've already interviewed Cactus Pryor, and he suggested that you'd be someone I ought to talk to about events that took place many years ago."

I didn't know what Carl had in mind, but anytime someone used my friend Cactus's name, I paid attention.

"I've got a video camera," Carl continued, "and I'll come over and sit down in your house and interview you."

He suggested a day and time that didn't work for me, and over the next few phone calls, we went back and forth until he said, "Why don't you come out here and I'll interview you at my place?"

He lived on a ranch out in the countryside a hundred miles southwest of Austin. I said, "No, I can't work that out."

Conspiracy theorist that he was, he believed that I was turning him down for reasons other than schedule conflicts. Finally, he sent me an email that said, "I don't know why you're refusing to talk to me. But here are the questions I'd like you to answer. You'll see why this interview is so important."

His long list of twenty or thirty questions was built around his conviction that I was involved in the Kennedy assassination. "What time did you arrive at that Murchison dinner? Who else was there? What were the specifics of your plot?" According to Carl, there was a meeting after the dinner—a smaller group that retired to another room.

"I have it on good authority that Vice President Lyndon Johnson was also at that meeting," Carl wrote in the email. "It was a group of right-wing people in Dallas who were planning to kill John F. Kennedy the next day."

Never mind that LBJ was 240 miles away that evening, appearing with President Kennedy in Houston.

Carl believed that Cactus Pryor was at the dinner as well. "I have it confirmed that you and Cactus were there, Neal," Carl wrote. "I want you to tell me who else was there and what you discussed."

In a subsequent phone conversation, Carl added, "I'll pay you $5,000 cash if you'll come out and let me interview you at the ranch." He was going to put a wad of bills in my hand to convince me to confess. "I'm sure you've kept this as a secret buried inside you all these years," he said, "and this will give you a chance to finally get it off your chest."

I was more perplexed than upset. I thought his theory was ridiculous, of course. I said, "I don't know why you think I was there." His response was, "I have it on the good authority of someone who was there, too. His name was Lex Dale Owens. Did you know Mr. Owens?"

"I knew him as an ambulance driver," I said. An ambulance driver, not an ambulance chaser. "He ran his own ambulance company back in the seventies and eighties."

Dale Owens was one of those Austin characters who seemed to be everywhere at once. He was elected as a justice of the peace, then started his ambulance company, and he was always running around with a camera, snapping pictures. On one occasion I was having serious back pain and my wife called for an ambulance to take me to the hospital. On the phone, she said, "Don't come out here with sirens blaring or anything like that. We just need a transport." So Dale himself roared up to the house with sirens blaring and lights flashing. I was lying in bed, moaning,

CELEBRITIES, POLITICIANS, AND A FEW RASCALS

"Oh it hurts, it hurts," and he grabbed my feet and said, "We'll take care of that," and pulled. I almost passed out from the pain.

"Dale was out at my place one day," Carl said, "looking through my notes on the Clint Murchison dinner and other stuff, and Dale said, 'You're working on this story? I was there!'"

When Carl asked him who else was there, Dale said, "Neal Spelce—and Cactus Pryor was there, too."

After hearing that nonsense, I wrote a meticulous email to Carl—so I'd have a written record of my response—informing him that I was on the air in Austin the night before President Kennedy was assassinated, which could easily be confirmed. I also told him that I knew for certain that Cactus Pryor was out at the LBJ Ranch making the arrangements for the entertainment portion of the Kennedys' upcoming visit to the ranch.

I included a quotation from the official obituary for Lex Dale Owens that ran in the *Austin American Statesman* in 2009. The obit was written by one of Dale's friends, and it began: "Lex Dale Owens was an embellisher, someone who friends said gently inflated the events of his life to the exact proportions of his self-image. Friends always saw through the exaggerations, knowing they weren't necessary."

Owens's friends knew he was an *embellisher*, I pointed out to Carl, and not someone to be taken too seriously. To Carl's credit, he replied, "My apologies, Neal. I accept the fact that you were not there in Dallas. I'm sorry, but I can't take your name out of the first edition of the book. It's already at the printer. But I will delete it from future editions."

Somewhere out there in the galaxy of self-published books by conspiracy theorists, I have dinner at Clint Murchison Sr.'s Dallas home on the night before President Kennedy was assassinated—even though at the time of the assassination, Clint Murchison hadn't lived in that house for many years.

FISHING WITH PRESIDENTS GEORGE AND GEORGE

When he served as governor of Texas, George W. Bush owned a rustic getaway cabin on Rainbo Lake, a relatively small and private lake surrounded by woods about eight miles southeast of Athens, Texas. At the time, it was his only residence outside of the Governor's Mansion in Austin. When I showed up at the lake just before daylight in January 1998 to interview both Bushes, father and son, together, George W. was still two years away from winning his first presidential election. They would become father-and-son presidents for only the second time in US history.

In early 1998, the momentum was already building for George W.'s candidacy. Pundits were speculating about him following in his daddy's footsteps, and a steady stream of Republican Party officials and power brokers were showing up at the Governor's Mansion, urging W. to run for president.

At that point in my career, I had returned to broadcast news as the main anchor at KEYE-TV (CBS) in Austin. We realized that a political father-son presidential rarity could be in the making, so we decided to explore the relationship between the two. We knew both men loved fishing, and after much schedule juggling, I was able to join them on a fishing trip in East Texas.

There's something wonderful about wandering through the woods by a serene lake in the early morning light. The three of us walked along drinking coffee and swapping tales about fishing, and I was struck by the bond between George H. W. and George W. as I listened to them trade one-liners and kid each other back and forth.

In a high-profile, wealthy family like the Bushes—always in the public spotlight because of their political power and historical impact on our nation—even their minor conflicts and differences are well chronicled. It comes with the territory. But on that morning, no policy disagreements were apparent when the two men were relaxing out in their bass boat, casting into the lake. We weren't there to talk politics or policy.

I crowded into their small bass boat, with seating for only two, and

In a rare interview, with me standing in a two-person fishing boat on an East Texas lake, both presidents Bush talked about their father/son relationship. *Photos courtesy Neal Spelce*

had to stand between them as our interview took place. I recalled LBJ's description of his presidential library: "It's all here with the bark off." It was the same there in the piney woods. I was seeing them with the bark off. There wasn't any pretense or posturing. They weren't trying to impress me. They were just two people who genuinely loved and respected each other, outdoors having fun, doing something they both enjoyed.

Even though I was there as a newsman, with a TV camera crew filming from another boat, I didn't have an agenda. I had never gone fishing with my father, who was absent for much of my childhood, but I'd lost a few lures paddling around in canoes with my son when he was a Boy Scout. On that cool, foggy morning at Rainbo Lake, I was more interested in how this father and son related to each other on a personal level.

In the grand old tradition of fishing in Texas (and elsewhere), quiet is important to anglers, few words are exchanged, and rarely does anyone holding a fishing rod engage in long political or philosophical dialogues. But I managed to evoke a few responses.

The elder Bush had been out of office for six years, and when I asked him if he missed life in the White House, he said, "It's not hard to adjust to being in private life as opposed to public. I don't do press conferences. . . . I don't think I've been to the Capitol since leaving the presidency. Very seldom go to Washington. You've just gotta shift gears. You can't always try to be what you used to be and hover around Washington." He added, "I miss some things. I miss the military, I miss friends, I miss the White House staff, who treated us like family."

George W. was candid about what it was like in those years when he was the son of a vice president and then the president: "The most difficult period for me was when people would criticize my dad. There was nothing in comparison, to see someone you love and respect, criticized."

At that point, George W. was running for a second term as the governor of Texas. I asked the elder Bush if he intended to stump around the state in support of his son's gubernatorial reelection campaign, which was already underway. He replied, "I don't think he needs help from his father. We can go, Barb and I, to fundraisers or something like that, not in the campaign in the sense of issues."

Karen Hughes, a longtime staffer for the Bushes, was monitoring our interview in one of the camera boats circling us (along with the ever-present Secret Service). When we pulled into shore after fishing, Karen told me that even though she'd served for many years as a Bush loyalist in

After the fishing outing, historian Mark Updegrove, who wrote the definitive biography on the two Bushes, told me he knew of only one other person who had interviewed the Bushes together. *Photo courtesy Neal Spelce*

formal and informal settings, she'd learned new things about the Bushes from my interview. (You can check that out for yourself. A transcript of the edited interview is included at the back of this book.)

As a reporter, I felt great personal satisfaction participating in that rare recorded conversation with two major figures in American history. Other writers have characterized their relationship as having "Shakespearean dimensions," but not on that morning in East Texas. They were simply father and son in a boat, enjoying the clean country air and their companionship. I was quite taken by the easy camaraderie of the two, their joking and self-deprecating humor. They had a deep father-son love for each other that I don't believe had manifested itself very often in public or in media coverage at the time.

It turned out to be a historic session. I've been told by Bush biographer Mark Updegrove, the author of *The Last Republicans: Inside the Extraordinary Relationship Between George H. W. Bush and George W. Bush*, that only one other interviewer ever sat down with the two of them together, and not in a relaxed, comfortable setting while bass fishing on a tranquil lake.

Incidentally, while they were casting their lines again and again, trying to snag a bass, both Bushes snagged me. Literally. Yes, each of them hit me with a hook as they flung their lines. They weren't very fond of the news media, in general, but I'm sure it wasn't intentional, right? Right?

JOURNALISM IS A DOING THING

With my three bachelor's degrees, I like to say that I was vaccinated by communications at the University of Texas, and sixty-odd years later I'm still doing what I was educated to do. On several occasions, I was deeply honored to be recognized for my achievements by the college whose training and instruction opened doors to what has been an incredibly fulfilling life.

In 1965, in the midst of my career as news director and anchor at KTBC, my old journalism professor, Norris Davis, called me and said UT was building a large complex to house the new School of Communication, which would include the three major departments of journalism, speech, and radio-television-film. "We've looked into it and discovered that you're the only UT graduate with a degree in all three disciplines," he said. "Would you like to be considered as dean of the new school?"

It was a query, not an offer. I was flattered, but I've never been the academic type. And if he'd looked at my transcripts, Professor Davis wouldn't have wasted a phone call.

The UT School of Communication was renamed the College of Communication in 1979 and the Moody College of Communication in 2013, following a $50 million gift from the Moody Foundation of Galveston.

I served a couple of terms (1985–1991 and 2000–2007) on the College of Communication Advisory Council, which is composed of alums who are industry leaders and other prominent figures who have strong ties to the world of media, public relations, and communications. The council meets regularly and gives advice about trends, developments, and best practices in the various professions, helping the college remain relevant and on the cutting edge of academic achievement.

I also served one term as the chairman of the advisory council. In 1990, during my tenure, Dean Bob Jeffrey formed a committee to plan the next twenty-five years of the college. I chaired that committee, but I had great staff help, which is always the key. Wayne Danielson had been the longtime dean of the college, and he provided institutional knowledge and wise counsel as we did our research and crafted a report that outlined several proposals for the college's future.

I was enormously pleased when I was asked to deliver the commencement address to the Moody College of Communication graduates in the fall of 2017. A commencement address is on a higher level than my usual invitations: "Hey, Neal, can you stand up here and say something?"

In my address I told a few jokes and had what I thought at the time were words of wisdom, but it wasn't earthshaking William Jennings Bryan oratory. The new graduates no doubt forgot my remarks the minute they walked out of the auditorium, happy to receive their degrees and focused on hugging their loved ones and getting on with their lives.

But my greatest honor came in 2016, when two friends of mine invited me to lunch—Mike Wilson, an assistant dean in the Moody College of Communication, and Tim McClure, one of the founders of the ad agency GSD&M. Halfway through a pleasant lunch, they said, "We've got something to ask of you." I thought, "Oh my, not another volunteer job. Or are they gonna ask me for money? I don't have any money."

They said they wanted to name in my honor a soon-to-be-renovated broadcast journalism studio in the Jesse H. Jones Communication Center on campus. I literally dropped my fork. The UT System Board of Regents required a person's permission to put his or her name on a permanent place, and so they were asking for my permission. I agreed with dumbfounded enthusiasm. Who wouldn't agree to that?

I left the restaurant floating on a cloud. It was a magnificent recognition. The university had been a huge part of my life, beginning when I was only sixteen years old, and having a campus facility named after me would be the greatest professional moment in my six decades of bleeding burnt orange.

But then months went by and I didn't hear anything more. I thought the Regents had killed the idea. Unbeknownst to me, Mike and Tim had asked for donations from Luci Johnson, Dan Rather, Bill Moyers, Roy Spence (cofounder of the GSD&M public relations group), Julian Read (press secretary for John Connally), Mike Myers (whose name is on the UT soccer field), Tom Johnson, and eighteen others.

When they invited me to lunch again, I walked in to find perhaps the most uplifting surprise of my professional life. They presented me with a mockup picture of the broadcast studio with my name on it. "Congratulations, Neal," they said, "you've earned this recognition."

The Neal Spelce Broadcast Journalism Studio named for me in UT's Moody College of Communication is a signal lifetime honor. *Photo courtesy UT Moody College of Communication*

The Neal Spelce Broadcast Journalism Studio is the perfect model of a real news studio, with a control room surrounded by multiple TV viewing screens, a bank of desktop computers, and a functioning news anchor desk. It rivals commercial TV news studios and gives students a "real world" broadcast experience.

The dedication ceremony took place in September 2016, and it began with a videotape of Roy Spence saying, tongue in cheek, "Smelling of rich mahogany, Neal Spelce is kind of a big deal because . . . he's a man of talent. He's a manly man"—a reference to the humorous character Ron Burgundy portrayed by Will Ferrell in the movie *Anchorman*.

Mike Wilson served as emcee, and during his introduction, when I facetiously asked him why my name was on the door in Scotch tape, he smiled and joked, "Certain checks haven't cleared yet."

The speakers included Jay Bernhardt, dean of the Moody College; R. B. Brenner, at that time the director of the School of Journalism; Catherine Robb, an Austin attorney, daughter of Lynda Johnson Robb, and granddaughter of LBJ and Mrs. Johnson; and Robin Rather, an environmental advocate and daughter of Dan Rather.

Dan was on an assignment and unable to attend, but he sent a videotape in which he thanked me for "being loyal when the heat was on." He said my "work was inspiring, and I mean that. Mark this well: His coverage of the Tower tragedy was one of the hallmark pieces of American journalism in the last half of the twentieth century." He ended the message by saying, "Neal, if you need help in any way, send up a flare. If you need bail money, call me."

Contrary to popular belief that news anchors can't get enough attention, I was overwhelmed by the adulation and had a hard time containing my emotions. I was comforted by the presence of my wife, Connie, several family members, including my two grandsons, and many dear friends and colleagues. It was truly a historic moment for me personally, a validation of a life spent "bearing witness when history happened," as R. B. Brenner said in his remarks. "Journalism is a *doing* thing," he continued, saying I was being recognized by the leaders of my revered alma mater for rushing toward trouble when wiser people were heading the other way.

The speakers were very generous in recalling that in my long career, I had endeavored to make sense of what I was witnessing and to share my insights with tens of thousands who were depending on me to get the story right. And now, six decades after I'd entered the University of Texas as a pimply-faced sixteen-year-old, I had come full circle back to those classroom days when I was taught to use timeless journalistic skills and practice the highest ethical standards in the pursuit of the truth. I was back home with my name on a door, and I couldn't have been prouder and more thankful.

I was especially pleased that Catherine Robb was there to represent the Lyndon Johnson family. In her remarks, she quoted her aunt Luci Johnson: "Lady Bird said that LBJ was 'a great man to have in a crisis.' Neal is that same kind of steady, thoughtful, decisive man. People could trust and believe Neal. . . . He was a local version of Walter Cronkite."

Those words of praise from the Johnson family touched my heart. In so many ways, it was LBJ and Mrs. Johnson who set me on the path to that "doing thing" called journalism, and I will forever be grateful to them for believing in me and taking me under their wing.

"TIME EQUALS TRUTH"

The esteemed LBJ biographer Robert Caro came to Austin in April 2019 to promote his new book entitled *Working*, his recollections about his life as a researcher and journalist. It was fitting that Caro be interviewed onstage at the LBJ Presidential Library auditorium, because he had quite possibly spent more time in the library's archives than any other researcher.

I was doubly interested in the event because my friend Stephen Harrigan—himself a distinguished journalist, novelist, and also an outstanding researcher—would interview the author widely considered to be the premier presidential biographer of our time.

Before the event began, I joined the long line of Caro devotees who were getting their books signed by the author as he sat with his wife, Ina, at a table in the lobby. When it was my turn to say hello to him and have my copy signed, someone told him that I'd known President Johnson personally and had worked for him and Mrs. Johnson for many years, starting at KTBC.

It didn't seem to make an impression on my fellow octogenarian Robert Caro. He was a nice, gracious man, but by that point in his life he'd met and interviewed hundreds of people who'd known LBJ, many of them within his closest inner circle. So what was meeting yet-another-white-haired LBJ associate at that point in his career? Caro had already published four of five planned volumes of *The Years of Lyndon Johnson*, which he'd begun working on in the 1970s. He probably felt he'd spoken with everyone who was anyone in LBJ's orbit.

Now bear with me for just a moment. My friends will tell you that I'm not a man given to excessive pride or arrogance. But as I waited for Robert Caro to sign his book, I couldn't help thinking he'd never even met Lyndon Johnson, much less spent countless hours with him in fascinating and extraordinary situations. But I had.

I'd been on the wrong end of the Johnson Treatment on a couple of occasions, having my butt chewed out royally. I'd carried on a conversation with The Man while he was getting an enema. I'd followed him into

Because my association with LBJ is a thread that has tied so much together in my life, I would be remiss if I didn't acknowledge key remaining "keepers of the LBJ flame": Larry Temple, Tom Johnson, LouAnn Temple, Bill Moyers, and Mark Updegrove. *Photo courtesy Headliners Club*

the jungles of Vietnam in 1961, at the very moment when our "advisers" were first deployed to aid the South Vietnamese government. It was the beginning of deeper US involvement in that tragic war.

I had wandered this building's nooks and crannies, and the library above them, with LBJ and Mrs. Johnson when we were planning the dedication ceremony of his presidential library.

And I'd held back tears when I oversaw the details as President Johnson was laid to rest on a cold winter's day at the family ranch, and years later when I helped out as his remarkable wife made her final journey to rest alongside him in that same sacred ground under the live oaks.

So eat your heart out, Brother Caro. I was actually there.

But let me be very clear: I am in no way in the same league as Pulitzer

Prize–winning Robert Caro as a writer and researcher. I was simply an eyewitness, a reporter, often at the right place at the right time.

In this memoir I rely on my own imperfect recollections—and the corroboration of a few friends and colleagues—to recount my professional interactions and eventual friendship with Lyndon Johnson, Lady Bird Johnson, and their family. I hope that what I lack in profundity, I make up with good humor and my rich personal memories.

As I sat up-front in the second row of the LBJ auditorium for the interview, I greeted a couple of old friends I've written about in these pages. Larry Temple was there to introduce the event, and Tom Johnson had flown in from Atlanta for the occasion. The numbers of those remaining from LBJ's circle are dwindling. I was happy to be there to hear the great presidential biographer discuss his craft, but I was also happy to represent those years that Larry, Tom, and I—and many others—had spent deeply engaged in Lyndon Johnson's life and long political career.

Once the interview began, Caro and Harrigan's words triggered more memories, much like a videotape playing and rewinding over and over again. I realized we would soon be celebrating the fiftieth anniversary of the dedication and opening of that massive library complex. I couldn't believe how quickly those years had flown by since I was in charge of that historic event.

To my surprise, all of those old anxieties came rushing back: Can this huge construction project be finished on time? How do I deal almost daily with the outsized LBJ personality? How do we handle the unprecedented number of VIPs invited to the event? What about the live TV coverage and the national media? Will antiwar protesters spoil the celebration? And what about the fact that President Nixon had asked me not to tell LBJ about his special gift—Do I lie to Nixon and tell LBJ anyway?

I was fascinated by a quote from the Caro book that Stephen Harrigan pointed out in the interview: "Time equals truth." Given Caro's credo, "Turn every page," I took the quote to mean that "the passage of time—with enough research—will bring the truth to light."

I wish I could say that in the sixty-five years since I first met Lyndon Johnson, when I was a young reporter at KTBC in 1956, I've uncovered startling revelations about him, and that in this book I have disclosed the absolute truth about that monumental figure in American history. But I really haven't.

LBJ presented me with this signed photograph the month before he died. He really liked this photo with his rugged features framed by his signature Stetson hat. He called it "my John Wayne picture." *Photo courtesy Neal Spelce*

What I hope I've done is to shine a little light and bring texture and a touch of humor to the oft-told tales of The Man. And I hope I've surprised, and maybe intrigued you and other readers with a few of the things I've witnessed firsthand that have never been told before.

If journalism is "the first rough draft of history," as Ben Bradlee of the *Washington Post* described it, consider this memoir a rough draft that adheres to the truth as best I remember it. In my more reflective moments, I can imagine LBJ himself throwing that long arm around my shoulders and saying, "Neal, every now and then you've effed things up, but you didn't this time."

He knows I told these stories with the bark off.

—Neal Spelce
Austin, Texas, 2020

-30-

POSTSCRIPT

I have intended this memoir to be enjoyable and informative, especially the frequent intersections with the lives of President Lyndon B. Johnson and Mrs. Johnson, five other US presidents, and three presidential wannabes.

If you would like to take a deeper dive, I am pleased to report that my archives have been donated to the Dolph Briscoe Center for American History at the University of Texas at Austin. Much more of this story remains there, including thirty-six boxes of my personal papers and photographs. The archives also contain the original film footage and audio recordings of the UT Tower shooting in 1966 and several hundred video vignettes from our nationally syndicated television productions of *An American Moment with Charles Kuralt* and *An American Moment with James Earl Jones* in the late 1990s. I intend to add the forty hours of Thomas Zigal's videotaped interviews with me, which have provided the background for this book.

The Briscoe Center is a distinguished history research center known worldwide for its collections in Texas history, congressional and political history, and photojournalism, and its vast archives related to the news media, including the papers of Walter Cronkite, Morley Safer, Dan Rather, Andy Rooney, Ann Richards, and Molly Ivins. I am deeply honored that my collections are housed alongside theirs.

ACKNOWLEDGMENTS

Y ou would not be holding this book in your hands, or reading it electronically, if it hadn't been for philanthropist Mickey Klein. Period. Paragraph.

I met Mickey a few years ago at a luncheon he attended for my daughter, Cile, when she was being honored as an outstanding graduate of Southwestern University in Georgetown, Texas. Between bites of food, Mickey peppered me with questions about my background. At the time, I thought it was just a "getting to know you" conversation. But he kept drawing stories out of me, even after we'd finished the luncheon, and finally he said what others have said: "You need to write a book."

I graciously demurred, as I usually did when that idea was expressed. But he persisted, saying I had an *obligation* to capture these never-before-told stories in print, especially about President Lyndon Johnson. *Obligation*—that got my attention.

I am deeply indebted to Mickey Klein for his encouragement and generous support. His positive reaction to the completed manuscript meant everything to me at a time when I was wondering if the three-year effort had any merit. He assured me it did.

While Mickey was the catalyst, the trigger, that got this project underway, Tom Johnson and members of the immediate LBJ family were instrumental in getting this memoir in your hands. Even though some of my observations may have been unflattering, they remained solidly behind my effort to relate these incidents with the bark off. In fact, after reading the final manuscript, LBJ's daughter Luci and Tom publicly praised the book.

Many others have expressed their approval of the book, first and foremost my family. Even though they've patiently listened to me tell these stories a thousand times over the years and would sometimes roll their eyes when I started a familiar retelling, they have been wonderfully supportive and very helpful in the crafting of these pages.

My wife, Connie, put up with the conversion of our dining room into a TV studio where my collaborator, Tom Zigal, interviewed me on videotape over several months. Connie shared her thoughts about the direction of the narrative and also coordinated the transcriptions of those videotapes, which formed the basis for this book. (My first wife, Sheila, died of ovarian cancer. Connie and I have been married for decades as of this writing.)

The entire family labored through various drafts with patience and care. Cile and her husband, Chris Elley—both Emmy Award–winning TV producers—gave us essential guidance in organizing the contents. My younger (by seventeen months) brother, Bennett, shored up my memory countless times and was an excellent proofreader. My son, Allen, and his wife, Kit, provided detailed memories and reassurance throughout.

Don Carleton, executive director of the University of Texas Dolph Briscoe Center for American History and a renowned historian and biographer (Walter Cronkite's bio, for one), is at the top of my list of those who made this book possible. He was an early proponent of the project, and he carefully reviewed every page and guided its publication. But more importantly, when we presented him with the first draft, he said, "It's too damn long, Spelce." And wonder of wonders, he agreed to break it in half and publish two books. The second book is in the works. Carleton's very able colleagues Dr. Holly Taylor, Alison Beck, and Erin Purdy have been real pros carrying out their respective responsibilities.

Tom Johnson, who appears many times in this book, vetted the entire manuscript, focusing especially on the LBJ and news media portions. Harsh critic that he is, Tom was most encouraging and enthusiastic. Larry Temple served with Tom in LBJ's White House as general counsel, and Larry, too, was helpful and supportive.

George Dillman's association with Lyndon Johnson's inner circle goes back to the 1950s, when he first worked with LBJ's trusted writer and adviser Horace Busby. That was when George became a friend of mine. He added valuable information to this memoir.

Mark Updegrove, a presidential historian and president and CEO of the LBJ Foundation, was an early reviewer of the Lyndon Johnson passages in the book. With Mark's kind approval, I knew I had avoided any serious errors in history. Even when I told LBJ's youngest daughter, Luci Johnson, that some of my references about her daddy were not flattering, she was still supportive. Special kudos go to LBJ Library staffers Anne Wheeler, who provided help with facts and details, and Jay Godwin, who supplied many of the great LBJ photos.

In his foreword, my old friend Dan Rather is generous and effusive about my career and our personal relationship, and for that I am greatly appreciative. We go way back, Dan and I, sharing many early pioneering endeavors in TV news. He was excited and happy for me as he followed this book to fruition.

Another longtime colleague in the world of television news and sports, Verne Lundquist, will be featured in my second memoir.

Gary Lavergne, the author of *A Sniper in the Tower* and the recognized authority on the UT Tower tragedy in 1966, confirmed my memories of that horrific event, corrected minor discrepancies, and gave his blessing to what I have written about my personal experiences on that fateful day. Keith Maitland, who produced the highly acclaimed documentary *Tower*, shared much of his original work with us as we shared original film footage with him of that dreadful day in 1966. For decades I have exchanged anecdotes and impressions with my good friends Forrest Preece, who narrowly missed getting shot by the sniper, and Gary Pickle, who braved the bullets to record amazing film footage that is still cited a half-century later for its visual chronicle under extreme duress. I value their friendship and the bond we share.

Two highly successful authors whom I admire greatly, Stephen Harrigan and Elizabeth Crook, have taken the time to encourage me to share my stories. To have them pat me on the back and say "go get 'em" meant so much.

My life and professional career have benefited enormously from the association and support of two people who worked side by side with me over the years—Ron Rogers, my partner in the radio business, and Howard Falkenberg, whom I trusted implicitly by giving up my title and naming him president of the Neal Spelce advertising and PR firm. They were indispensable with details and background for this book.

I walked alongside many others in those old stomping grounds of advertising and public relations. I am thankful for my friendship with Julian Read, a PR man extraordinaire, with whom I alternately competed and cooperated for decades (RIP, Julian). Tuck Kamin, a branding and marketing expert who worked for my ad agency back in the day, was quite persistent in keeping after me on this book project. Likewise, editor Tim Taliaferro of *Texas Monthly* and *Alcalde* magazine was most encouraging when he heard what I was writing.

Tim McClure, Jay Bernhardt, and Mike Wilson—the three people who spearheaded the effort to name the Neal Spelce Broadcast Journalism Studio in UT's Moody College of Communication in my honor—deserve special mention and my sincerest gratitude. As do the stalwarts of the Headliners Club (where a room is set aside to feature books written by the club's members) Sue Meller, Mark Morrison, and Brian Greig.

A special shout-out goes to Bill and Christie Nalle, who provided me with storytelling companionship and the best place possible for writing—a lakeside home inside the Nalle Bunny Run Wildlife Preserve in Austin, where majestic views of the limestone cliffs were matched by an amazing array of birds and other wildlife (yes, snakes too).

I also want to acknowledge several friends who have aided me in many ways over the past two years as I have progressed through this book-writing process: John Selman, Charlie Betts, C. W. Hetherly Jr., Alden Smith, Sam Perry, Dusty Rhodes, Les Gage, Jim Howard, Alan Bergstrom, Carlos Klutts (RIP, Carlos), Dan Burck (RIP, Dan), Merritt Belisle, Hagen McMahon, Terrell Blodgett, Lee Cooke, Matt Mathias, Sandy Gottesman, and a host of others I probably should include. Please forgive me if I have failed to mention you by name. I will buy you an old-fashioned at the Headliners Club.

Finally, and most importantly, I want to thank Thomas Zigal, already an accomplished author and invaluable as my collaborator. Yes, I had written an average of 1,500 words a week for forty years in my newsletter, plus countless TV news stories and radio reports, but never a book. Tom's background, research, inquisitiveness, and ability to take my words, improve them, and build a narrative arc through a 94,907-word manuscript continually amazed me. Not only that, he was a delight to work with and to share stories with (over an old-fashioned or two or three) even if they sometimes didn't make it into the book. Our videotape gaffes alone are worthy of a book of humor. As they used to say on my grandparents' Arkansas farm—Tom and I "gee-d and haw-ed" together really well.

Tom and I wish to thank his stepson Esteban Gonzales and partner Janet Wagner, who were home from college the first summer and transcribed our early videotapes before we found an Internet source. Tom's son, Danny, pieced together the eight hundred pages of transcriptions into a reasonable order.

I will be forever grateful to everyone mentioned in these acknowledgments. They helped me accomplish what I've always dreamed of doing: writing and publishing a book that captures what I saw and heard and did over the eighty-plus years of my life. Not every moment was noteworthy, of course, but as I learned from my mother at an early age, it was important to do something for the public good—and along the way, to conduct yourself with honesty, empathy, and dignity in pursuit of those things that make all of our lives more fully human. And so thank you most of all to my first and most memorable inspiration, Fannie Lou Spelce.

APPENDIX A

Dear Neal:

You gave us a successful beginning to what we hope will prove to be a worthy project. The good memories of May twenty-second are going to stay with us always, and whenever we turn our thoughts to that day, we are going to be thinking of you, too, with gratitude and admiration. You did an outstanding job arranging everything for the dedication ceremonies, tying a thousand and one details together during days we know were never long enough.

Our friends have warmly complimented us—both in person and in writing—about the hospitality they found awaiting them here and of how well coordinated the entire weekend was. We have heard only kind words about it . . . again and again.

Mrs. Johnson and I thank you on behalf of all the guests who were here, and most of all, we thank you on our behalf for a perfectly planned day.

Sincerely, LBJ

Dear Neal:

I know you must be exhausted, but I hope you are happy, because the Dedication couldn't have been better and you deserve a lion's share of the credit. Everyone has been singing your praises and if you're not careful you're going to be putting on every dedication that's held in Texas or any other place for that matter!

To say we couldn't have done it without you is an understatement, but I'm sure you have heard every superlative by now. Please know that Lyndon and I will never forget all you did and will be forever grateful.

Sincerely, Lady Bird

Dear Neal:

The opportunity to come to Austin for the dedication ceremonies was an especially exciting one for the Nixons, and I just wanted to get this note off to thank you for your many excellent arrangements, not only in connection with our visit, but also for the entire dedication. The Library tour was certainly one of the highlights of the day, and I think you have every reason to take great pride in the work you did to make this occasion the success that it was.

Mrs. Nixon joins me in sending our best wishes.

Sincerely, Richard Nixon

Dear Mr. Spelce:

Mrs. Agnew and I deeply appreciate your assistance in arranging our recent visit to Austin. It was a memorable day for us, and we were honored to be a part of the dedication.

You can be justly proud of your work as Director of the Dedication Office. It must have been hectic; but from what we see, the results were well worth the effort.

Warm Regards, Spiro T. Agnew

APPENDIX B

Presidents George and George: Father and Son at Rainbo Lake

The following are excerpts from my interview with George H. W. Bush and George W. Bush, which appeared in segments on KEYE-TV Austin in February 1998.

Neal Spelce: For the first time ever, President Bush and Governor Bush invited a journalist along on a fishing trip. We spent a few hours fishing on a small lake in East Texas. They have been asked every question imaginable about policy and politics, but they've never allowed a television crew to capture this personal moment between a father and his son, who just happen to share a love of fishing. We talked about a lot of things that these two men normally don't discuss in public. It's rare in the history of the United States that the son of a president is elected governor of a state. Yet no reporter has had the opportunity to discuss the influence of that relationship in such an informal, lengthy session. I think you're going to see a side of the president, and the governor, that you've never seen before.

Neal Spelce: Good to see you this morning, sir.

George, the father: How are you, Neal?

Neal Spelce: Great, thank you. Good morning, Governor.

George, the son: Good to see you.

Neal Spelce: [Voice-over] This is the governor's private sanctuary.

George, the son: This is my place to get away.

Neal Spelce: [Voice-over] This is the only property the governor owns in Texas, a home only his family and closest friends ever come inside. . . . The governor loves it here, and he savors moments like these with his dad. They come around only three or four times a year, just him and his dad, a fishing pole, and a tackle box full of lures.

GEORGE, THE SON: See this bait here, Neal. What's fun is to fool around with the bait. See that bait? It's spinner bait.

GEORGE, THE FATHER: We're trying everything here.

NEAL SPELCE: *[Voice-over]* For a couple of hours, we talked about fishing, family, and life. I asked about President Bush's life after the White House.

GEORGE, THE FATHER: It's not hard to adjust to be in private life as opposed to public. I don't do press conferences. . . . I don't think I've been to the Capitol since leaving the presidency. Very seldom go to Washington. You've just gotta shift gears. You can't always try to be what you used to be and hover around Washington. I miss some things. I miss the military, I miss friends, I miss the White House staff, who treated us like family.

NEAL SPELCE: *[Voice-over]* I asked the former president if he ever sought his son's advice, and I asked the governor if he ever asked his dad for guidance.

GEORGE, THE FATHER: We're not in the advice-giving business. I wouldn't begin to give George advice.

NEAL SPELCE: *[Voice-over]* Except maybe when it comes to picking the right bait. While the president may not offer advice, I found out his kids and grandkids aren't opposed to speaking up. Take, for instance, Governor Bush's twin sixteen-year-old daughters.

NEAL SPELCE: Do they try to tell you what to do? Do they say, "Dad, you ought to do this, Dad you ought to do that?"

GEORGE, THE SON: Yes, sure.

NEAL SPELCE: Did you do that to the president?

GEORGE, THE SON: Yeah, as often as he would let me.

GEORGE, THE FATHER: These girls are pretty intelligent. Three years ago, I was sitting with them when they came up on vacation. They said,

"All right, we want to know the truth, Grampy," and I said, "What are you talking about?" "You were head of the CIA, weren't you?" I said, "Yeah." They said, "Okay, what did you do with those aliens that you froze and kept?" I said, "Look, I'm a busy guy, don't give me this stuff." "We're serious!" I said, "Yeah, hell with you."

NEAL SPELCE: Mr. President, what *did* you do with those aliens?

GEORGE, THE FATHER: That's what they kept asking.

GEORGE, THE SON: They're playing for the Texas Rangers next year.

NEAL SPELCE: *[Voice-over]* Even on the lake, the demands and pressures of public office, something both these men relate to, never seem far away. While we fished, convicted killer Karla Faye Tucker begged the governor to spare her life.

GEORGE, THE SON: I heard her case is working its way through the courts now. I explained to my girls what due process means and the appeals process and how on death row, everybody's entitled to a full hearing.

GEORGE, THE FATHER: George, may I point out you can't catch a fish if the hook is not in the water.

GEORGE, THE SON: Sir, it is in the water, it's just not . . .

NEAL SPELCE: *[Voice-over]* Of course, the president is quick to remind us that this trip is about fishing.

GEORGE, THE FATHER: Can't you talk and fish at the same time?

GEORGE, THE SON: Well, if you had to put it that way, sir, absolutely.

GEORGE, THE FATHER: Pretty out here today, Junior.

GEORGE, THE SON: It is beautiful.

NEAL SPELCE: I don't guess there's a more stressful occupation than being in government and politics, with flak coming all the time, and you have pressures everywhere. So this must be the ideal way to relax when you get out.

GEORGE, THE FATHER: Yeah, it really is.

GEORGE, THE SON: It's peaceful.

GEORGE, THE FATHER: Total relaxation, and then you've got the beauty of [the surroundings]. Most places you fish are beautiful, not all, but most. Here you have the natural beauty to go with just the plain R&R of it all.

NEAL SPELCE: But I wonder, who's the best fisherman in this group?

GEORGE, THE SON: In the whole family?

NEAL SPELCE: Yeah.

GEORGE, THE SON: I'd say Dad is.

GEORGE, THE FATHER: I don't know.

NEAL SPELCE: Is the patriarch of the family the [best]?

GEORGE, THE SON: Yes, he is first.

GEORGE, THE FATHER: He's the one that's spent the most time at it these days.

GEORGE, THE SON: After all, he's got the most experience.

GEORGE, THE FATHER: Yes. Yes.

GEORGE, THE SON: Dad's a good fisherman. Part of fishing is the love of fishing.

GEORGE, THE FATHER: Yeah, that's all it is.

NEAL SPELCE: Who's the biggest liar, though?

GEORGE, THE FATHER: I would be, of course.

NEAL SPELCE: *[Voice-over]* On this morning, tensions build in the Persian Gulf, controversy embroils the White House, and a convicted killer pleads with the governor to spare her life. But talk here is about simpler things.

GEORGE, THE FATHER: Do you do any good with crankbait up here?

GEORGE, THE SON: Yeah.

GEORGE, THE FATHER: Have ya?

GEORGE, THE SON: I did the other day.

NEAL SPELCE: *[Voice-over]* Just two guys fishing. Two guys who share a famous last name. A father and a son who dedicated their lives to public service. Two friends who share a sense of humor.

GEORGE, THE FATHER: Let me know when you start trying to catch them.

GEORGE, THE SON: I need a little leadership as to where to put this thing.

GEORGE, THE FATHER: See that pole right there? Next to that, that's where they are.

GEORGE, THE SON: I hope so, sir.

NEAL SPELCE: So you were trying to hit the pole, were you not?

GEORGE, THE FATHER: Yeah, absolutely.

GEORGE, THE SON: It's more important to hit the fish, but . . .

GEORGE, THE FATHER: I'm going to hang up against these poles.

GEORGE, THE SON: Then do.

GEORGE, THE FATHER: See that? It hit that pole again.

NEAL SPELCE: That's two in a row.

GEORGE, THE FATHER: I'm not trying to brag or anything.

GEORGE, THE SON: I'll tell you one thing, you must be scaring the heck out of the fish by hitting that pole because they're running the other way.

NEAL SPELCE: *[Voice-over]* There are moments when you forget you're fishing with President Bush and Governor Bush. It's just George and George.

GEORGE, THE FATHER: Do you have a hit?

GEORGE, THE SON: I think so.

GEORGE, THE FATHER: Got a fish?

GEORGE, THE SON: Yeah, I hope so.

GEORGE, THE FATHER: Record this!

NEAL SPELCE: You have a weed? Weed or fish?

GEORGE, THE SON: Little fish.

NEAL SPELCE: Little guy?

GEORGE, THE SON: No, not so little.

GEORGE, THE FATHER: That's nice. Oh, you gill-hooked it. Very hard to do. Very hard. Very hard. A gill . . .

NEAL SPELCE: Look at that.

GEORGE, THE FATHER: The seldom-used gill hook.

GEORGE, THE SON: Mr. President.

GEORGE, THE FATHER: I'm not going to bring it up for anybody, but it's nice to try to get him in the mouth.

GEORGE, THE SON: Mr. President, would you like to hold the fish?

GEORGE, THE FATHER: No thanks. No, not that little fellow.

GEORGE, THE SON: See what it feels like?

NEAL SPELCE: [Voice-over] The Bushes cherish and protect these private moments. It's not always easy when you live in the public eye. President Bush's public life started in 1966 when he was elected to the US House of Representatives. About the time his dad headed to Washington, George W. headed to college.

NEAL SPELCE: How is it growing up in such a fishbowl, Governor?

GEORGE, THE SON: In my case, the fishbowl really began when Dad became vice president in 1980, so I was thirty-four.

NEAL SPELCE: [Voice-over] When Dad became president, private moments like these became more rare. But a devoted father squeezed precious family time in between the constant demands of [public office].

GEORGE, THE FATHER: Remember those volleyball games?

GEORGE, THE SON: Oh, we had great fun. The thing about fishing is there's a certain sense of envy during slow moments.

GEORGE, THE FATHER Actually, it's a team sport in a boat like this. One guy catches and we all rejoice.

NEAL SPELCE: *[Voice-over]* It gets tough when the criticism comes from the outside, at least when it's about his dad.

GEORGE, THE SON: The most difficult period for me was when people would criticize my dad. There was nothing in comparison, to see someone you love and respect, criticized.

GEORGE, THE FATHER: I don't think I was a favorite at CBS News. You can either leave this in or edit it out, whatever you want. They do all these surveys at the end of the election cycle. I'm afraid I was not their favorite person on those surveys. However, life goes on. Look how happy we are.

NEAL SPELCE: *[Voice-over]* The good life of a proud father, grandfather, and avid fisherman.

GEORGE, THE SON: Let's go back in that cove and we'll give it one more run.

GEORGE, THE FATHER: Where we started?

GEORGE, THE SON: Yes.

NEAL SPELCE: *[Voice-over]* The commander in chief and his loyal captain.

GEORGE, THE SON: Crank up the boat, men.

GEORGE, THE FATHER: One last cast before we go.

NEAL SPELCE: *[Voice-over]* But you can fish and talk about family, and nothing is more important to the Bushes.

NEAL SPELCE: What about holidays? Thanksgiving? Do you guys get all your families together at that time?

GEORGE, THE FATHER: We used to.

GEORGE, THE SON: Not anymore.

GEORGE, THE FATHER: Now they're all spread out. George's in Austin, Neil's in Houston, Marvin's up in Virginia. Dorothy is in Maryland and Jeb is in Florida. So it's hard to get everyone together. We used to do it at Camp David when I was president.

NEAL SPELCE: Mr. President, are you gonna help campaign for [George W.'s gubernatorial] reelection now?

GEORGE, THE FATHER: I don't think he needs help from his father. We can go, Barb and I, to fundraisers or something like that, not in the campaign in the sense of issues.

GEORGE, THE SON: One of the interesting initiatives that I'm gonna work with the legislature on is we've got to find a way to refurbish our courthouses, starting with those built prior to 1911. Why I'm so fascinated by . . . First of all, I love Texas history. I understand what small-town Texas means to Texas and its identity and history. I also understand what the courthouse means. It's the center of community. Many of these courthouses are masterpieces [of architecture], and we need to save them and preserve them.

GEORGE, THE FATHER: Push to that bank over there, see if we can get some fish.

GEORGE, THE SON: There I was on the courthouse planning and he interrupted me.

GEORGE, THE FATHER: It's very interesting. I respect your view on it and certainly would not try to argue the issue. But I would like to catch some bass.

NEAL SPELCE: [Voice-over] This former president loves to fish, but he'll tell you there is more to retirement.

NEAL SPELCE: The book you're working on now is . . . ?

GEORGE, THE FATHER: Is letters that I've written over the many years.

NEAL SPELCE: Personal letters?

GEORGE, THE FATHER: Yeah. One of the great letters [is to my family] prior to Desert Storm.

GEORGE, THE SON: Actually, it's on display now at the [George H. W. Bush Presidential] library [in College Station, Texas].

NEAL SPELCE: *[Voice-over]* A letter written December 31, 1990, as a devoted dad prepared to lead America's sons and daughters into war.

GEORGE, THE SON: This is going to blow your mind. I'm just looking at my watch. We've been out here for an hour and a half. It feels like about thirty minutes.

NEAL SPELCE: Time really does fly when you're fishing.

GEORGE, THE FATHER: George, so you think I might ought to forget lunch I had planned in Houston?

NEAL SPELCE: *[Voice-over]* The president and the governor decided it was time to get back to work. Knowing how rare these precious private moments are for this dad and son, it's a little tough leaving.

GEORGE, THE FATHER: That's a gray crane talking. Yes, the call of the crane. Hits [me] every time I hear that. I think how fortunate we are in this country to hear the call of the great crane. You like that, George? [When] I'm sitting alone on the dock, listening to the call of the crane.

GEORGE, THE SON: No, sir. I always know when I catch you on the dock, sitting there by yourself, talking to the crane . . .

GEORGE, THE FATHER: How far away is the psychiatric ward?

GEORGE, THE SON: Yes. We love you, Dad, but . . .

GEORGE, THE FATHER: There he is again. Where is my father? Well, he was a fine fella in his time, but he's down there . . .

GEORGE, THE SON: Talking to the cranes.

APPENDIX C

Excerpts from the Dedication of the Neal Spelce Broadcast Journalism Studio in September 2016

Dean Jay Bernhardt, Moody College of Communication:

"Neal is a communications visionary, community leader, and one of Moody College's most accomplished alums."

"He practiced his reporting with the ethics and skills and rigor he acquired at this university."

"The leaders and practitioners of tomorrow will learn their trade in this studio named in his honor."

Catherine Robb, attorney and Johnson family member:

Quoting her Aunt Luci Johnson: "Lady Bird said that LBJ was 'a great man to have in a crisis.' Neal is that same kind of steady, thoughtful, decisive man."

"People could trust and believe Neal . . . He was a local version of Walter Cronkite."

R. B. Brenner, director of the UT School of Journalism:

"Journalists bear witness . . . to be present when history happens, to serve as the eyes and ears of the public. The Tower showed Neal's poise, bravery, and professionalism."

Robin Rather, environmental advocate:

"Neal transcends the white light of the media vortex."

"Neal is the classiest, most loving, most loyal friend to the Rather family and an unbelievably great human being."

"Only one TV anchor can be friends with another anchor's family—it's the 'one family, one anchor' rule."

DAN RATHER VIDEO:

"Neal was loyal when the heat was on."

"His work was inspiring, and I mean that. Mark this well: His coverage of the Tower tragedy was one of the hallmark pieces of American journalism in the last half of the twentieth century."

"Neal, if you need help in any way, send up a flare. If you need bail money, call me."

INDEX

Italicized page numbers denote pictures.

Austin and, 14, 77
Pickle Express, 79
Piedras Negras jailbreak, 259–60
"Point-Counterpoint" segment of *60 Minutes*, 97–98
polarization, 96–98
polling, 98–99
Portman, Rob, 237
Powers, Bill, 137
Powers, Francis Gary, 45
Preece, Forrest, 137
presidential biographers. *See* Caro, Robert; Updegrove, Mark
presidential election, 2016, 98–99
presidential succession, 88
press and elections, 98–99
press at LBJ Ranch, 60, 86, 91–94, *92*
Pryor, Richard S., Jr. "Cactus": entertainment roots and comedic genius of, 26–28; at the Headliners Club, *83, 84*; JFK assassination conspiracy theory involving, 261–63; Johnson family and, 202; as KTBC program director, 21, 22, 31; "thermostrockimortimer" saying of, 202
Pryor, Richard S., Sr. "Skinny," 27
Pryor, Wally, 247, 249

Q
Q-Rating, Walter Cronkite's, 252

R
Rainbo Lake, 264–67, *265, 267*
Randolph, Frankie, 74
Ransom, Harry, 122
Rather, Dan: Bush-documents affair and, 258–59; career trajectory of, 31, 47–48, 250; at CBS, 47–48, 258–59; courage of, 259; Dolly Parton interview by, 258; foreword by, xi–xiii, *x*; at the Headliners Club's 60th anniversary gala, *84*; music affinity of, 257–58; on Neal Spelce and his body of work, xi, xiii, 272, 293; Neal Spelce Broadcast Journalism Studio, 270; Neal Spelce's 2012 Texas Book Festival interview of, 256–57, *257*; on- and off-camera personalities of, 255–56; origin and

family life of, 255; *Rather Outspoken: My Life in the News,* 256; tenacity as a news reporter of, 32–33, 255; Watergate reporting of, 255; Zapruder film and, 69
Rather, Robin, 272, 292–93
"Rathergrams," 255
Rayburn, Sam, 24, 26, 76
Read, Julian, 64, *65*, 270
Reagan, Nancy, 206, *207*
real estate bust of the late 1980s, 212
Reddick, DeWitt, 18, 19
Redford, Robert, 259
Red Rovers (KTBC mobile units), 103–4, *104, 105, 126*
Reedy, George, 91
reelection of LBJ in 1964, 72
Reid, Jan, 219, 240, 261
Republican National Convention, 2008, 227
Republican Party in Texas, 73
Richards, Ann: 1988 Democratic National Convention speech of, 220–23, *221*; Neal Spelce as speech adviser to, 219–21; Texas governor victory of, 223–24; Texas state treasurer race and victory of, 219; Walter Cronkite and 1988 Democratic National Convention speech of, 223
Riverbend Church, 206–8
Robb, Catherine, 271–72, 292
Robert Mueller Airport, 77
Roddy, Joe, 103, 111, 124, 127, 138
Rogers, Lorene, 132
Rogers, Mary Beth, 219
Rogers, Ron, 153–59
Rogers, William, 170, *175*
Rogers Spelce Company, 157
Roosevelt, Eleanor, 45, *46*
Roosevelt, Franklin, 13
Rose, Howard, 64
Royal, Darrell: Austin affinity of, 242, *244*; college and early coaching career of, 240; country music and, 241–42; down-to-earth nature of, 243–45; LBJ on leadership skills of, 246–47; Marriott Hotel fiasco and, 245–46; misadventure with Willie Nelson, Neal